Reincarnated a Sword

3

story by
YUU TANAKA

art by
TOMOWO MARUYAMA

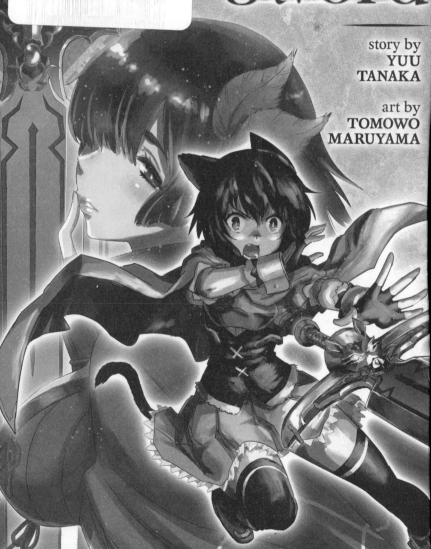

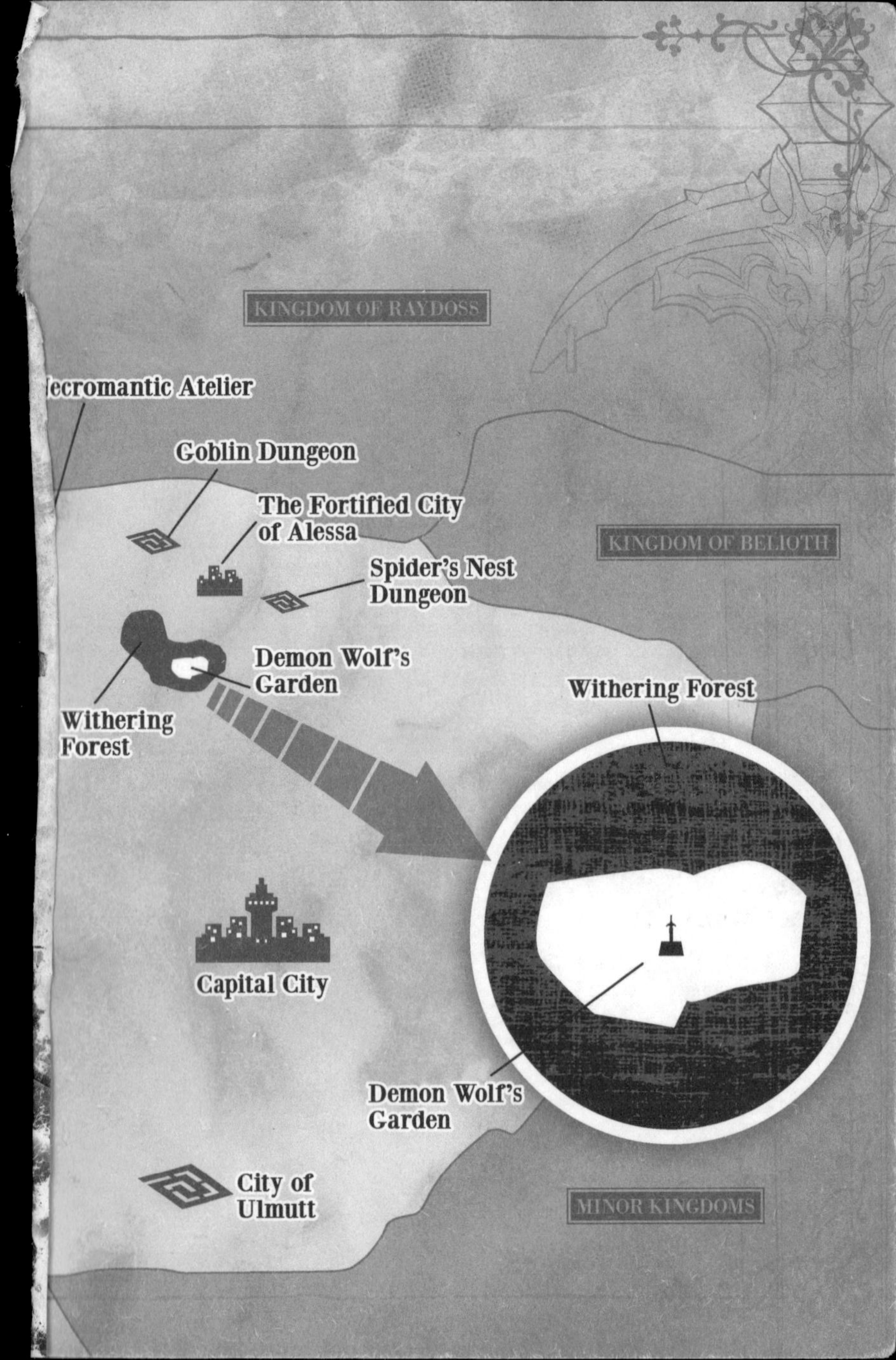

KINGDOM OF RAYDOSS
ecromantic Atelier
Goblin Dungeon
The Fortified City of Alessa
KINGDOM OF BELIOTH
Spider's Nest Dungeon
Demon Wolf's Garden
Withering Forest
Withering Forest
Capital City
Demon Wolf's Garden
City of Ulmutt
MINOR KINGDOMS

WORLD MAP

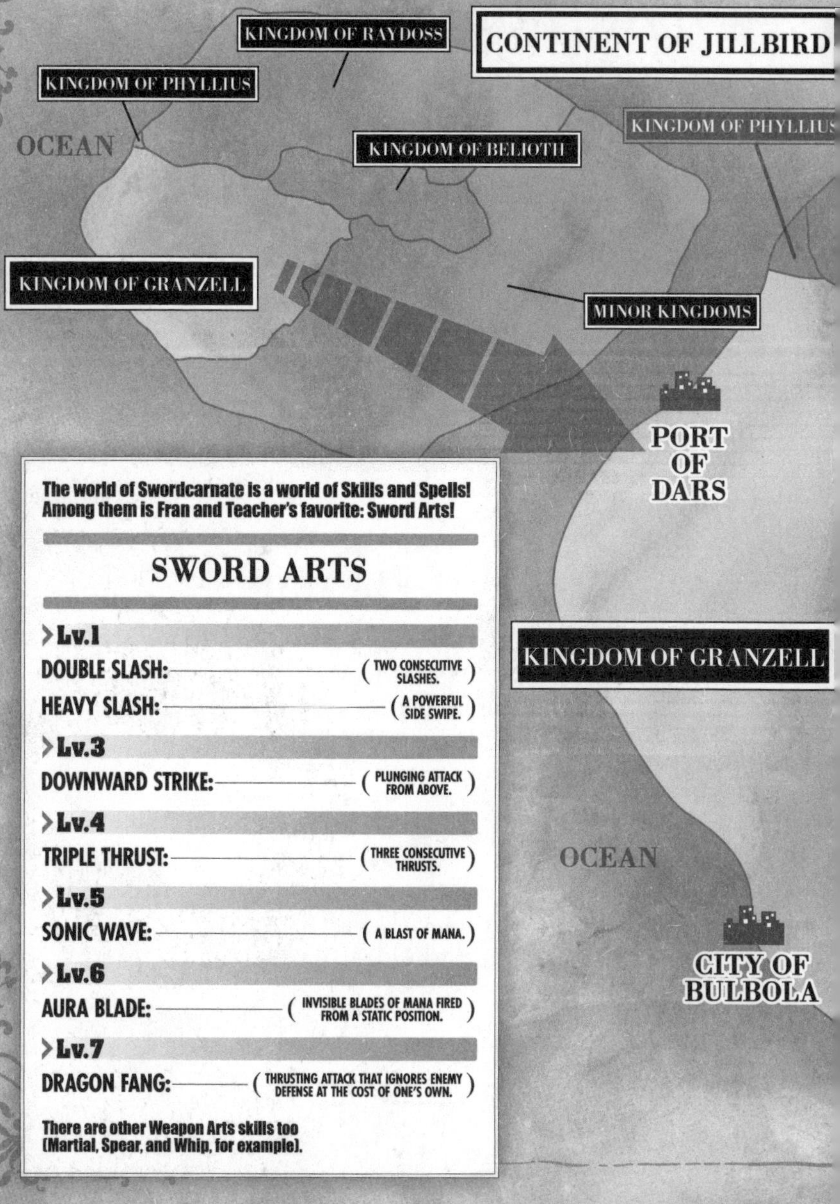
KINGDOM OF RAYDOSS
CONTINENT OF JILLBIRD
KINGDOM OF PHYLLIUS
OCEAN
KINGDOM OF BELIOTH
KINGDOM OF PHYLLIUS
KINGDOM OF GRANZELL
MINOR KINGDOMS
PORT OF DARS
KINGDOM OF GRANZELL
OCEAN
CITY OF BULBOLA

The world of Swordcarnate is a world of Skills and Spells! Among them is Fran and Teacher's favorite: Sword Arts!

SWORD ARTS

› Lv.1

DOUBLE SLASH: (TWO CONSECUTIVE SLASHES.)

HEAVY SLASH: (A POWERFUL SIDE SWIPE.)

› Lv.3

DOWNWARD STRIKE: (PLUNGING ATTACK FROM ABOVE.)

› Lv.4

TRIPLE THRUST: (THREE CONSECUTIVE THRUSTS.)

› Lv.5

SONIC WAVE: (A BLAST OF MANA.)

› Lv.6

AURA BLADE: (INVISIBLE BLADES OF MANA FIRED FROM A STATIC POSITION.)

› Lv.7

DRAGON FANG: (THRUSTING ATTACK THAT IGNORES ENEMY DEFENSE AT THE COST OF ONE'S OWN.)

There are other Weapon Arts skills too (Martial, Spear, and Whip, for example).

Reincarnated as a Sword

3

Chapter 12: Trump Card

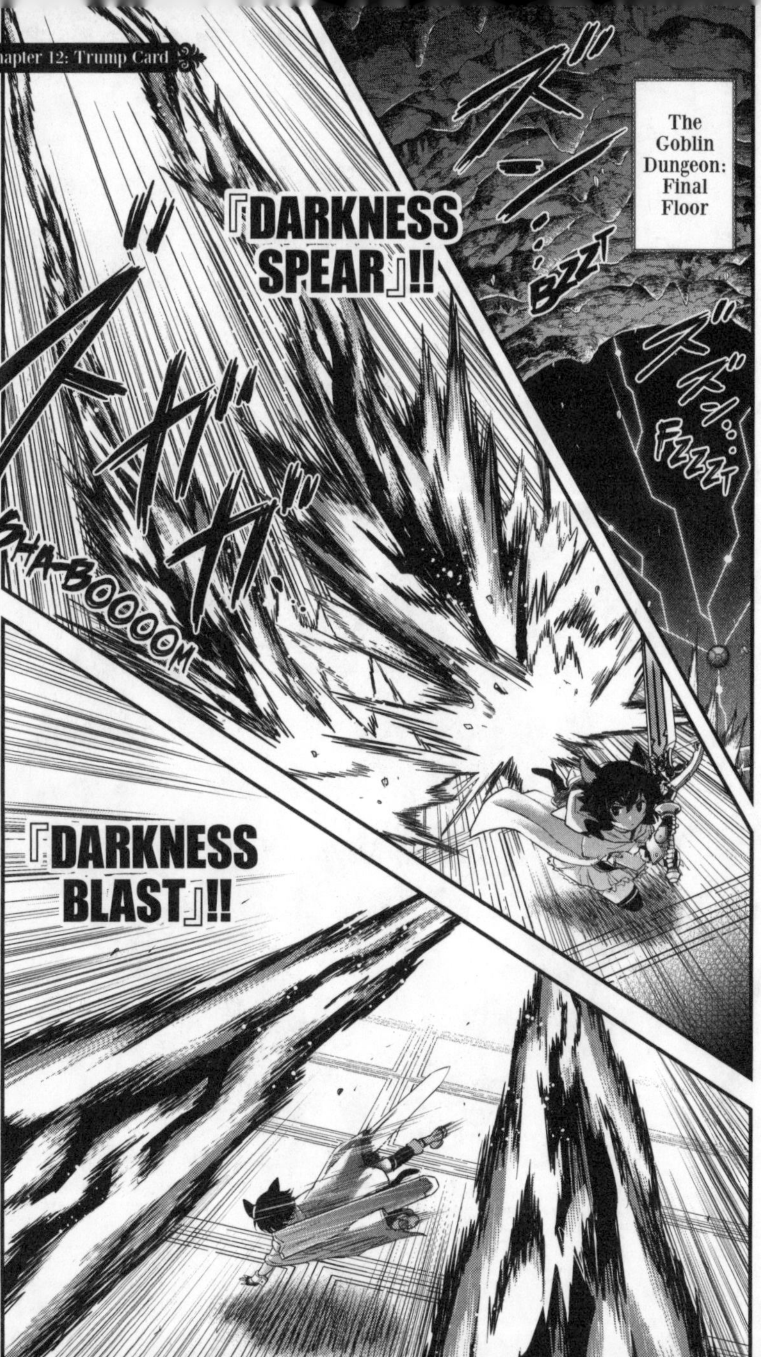
The Goblin Dungeon: Final Floor
BZZT
FZZZT
『DARKNESS SPEAR』!!
SHA-BOOOOOM
『DARKNESS BLAST』!!

Chapter 12: Trump Card

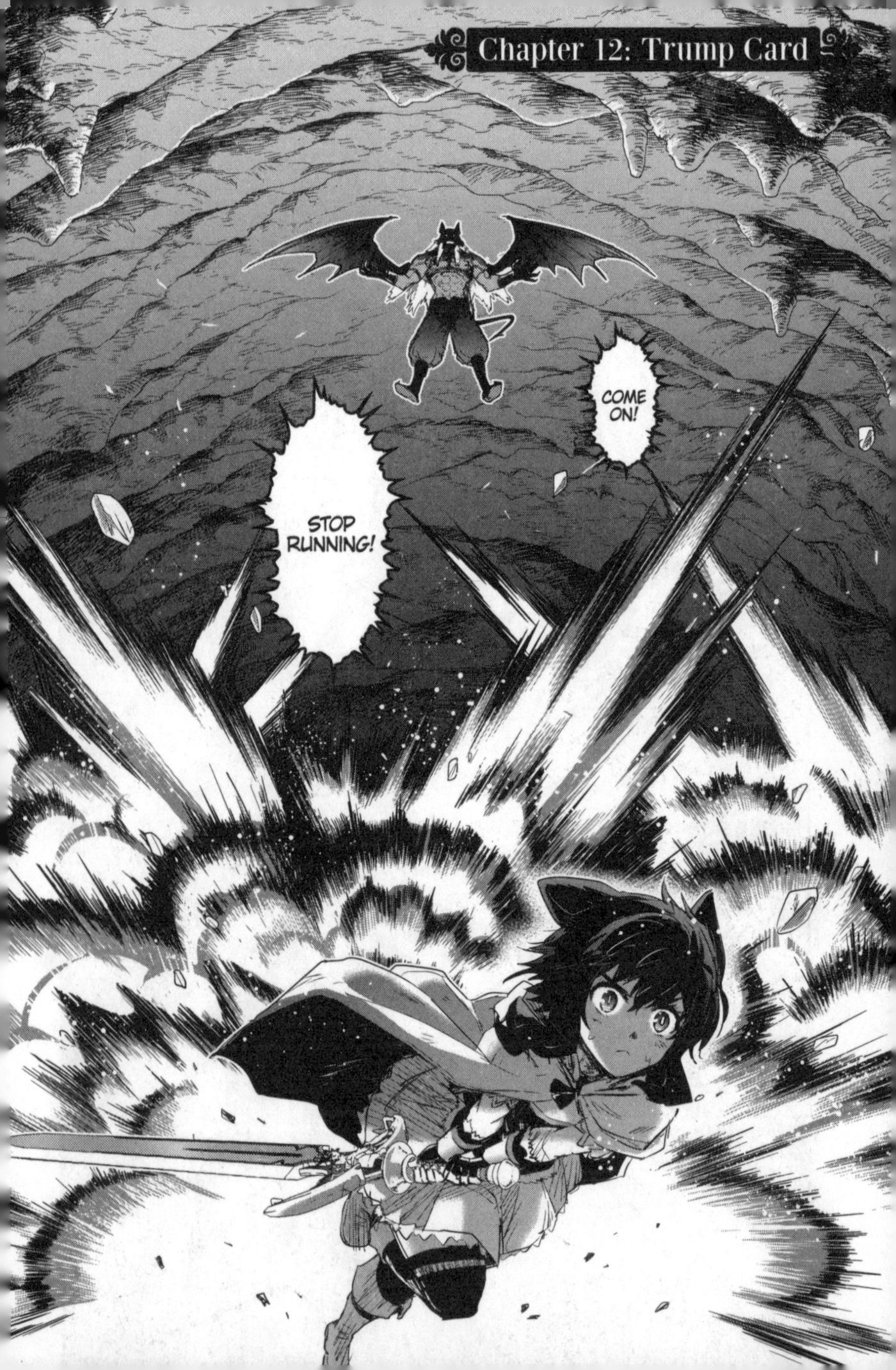
COME ON!
STOP RUNNING!

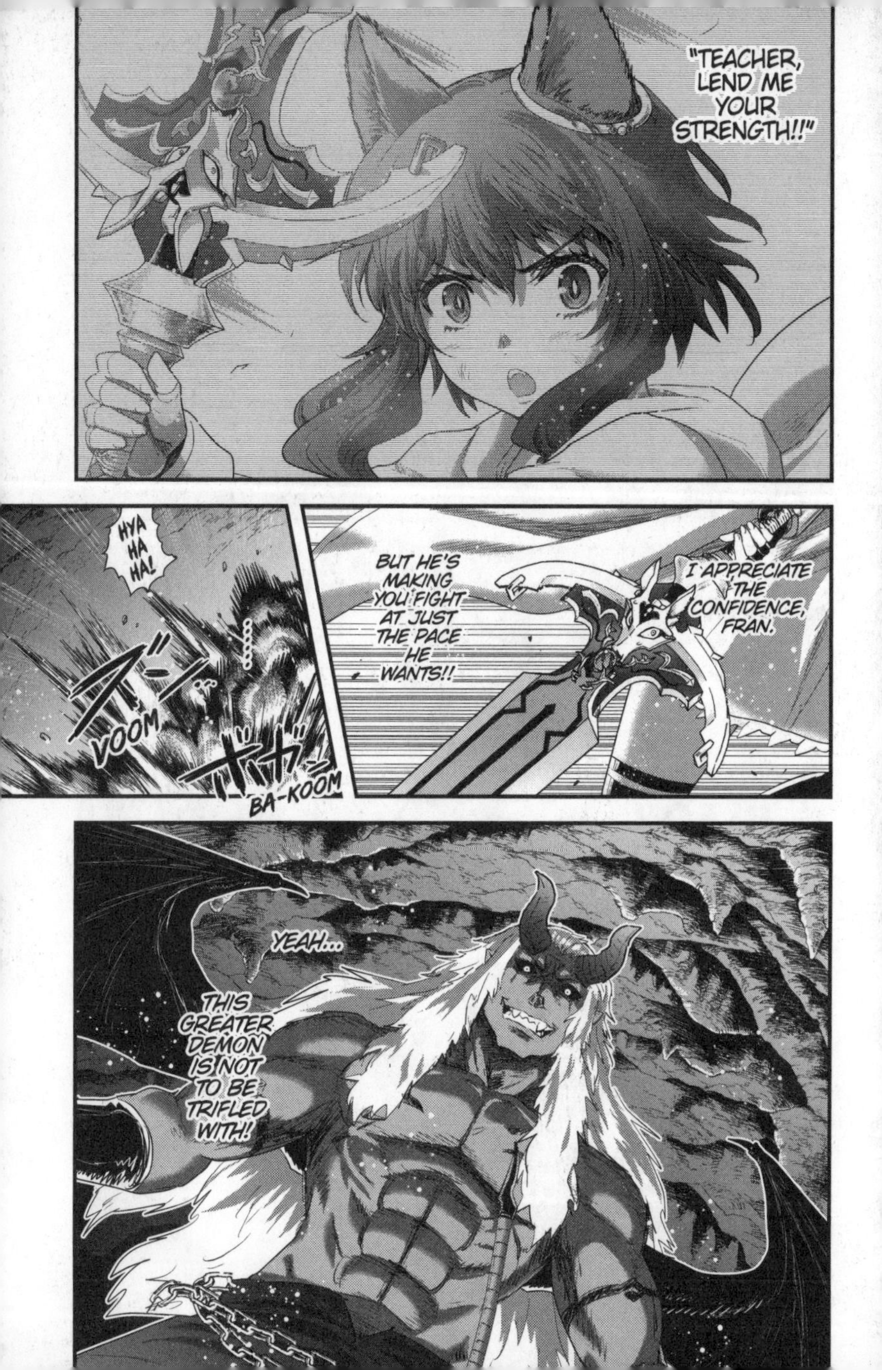
"TEACHER, LEND ME YOUR STRENGTH!!"
I APPRECIATE THE CONFIDENCE, FRAN.
BUT HE'S MAKING YOU FIGHT AT JUST THE PACE HE WANTS!!
HYA HA HA!
......
VOOM
BA-KOOM
YEAH...
THIS GREATER DEMON IS NOT TO BE TRIFLED WITH!

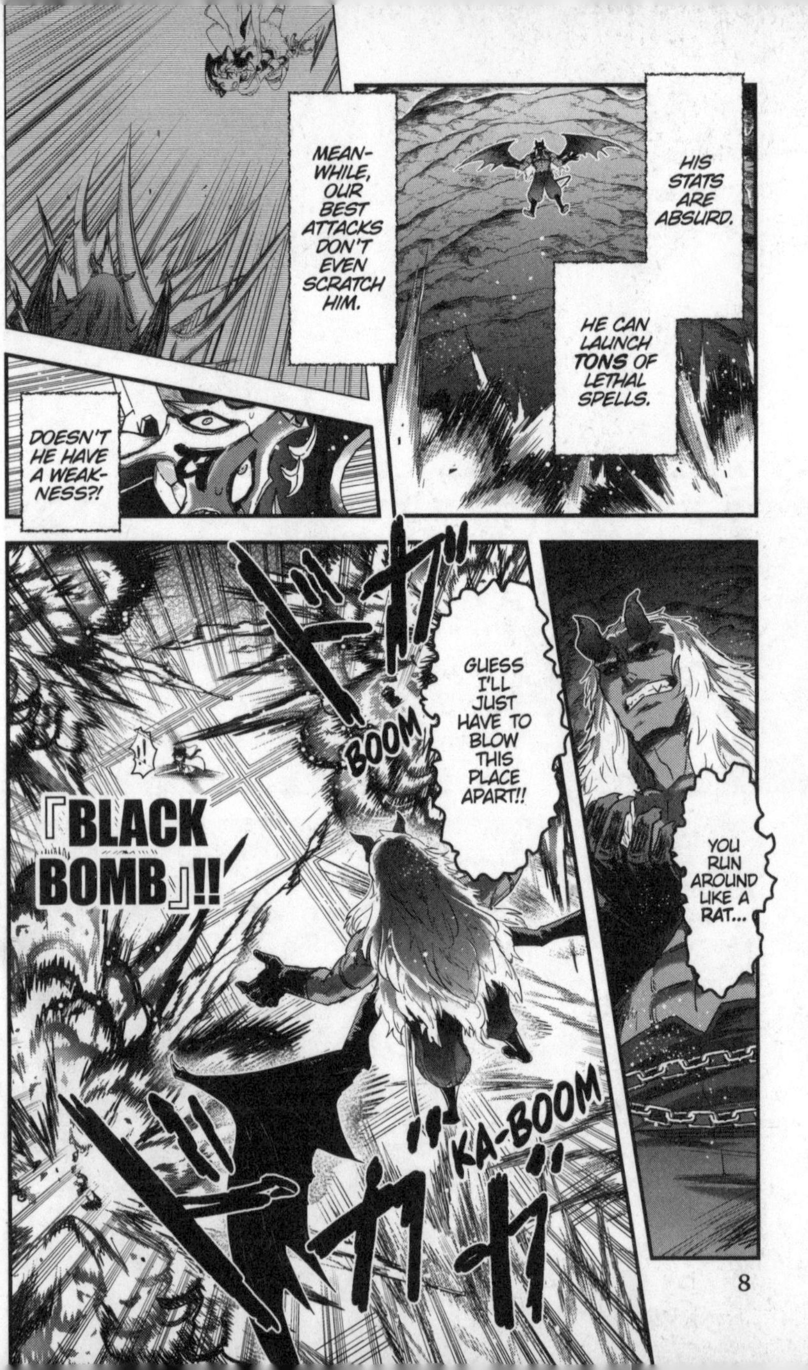
HIS STATS ARE ABSURD.
HE CAN LAUNCH TONS OF LETHAL SPELLS.
MEAN-WHILE, OUR BEST ATTACKS DON'T EVEN SCRATCH HIM.
DOESN'T HE HAVE A WEAK-NESS?!
YOU RUN AROUND LIKE A RAT...
GUESS I'LL JUST HAVE TO BLOW THIS PLACE APART!!
BOOM
!!
『BLACK BOMB』!!
KA-BOOM

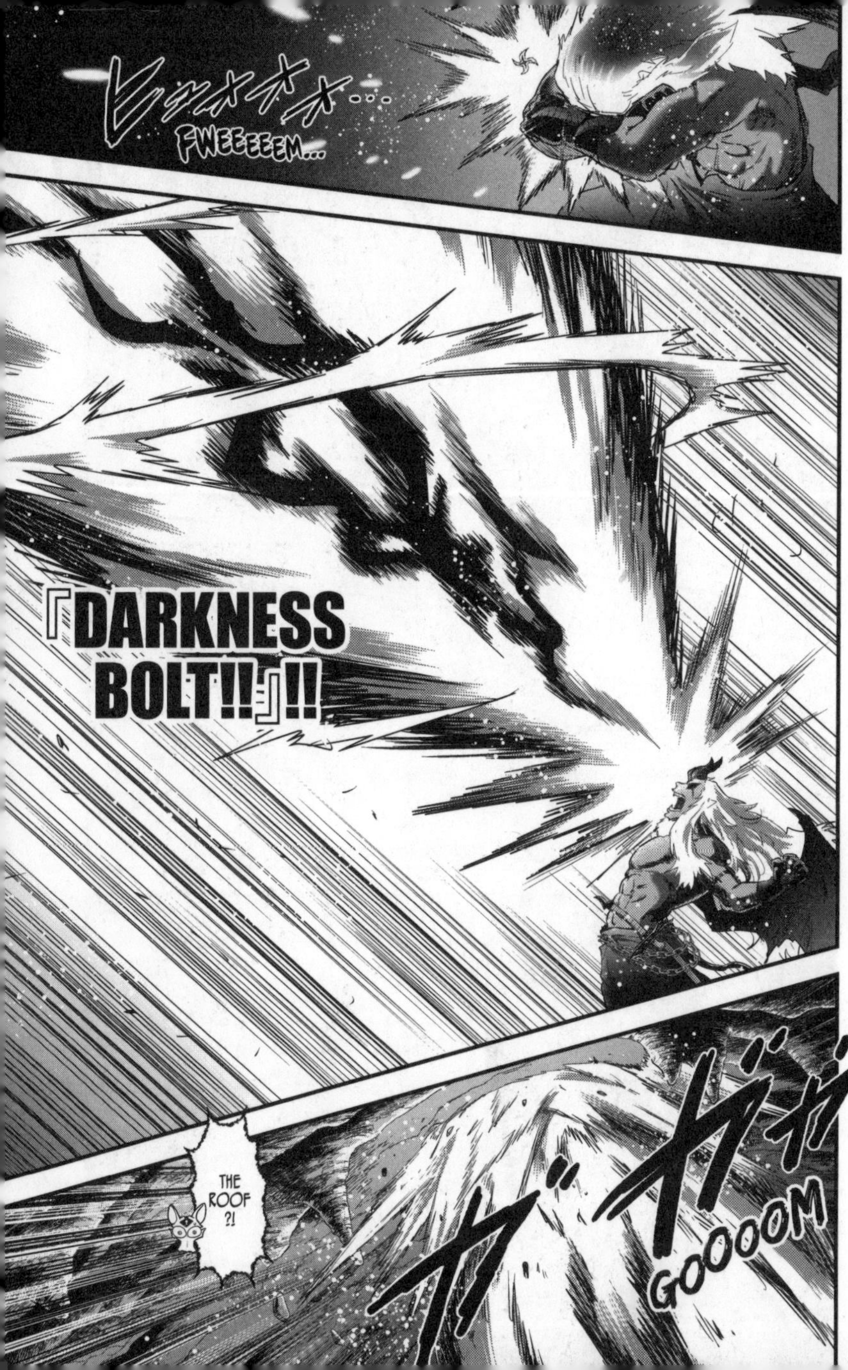
FWEEEEEM...
『DARKNESS BOLT!!』!!
GOOOOM
THE ROOF ?!

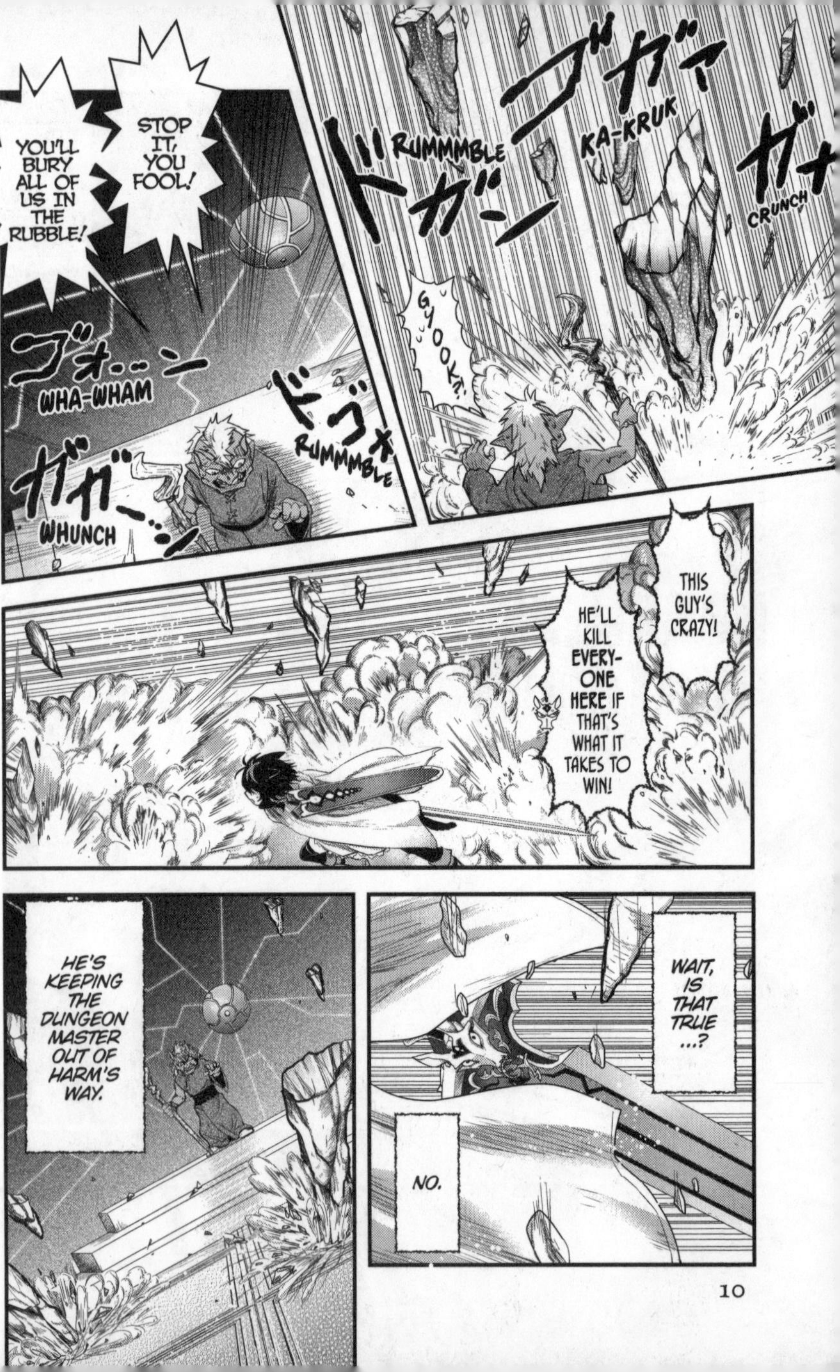
RUMMMBLE
KA-KRUK
CRUNCH
GYOOOK?!
STOP IT, YOU FOOL!
YOU'LL BURY ALL OF US IN THE RUBBLE!
WHA-WHAM
RUMMMBLE
WHUNCH
THIS GUY'S CRAZY!
HE'LL KILL EVERYONE HERE IF THAT'S WHAT IT TAKES TO WIN!
WAIT, IS THAT TRUE...?
NO.
HE'S KEEPING THE DUNGEON MASTER OUT OF HARM'S WAY.

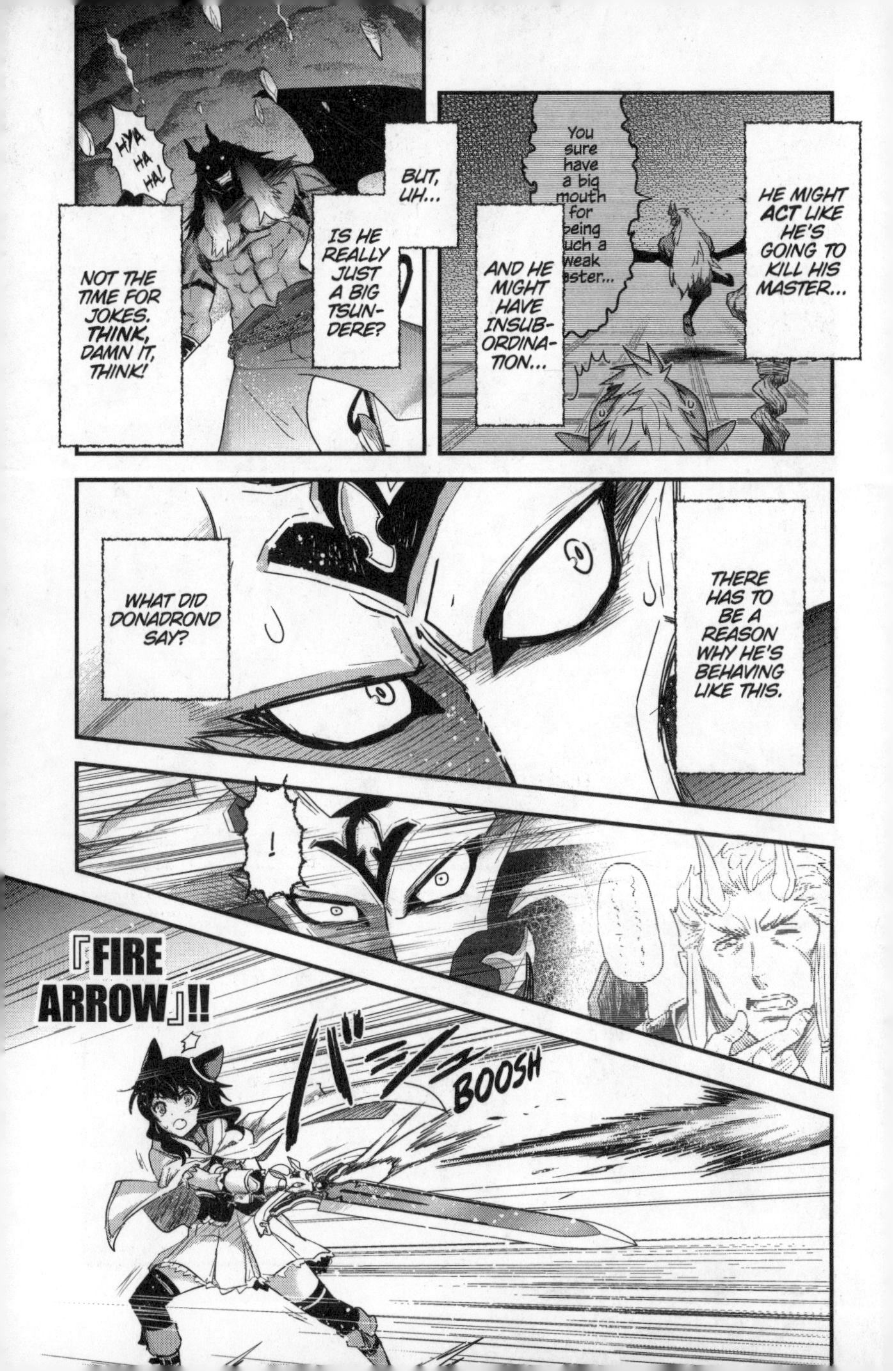
HE MIGHT ACT LIKE HE'S GOING TO KILL HIS MASTER...
You sure have a big mouth for eing uch a weak aster...
AND HE MIGHT HAVE INSUBORDINATION...
BUT, UH...
IS HE REALLY JUST A BIG TSUNDERE?
HYA HA HA!
NOT THE TIME FOR JOKES. THINK, DAMN IT, THINK!
THERE HAS TO BE A REASON WHY HE'S BEHAVING LIKE THIS.
WHAT DID DONADROND SAY?
!
『FIRE ARROW』!!
BOOSH

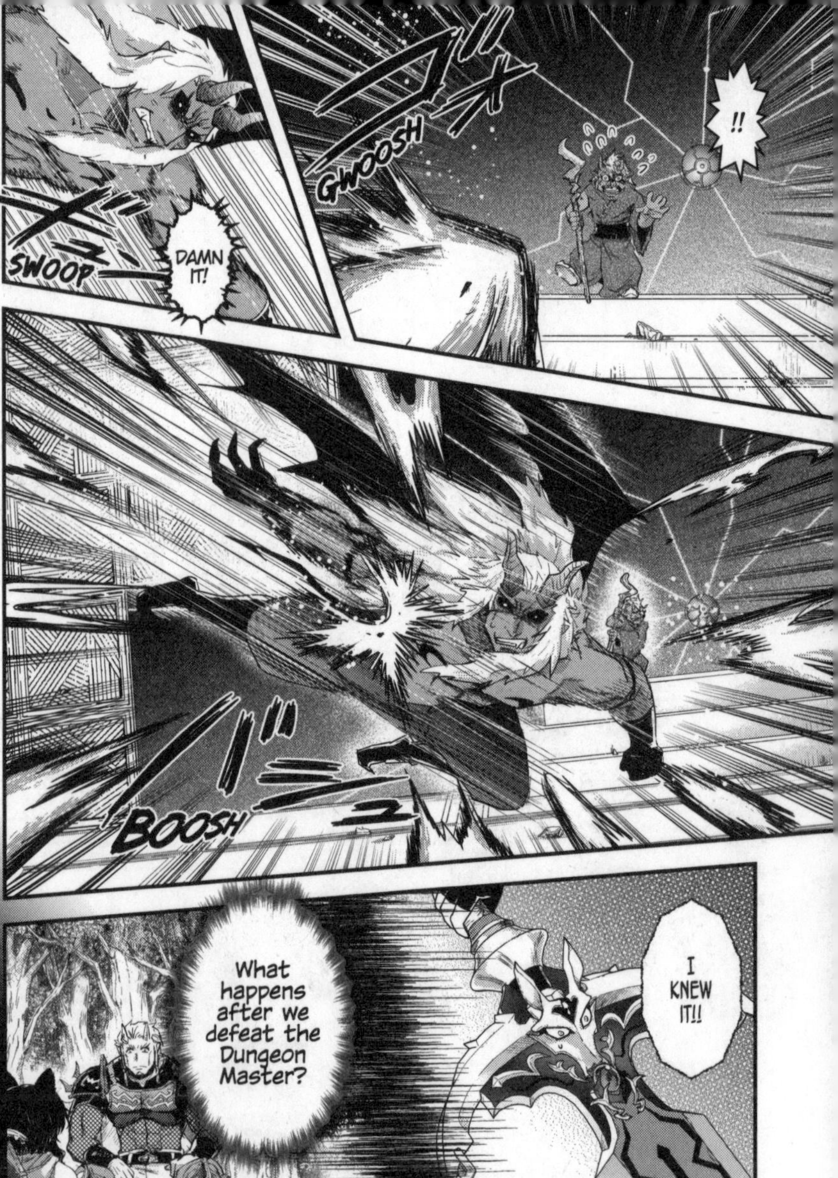

GWOOSH
!!
SWOOP
DAMN IT!
BOOSH
I KNEW IT!!
What happens after we defeat the Dungeon Master?

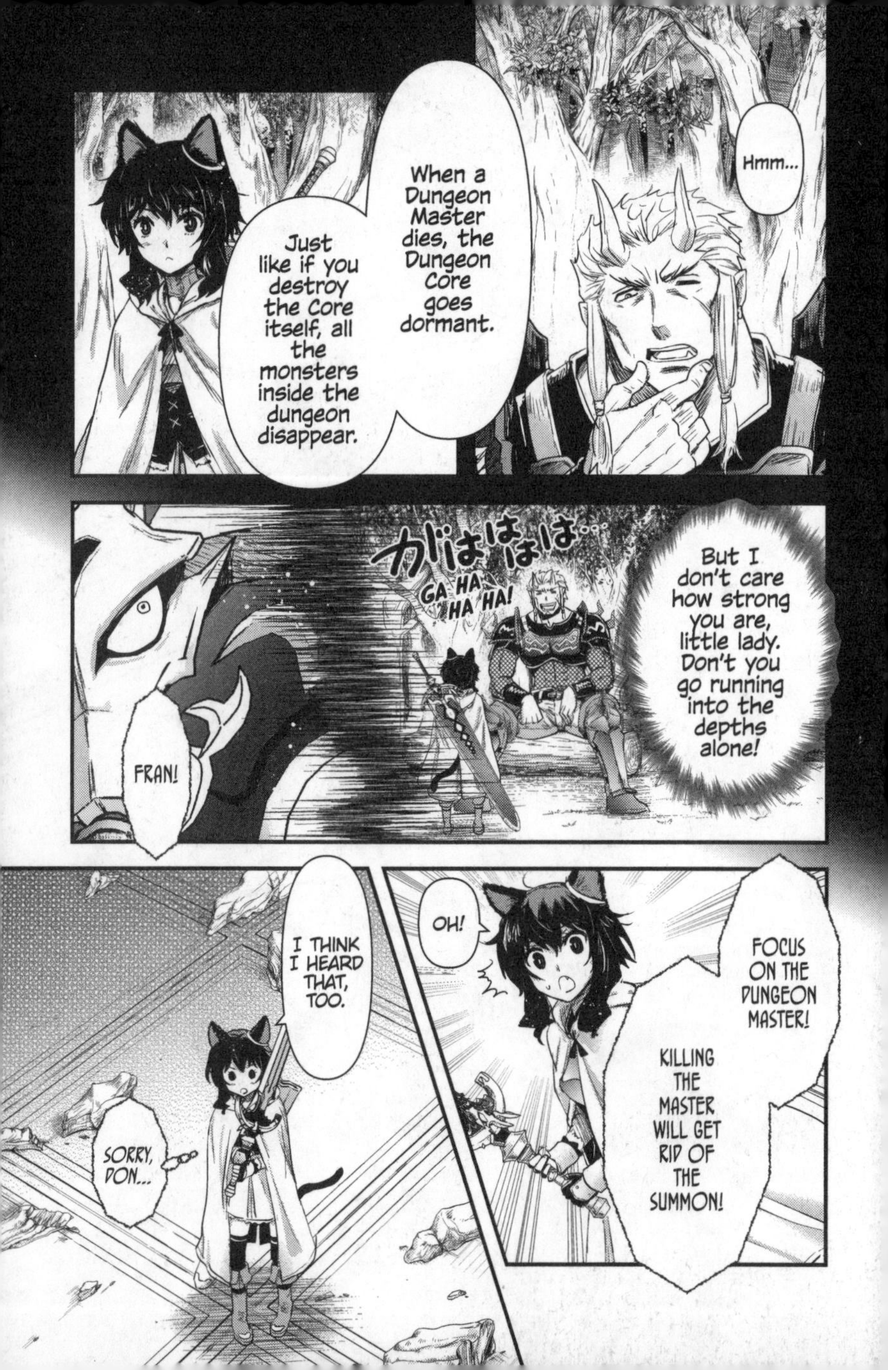
Hmm...
When a Dungeon Master dies, the Dungeon Core goes dormant.
Just like if you destroy the Core itself, all the monsters inside the dungeon disappear.
But I don't care how strong you are, little lady. Don't you go running into the depths alone!
ガははは…
GA HA HA HA!
FRAN!
FOCUS ON THE DUNGEON MASTER!
KILLING THE MASTER WILL GET RID OF THE SUMMON!
OH!
I THINK I HEARD THAT, TOO.
SORRY, DON...

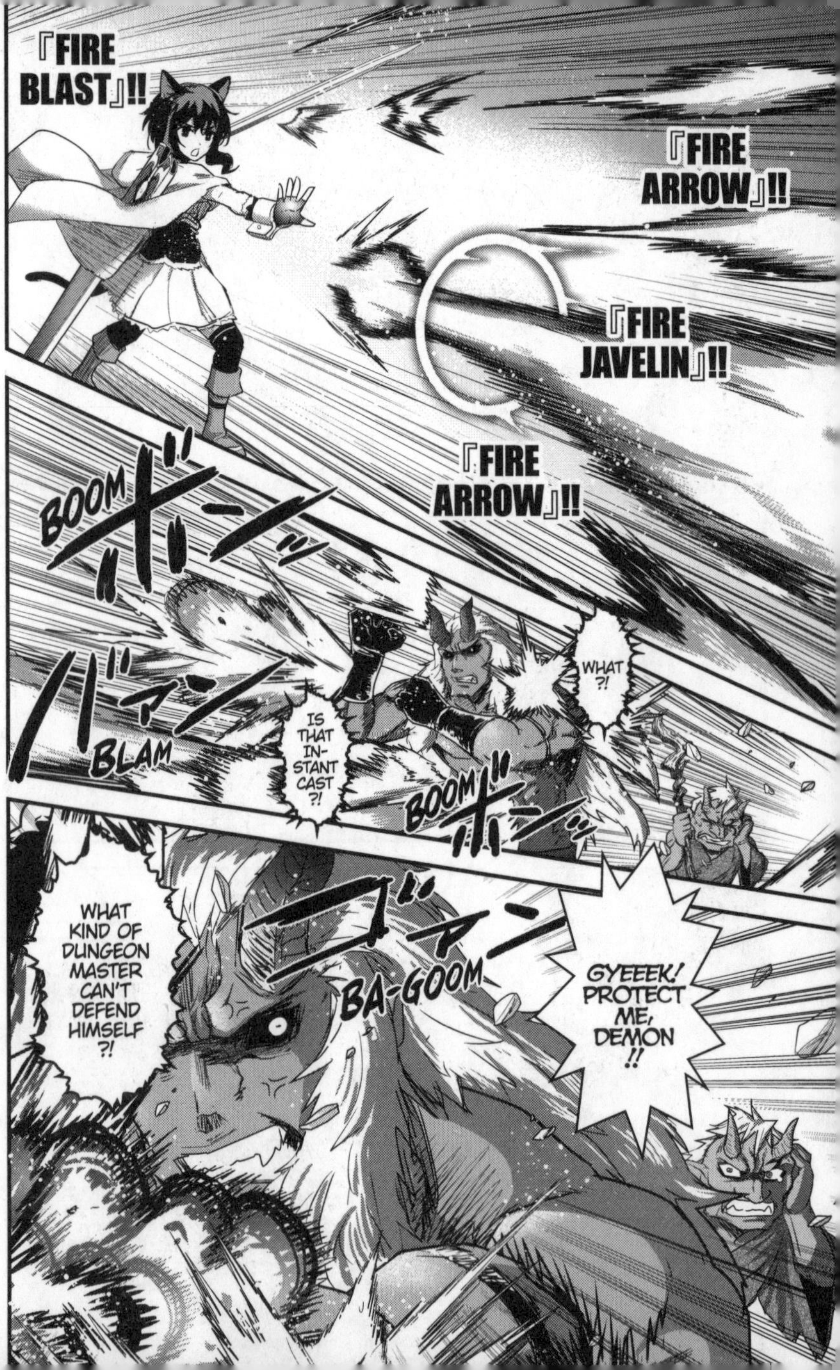
『FIRE BLAST』!!
『FIRE ARROW』!!
『FIRE JAVELIN』!!
『FIRE ARROW』!!
BOOM
WHAT ?!
IS THAT IN-STANT CAST ?!
BLAM
BOOM
GYEEEK! PROTECT ME, DEMON !!
BA-GOOM
WHAT KIND OF DUNGEON MASTER CAN'T DEFEND HIMSELF ?!

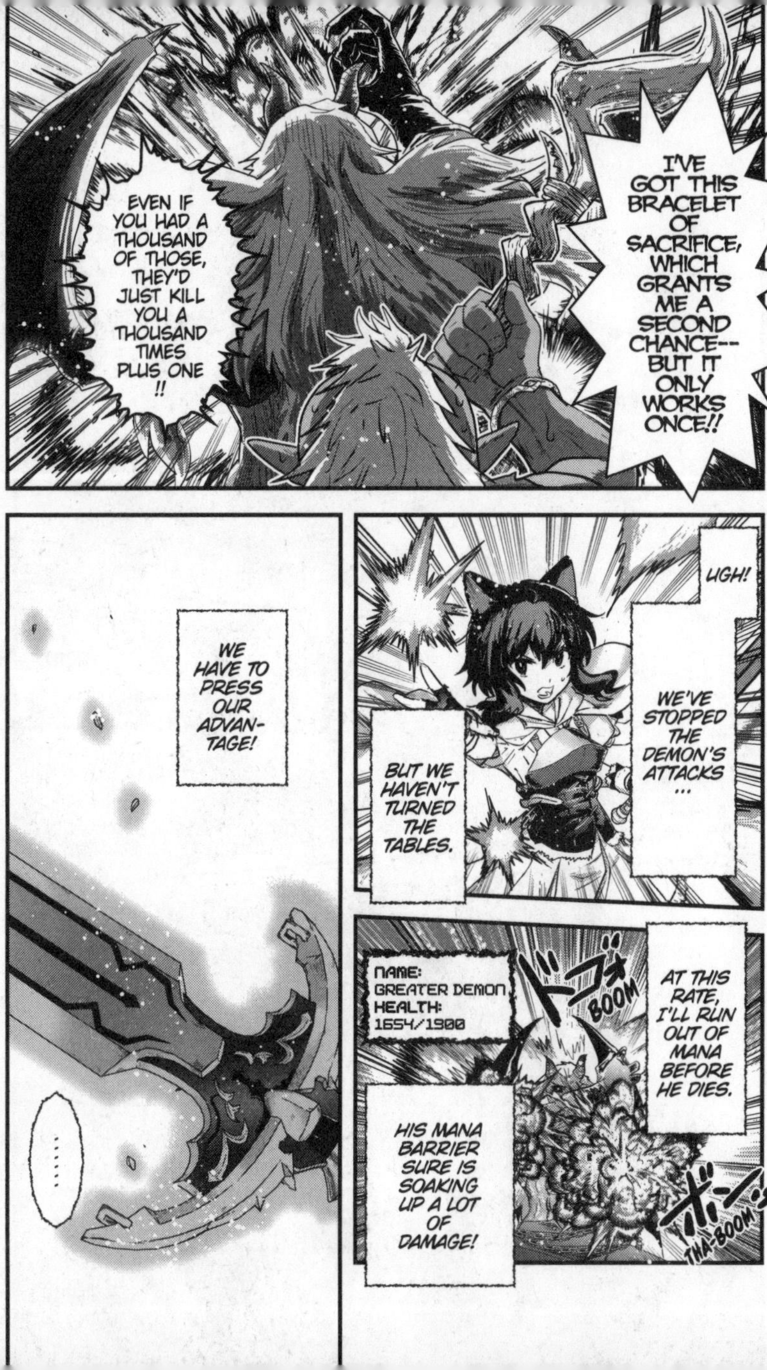
I'VE GOT THIS BRACELET OF SACRIFICE, WHICH GRANTS ME A SECOND CHANCE-- BUT IT ONLY WORKS ONCE!!
EVEN IF YOU HAD A THOUSAND OF THOSE, THEY'D JUST KILL YOU A THOUSAND TIMES PLUS ONE !!
UGH!
WE'VE STOPPED THE DEMON'S ATTACKS ...
BUT WE HAVEN'T TURNED THE TABLES.
AT THIS RATE, I'LL RUN OUT OF MANA BEFORE HE DIES.
NAME: GREATER DEMON HEALTH: 1654/1900
BOOM
HIS MANA BARRIER SURE IS SOAKING UP A LOT OF DAMAGE!
THA-BOOM
WE HAVE TO PRESS OUR ADVANTAGE!
......

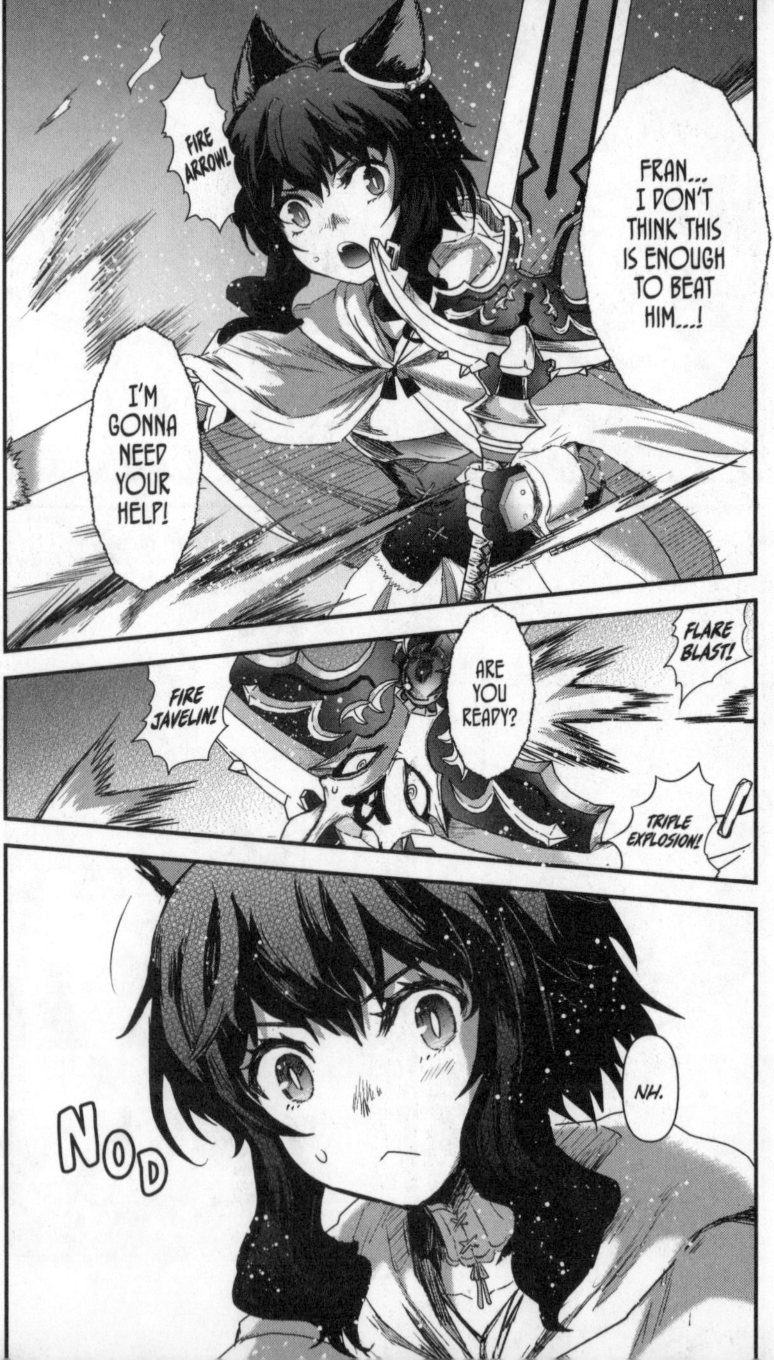
FRAN... I DON'T THINK THIS IS ENOUGH TO BEAT HIM...!
FIRE ARROW!
I'M GONNA NEED YOUR HELP!
FLARE BLAST!
ARE YOU READY?
FIRE JAVELIN!
TRIPLE EXPLOSION!
NH.
NOD

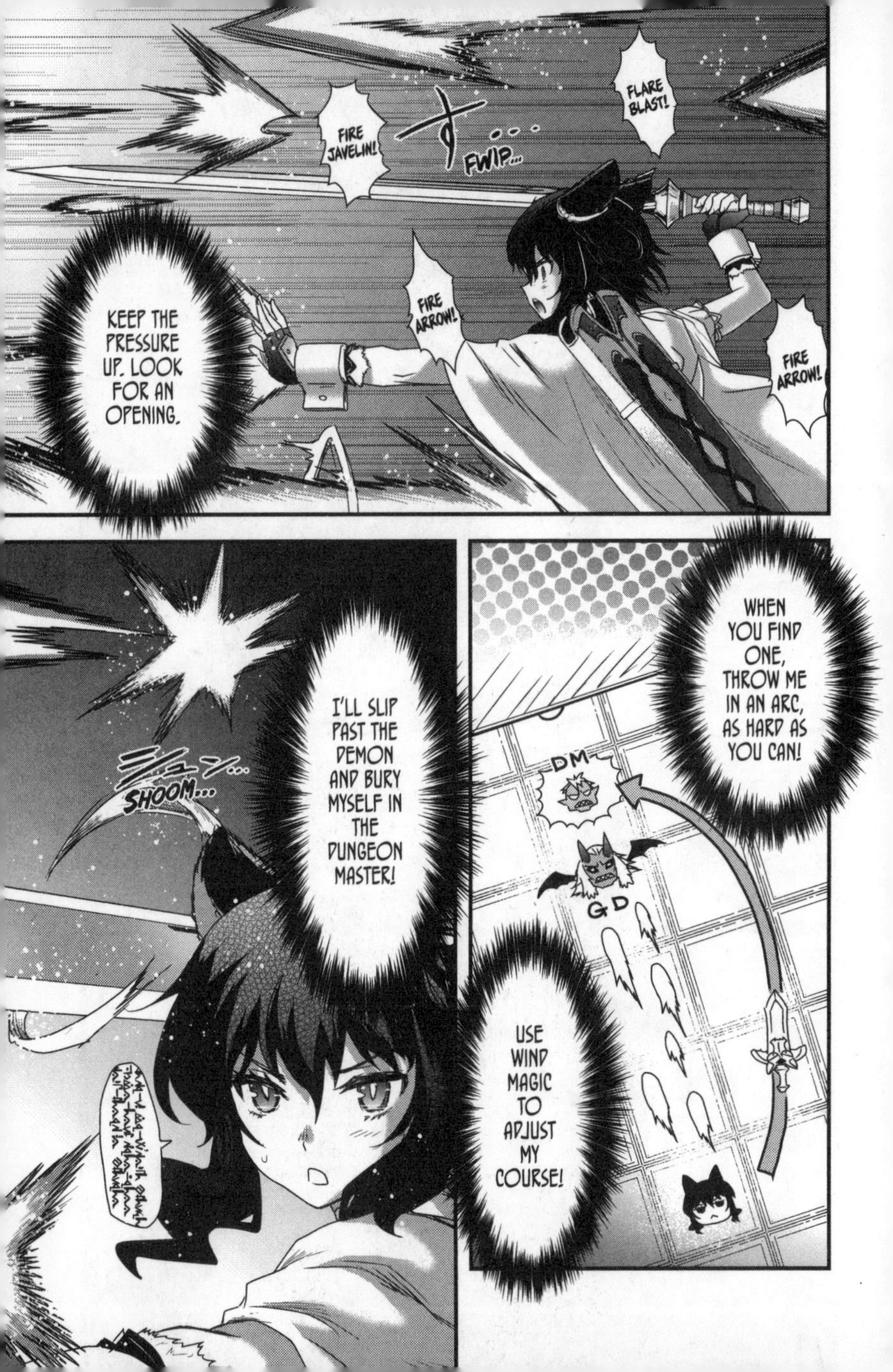
FLARE BLAST!
...
FWIP...
FIRE JAVELIN!
FIRE ARROW!
FIRE ARROW!
KEEP THE PRESSURE UP. LOOK FOR AN OPENING.
WHEN YOU FIND ONE, THROW ME IN AN ARC, AS HARD AS YOU CAN!
DM
GD
USE WIND MAGIC TO ADJUST MY COURSE!
I'LL SLIP PAST THE DEMON AND BURY MYSELF IN THE DUNGEON MASTER!
SHOOM...

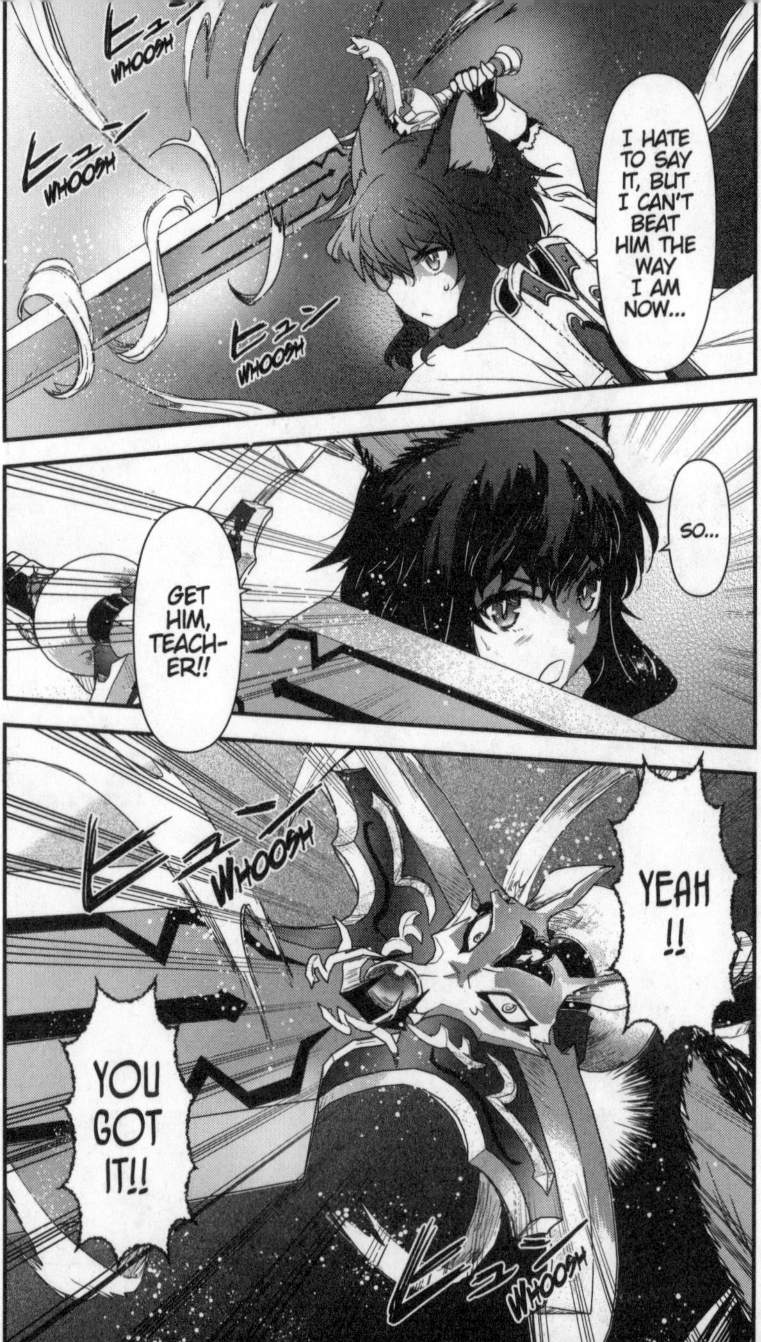
I HATE TO SAY IT, BUT I CAN'T BEAT HIM THE WAY I AM NOW...
ヒュン WHOOSH
ヒュン WHOOSH
ヒュン WHOOSH
SO...
GET HIM, TEACHER!!
YEAH!!
WHOOSH
YOU GOT IT!!
WHOOSH

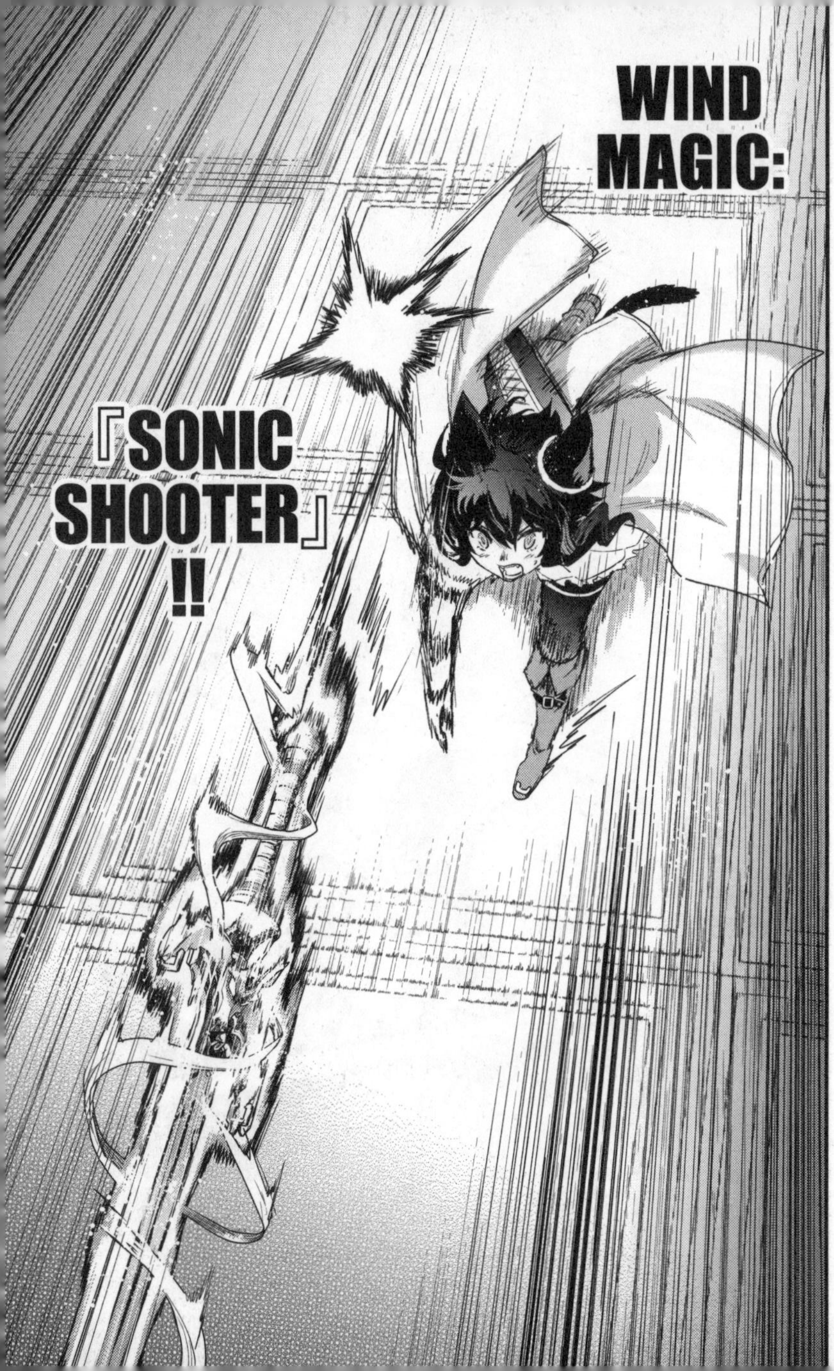
WIND MAGIC:
『SONIC SHOOTER』!!

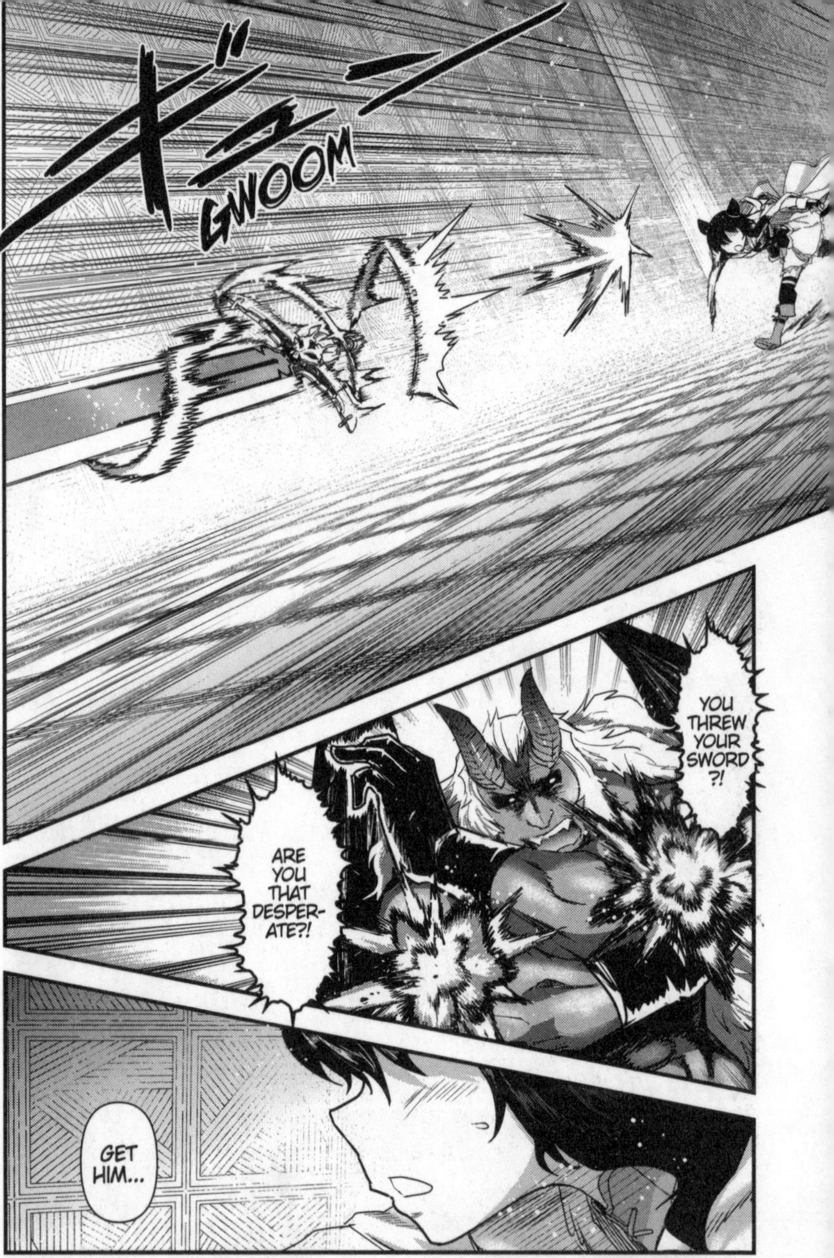
GWOOM
YOU THREW YOUR SWORD?!
ARE YOU THAT DESPERATE?!
GET HIM...

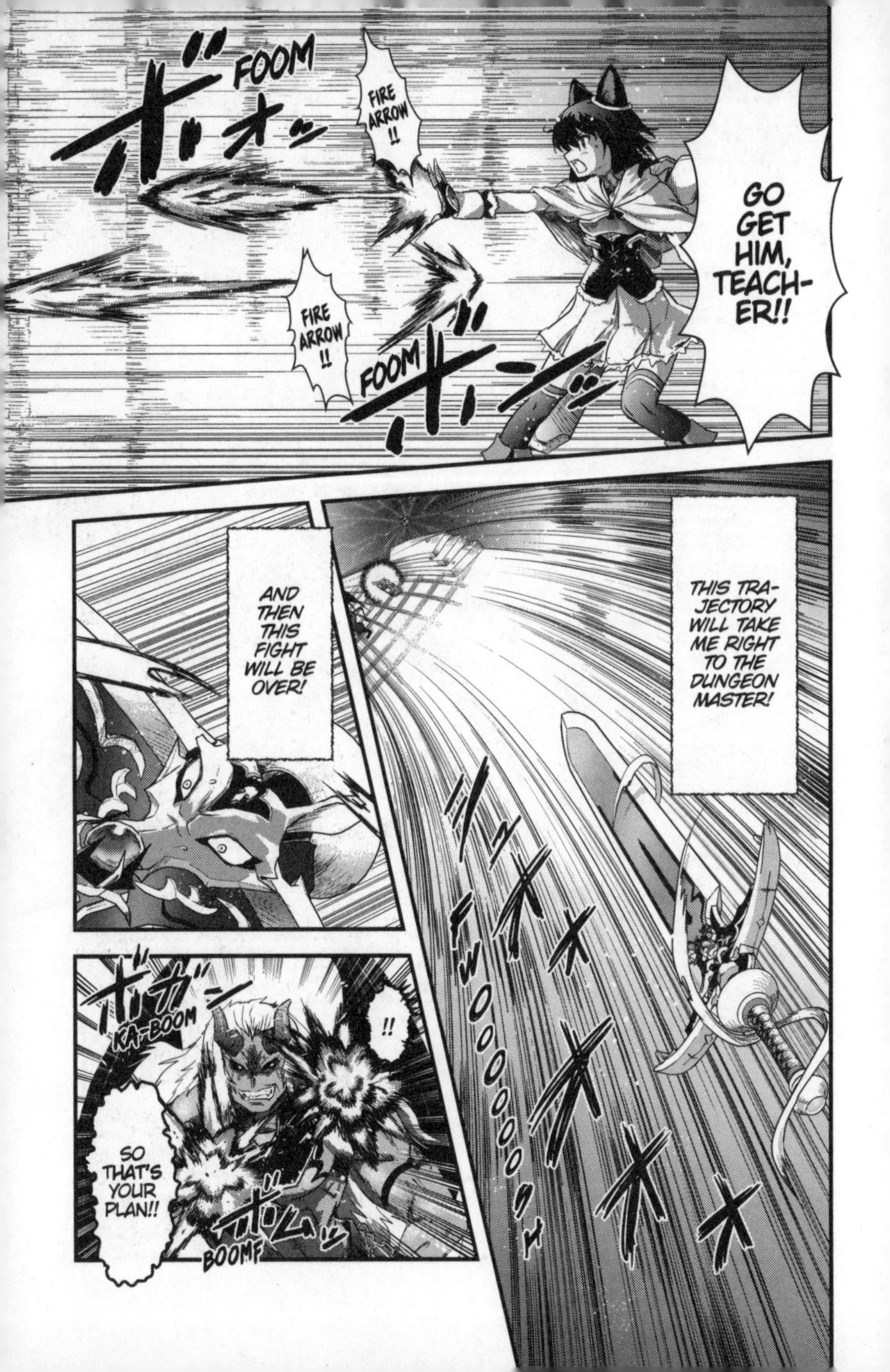
GO GET HIM, TEACHER!!
FIRE ARROW!!
FOOM
FIRE ARROW!!
FOOM
THIS TRAJECTORY WILL TAKE ME RIGHT TO THE DUNGEON MASTER!
AND THEN THIS FIGHT WILL BE OVER!
!!
KA-BOOM
SO THAT'S YOUR PLAN!!
BOOMF

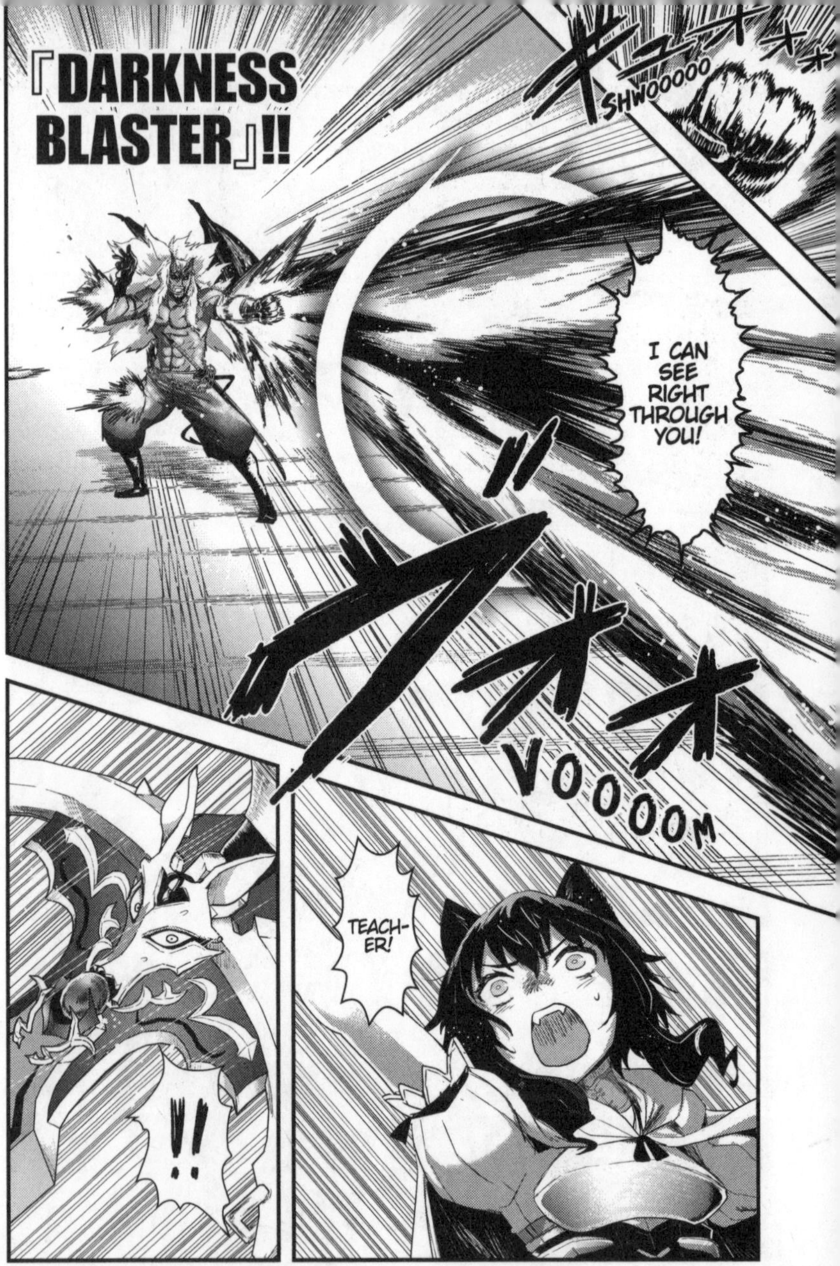
『DARKNESS BLASTER』!!
SHWOOOOO
I CAN SEE RIGHT THROUGH YOU!
VOOOOOM
TEACH-ER!
!!

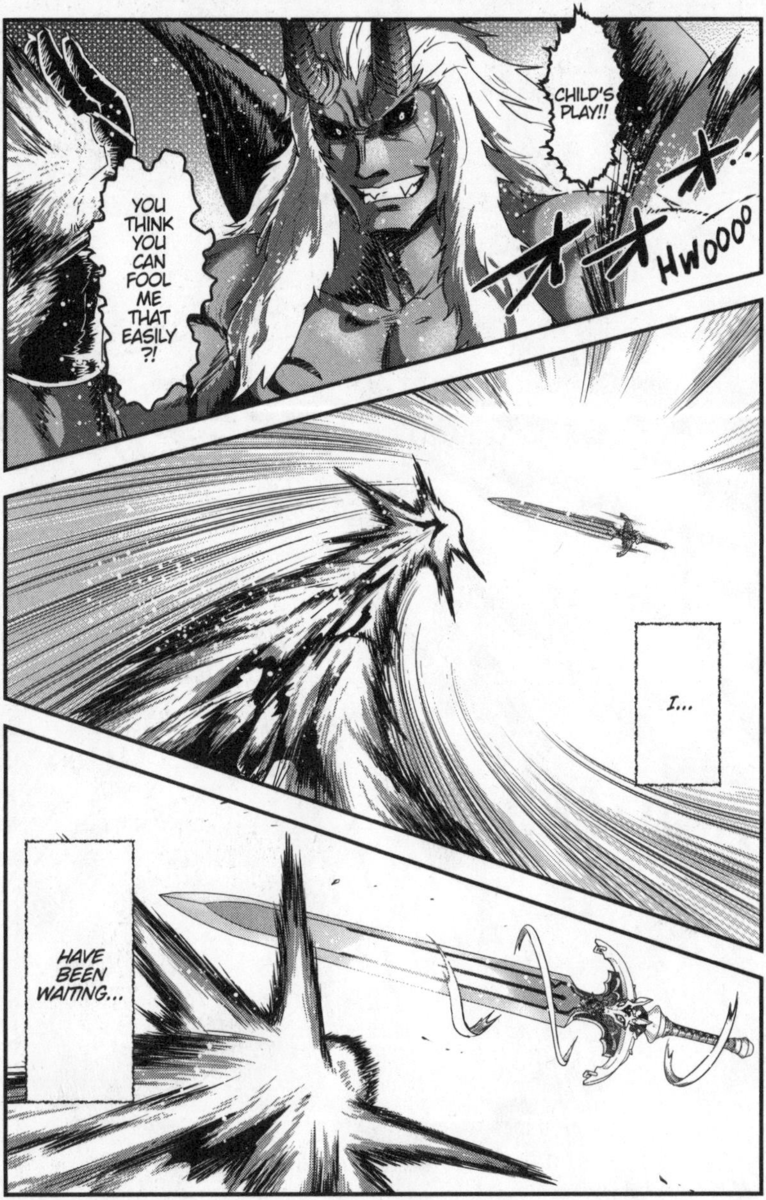
CHILD'S PLAY!!
オオオ..
HWOOOO
YOU THINK YOU CAN FOOL ME THAT EASILY ?!
I...
HAVE BEEN WAITING...

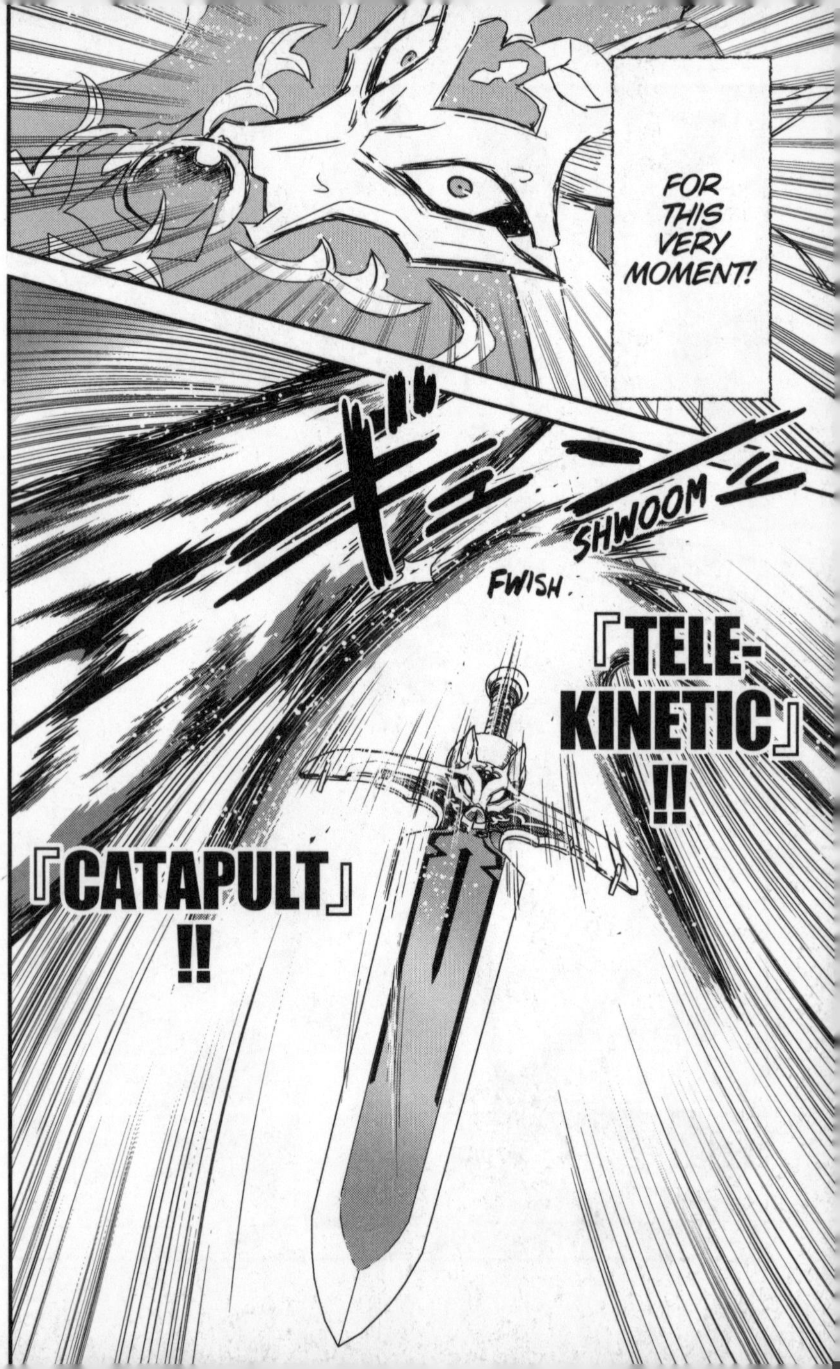
FOR THIS VERY MOMENT!
SHWOOM
FWISH
『TELE-KINETIC』!!
『CATAPULT』!!

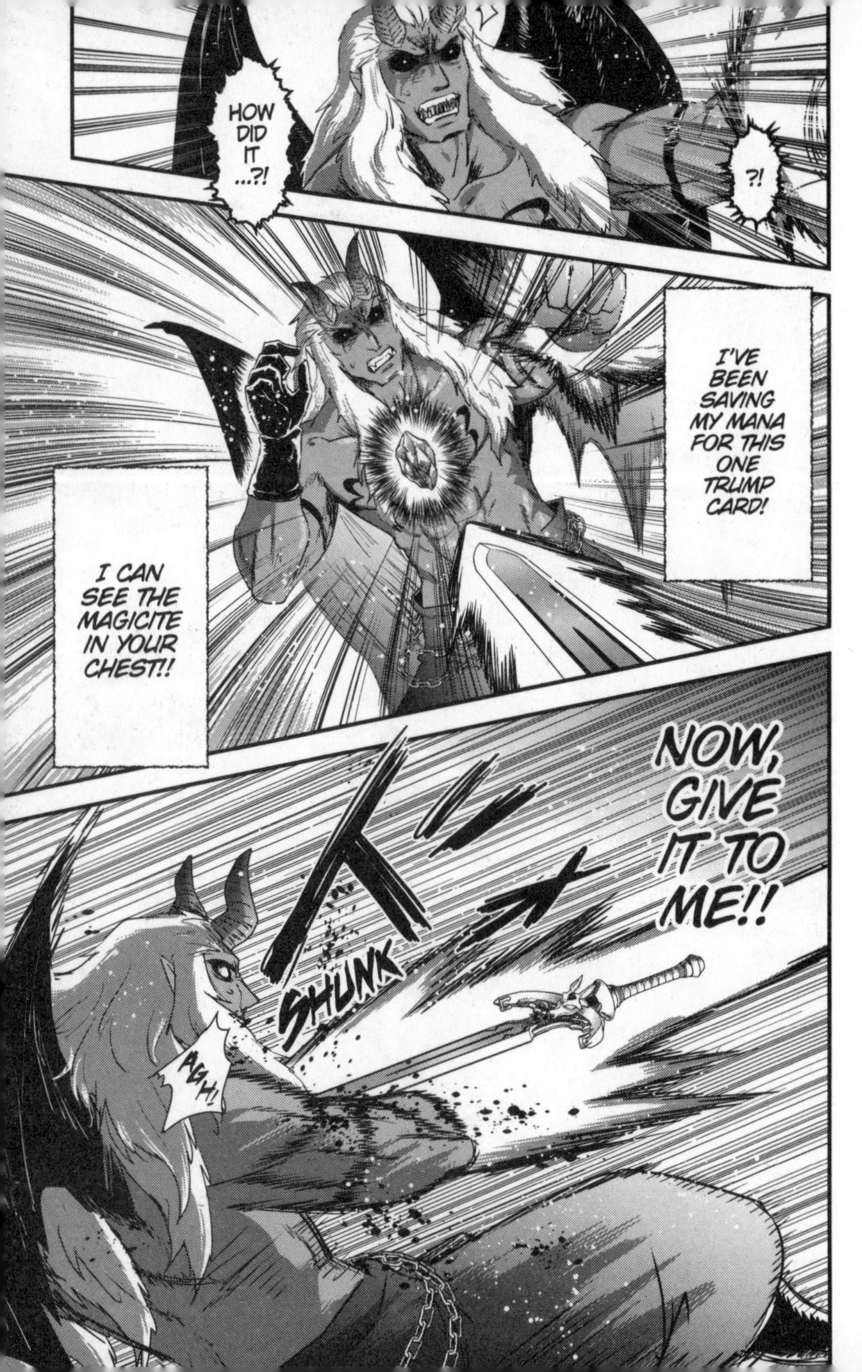
?!
HOW DID IT ...?!
I'VE BEEN SAVING MY MANA FOR THIS ONE TRUMP CARD!
I CAN SEE THE MAGICITE IN YOUR CHEST!!
NOW, GIVE IT TO ME!!
SHUNK
AGH!

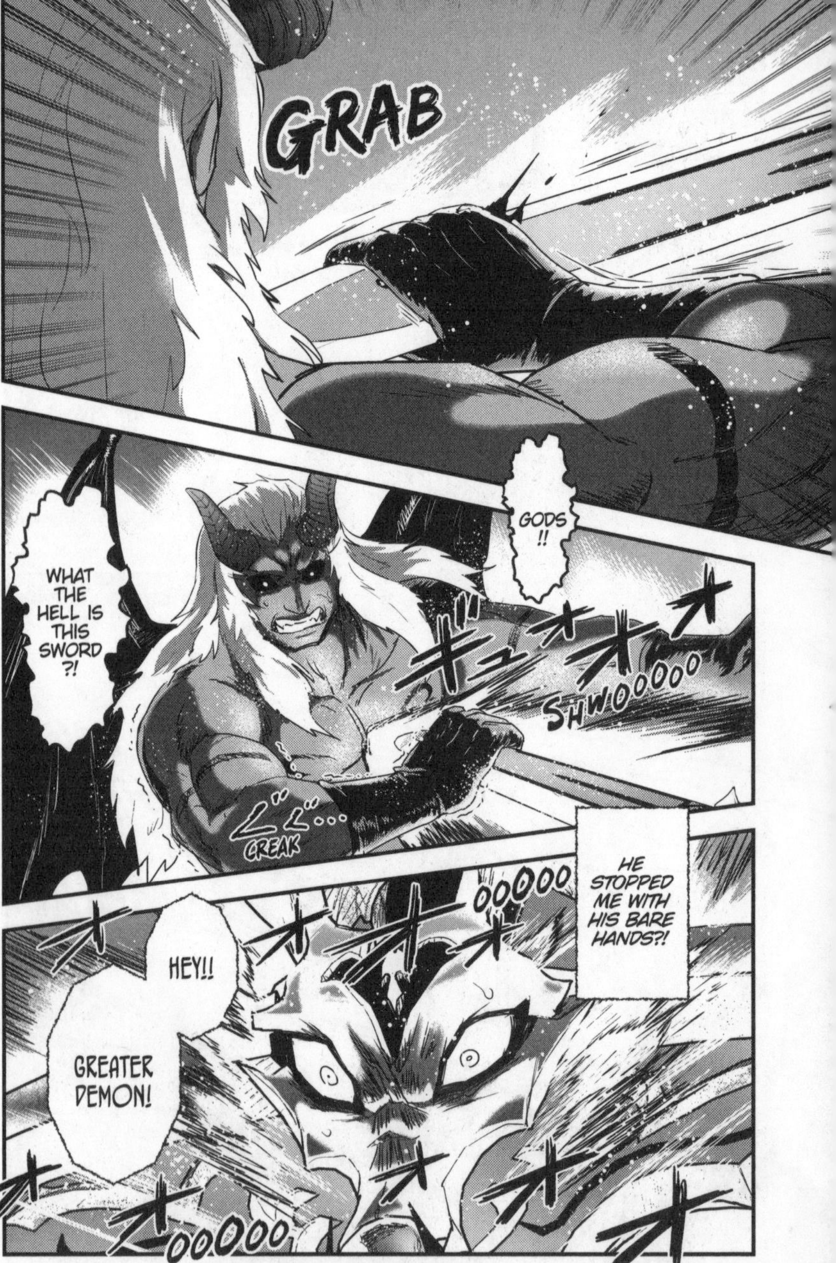
GRAB
GODS!!
SHWOOOOO
WHAT THE HELL IS THIS SWORD?!
CREAK
HE STOPPED ME WITH HIS BARE HANDS?!
OOOOO
HEY!!
GREATER DEMON!
OOOOO

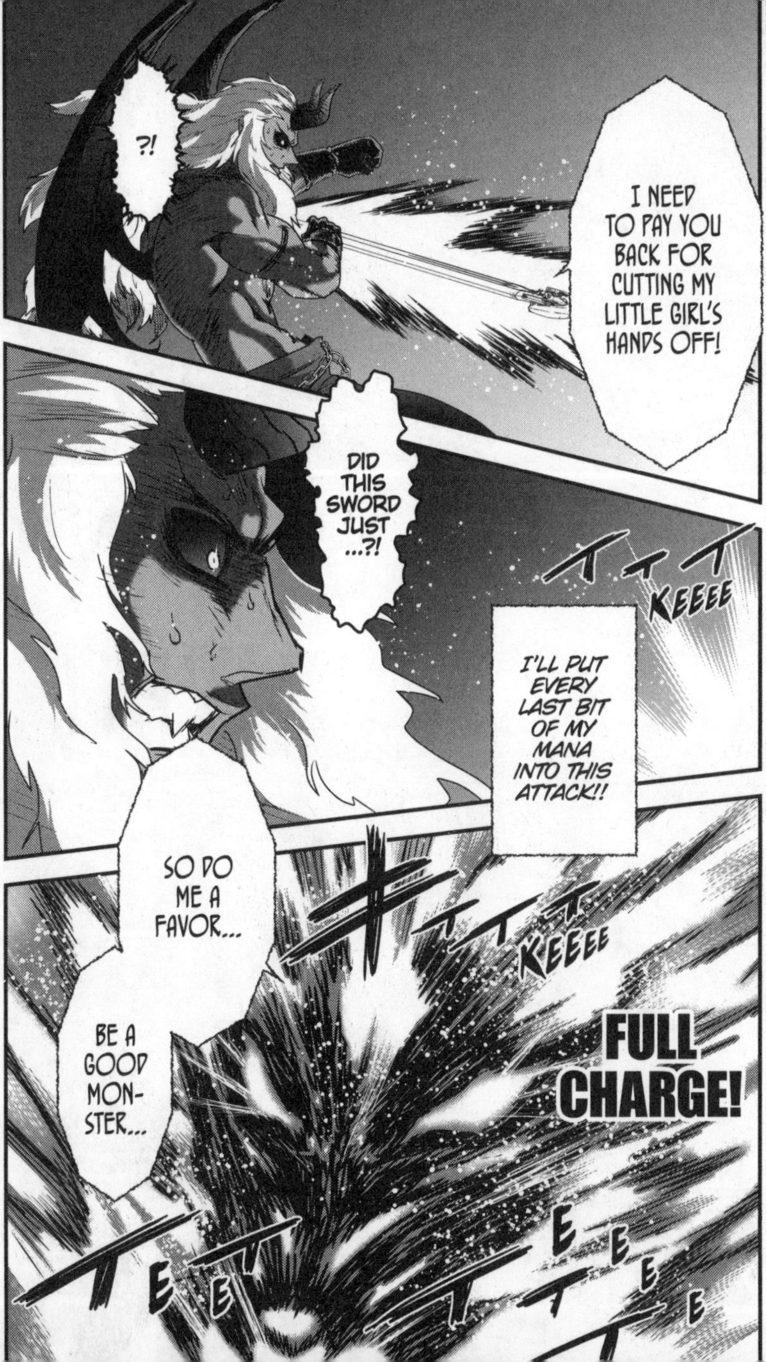
I NEED TO PAY YOU BACK FOR CUTTING MY LITTLE GIRL'S HANDS OFF!
?!
DID THIS SWORD JUST ...?!
KEEEE
I'LL PUT EVERY LAST BIT OF MY MANA INTO THIS ATTACK!!
KEEEE
SO DO ME A FAVOR...
FULL CHARGE!
BE A GOOD MON-STER...
EEEEE

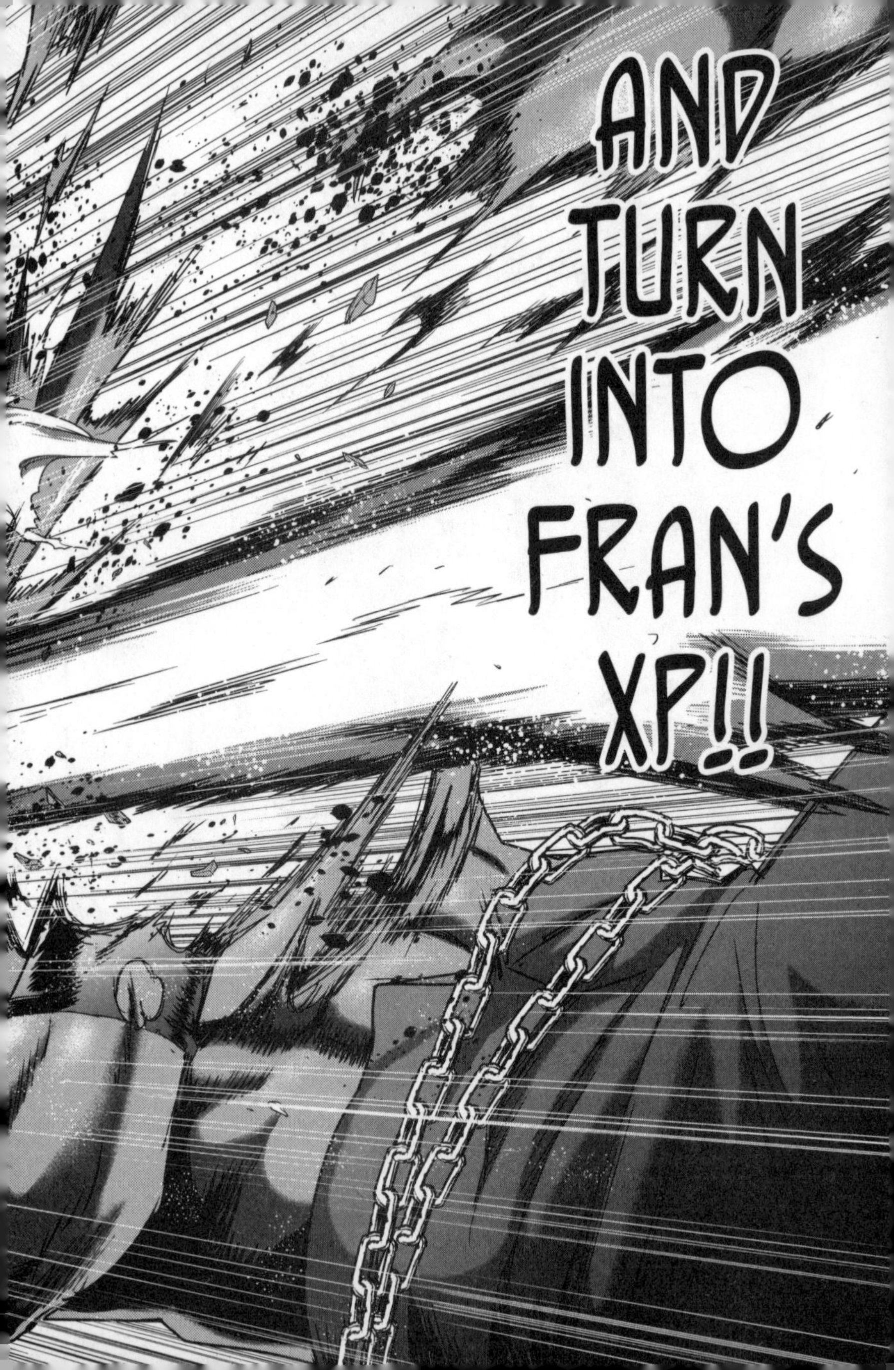
AND TURN INTO FRAN'S XP!!

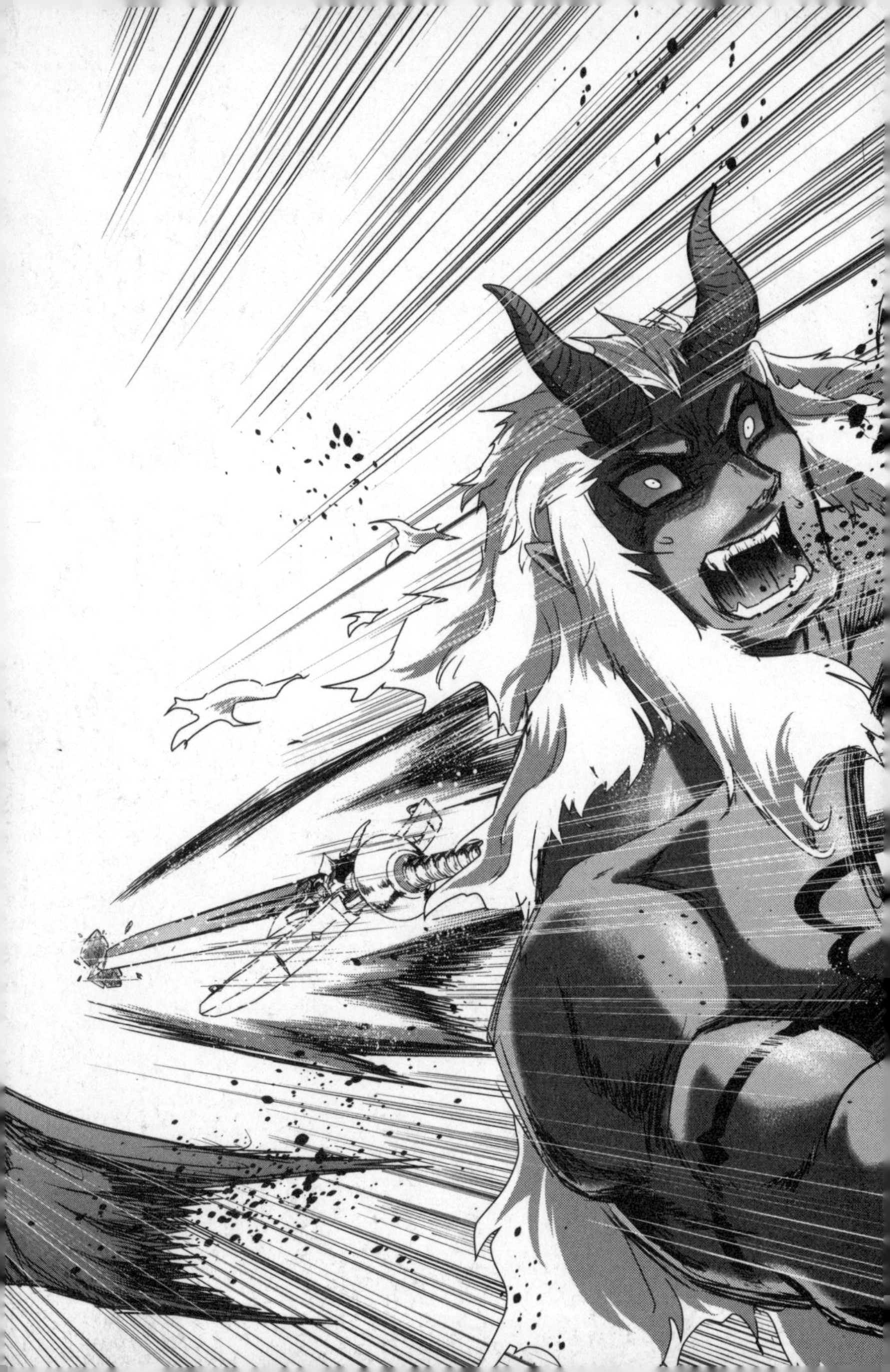

Reincarnated
as a sword

Chapter 13: Demon Killer

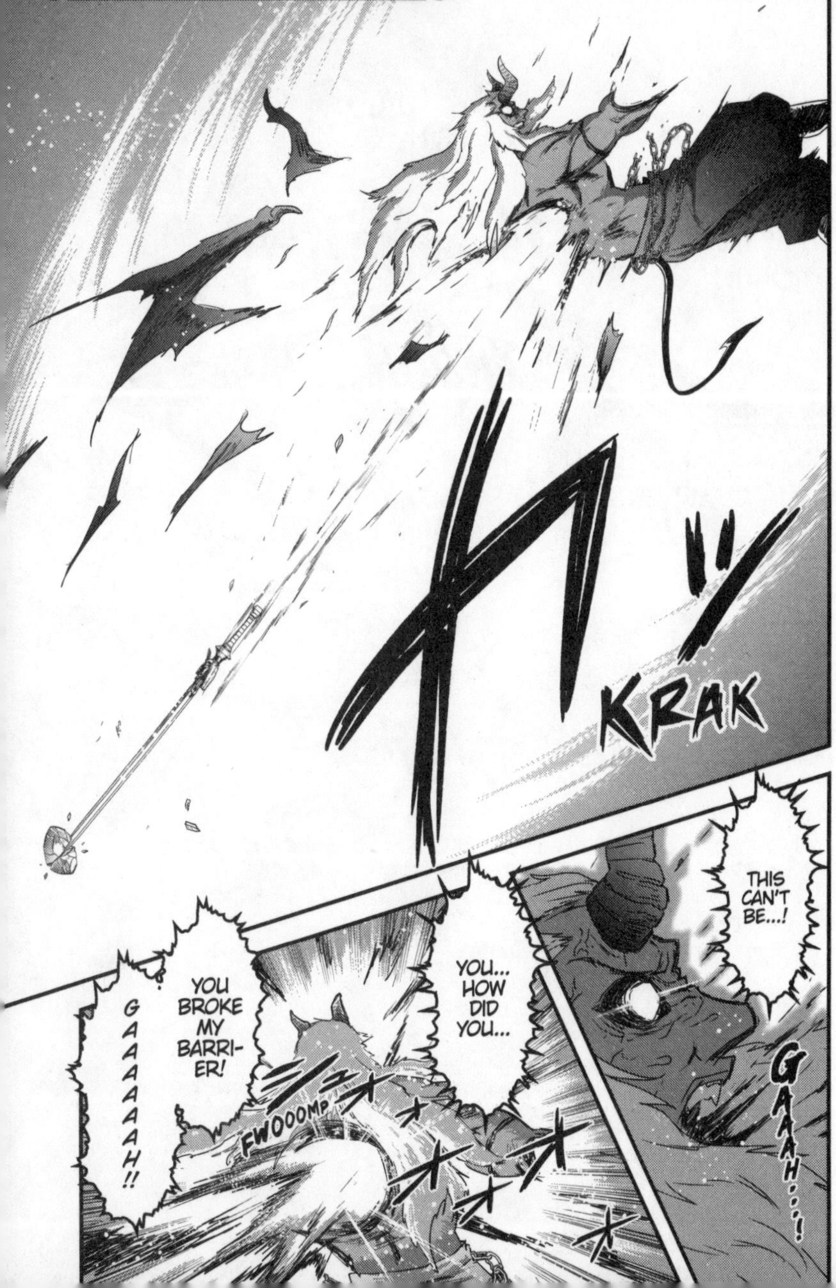
KRAK
THIS CAN'T BE...!
GAAAH...!
YOU... HOW DID YOU...
YOU BROKE MY BARRI-ER!
GAAAAAAAH!!
FWOOOMP

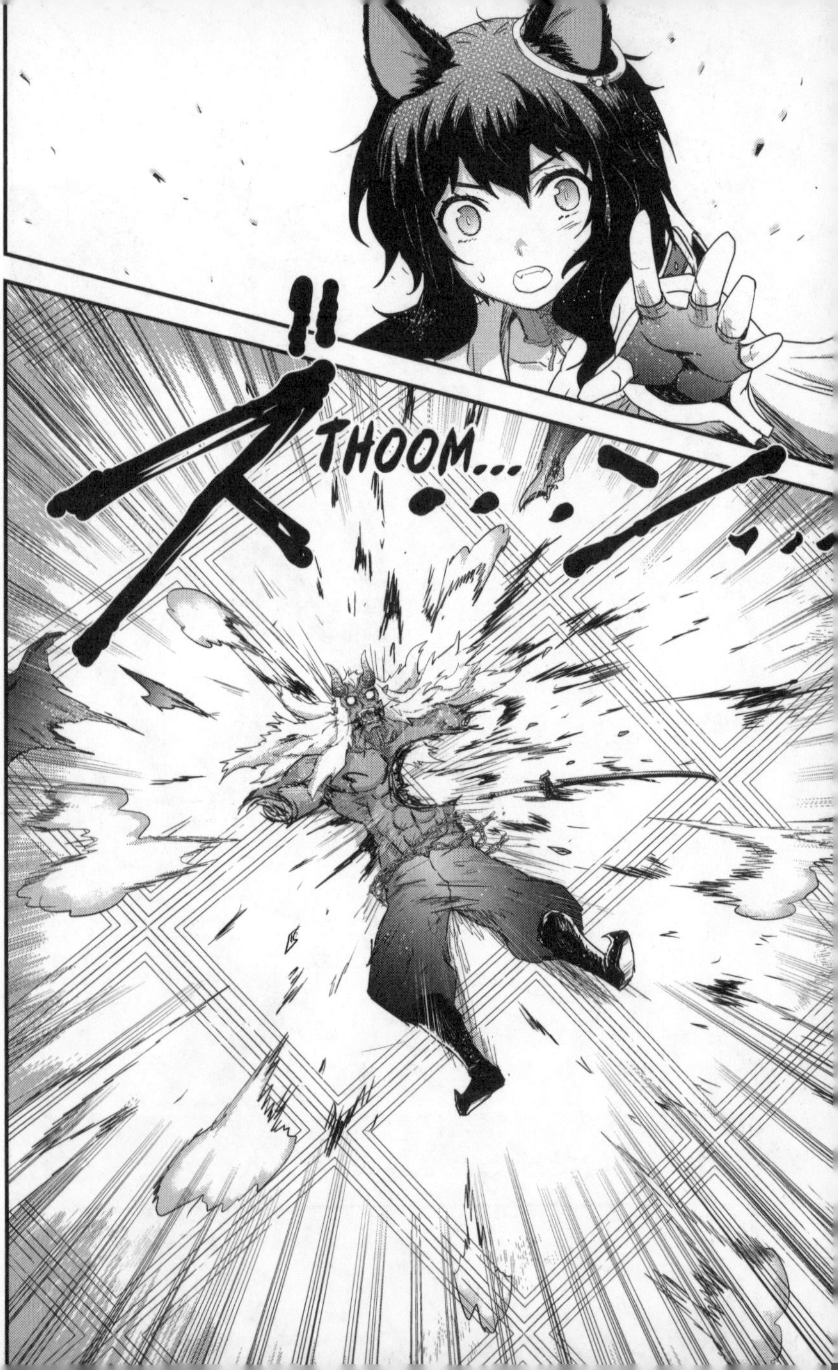
THOOM...

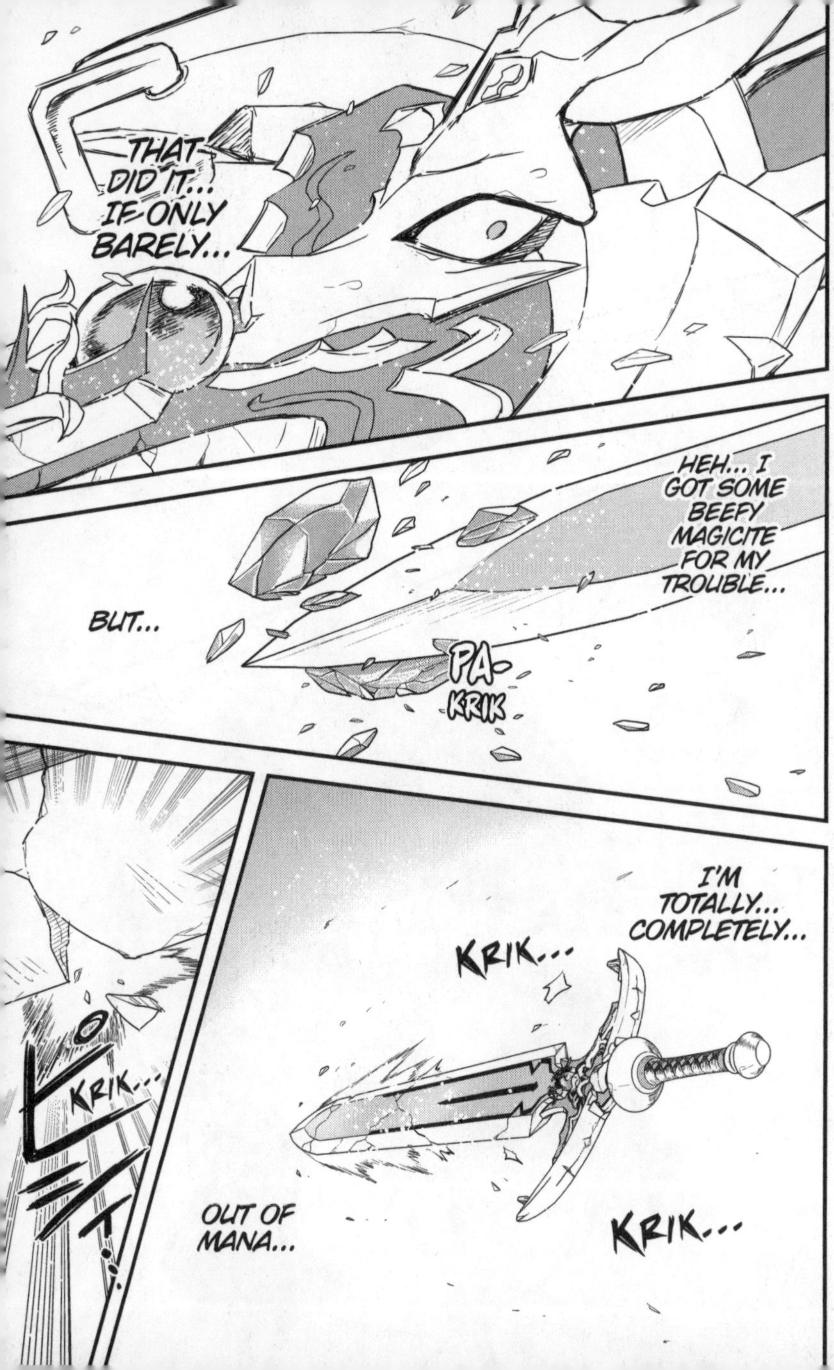
THAT DID IT... IF ONLY BARELY...
HEH... I GOT SOME BEEFY MAGICITE FOR MY TROUBLE...
PA-KRIK
BUT...
I'M TOTALLY... COMPLETELY...
KRIK...
KRIK...
OUT OF MANA...
KRIK...

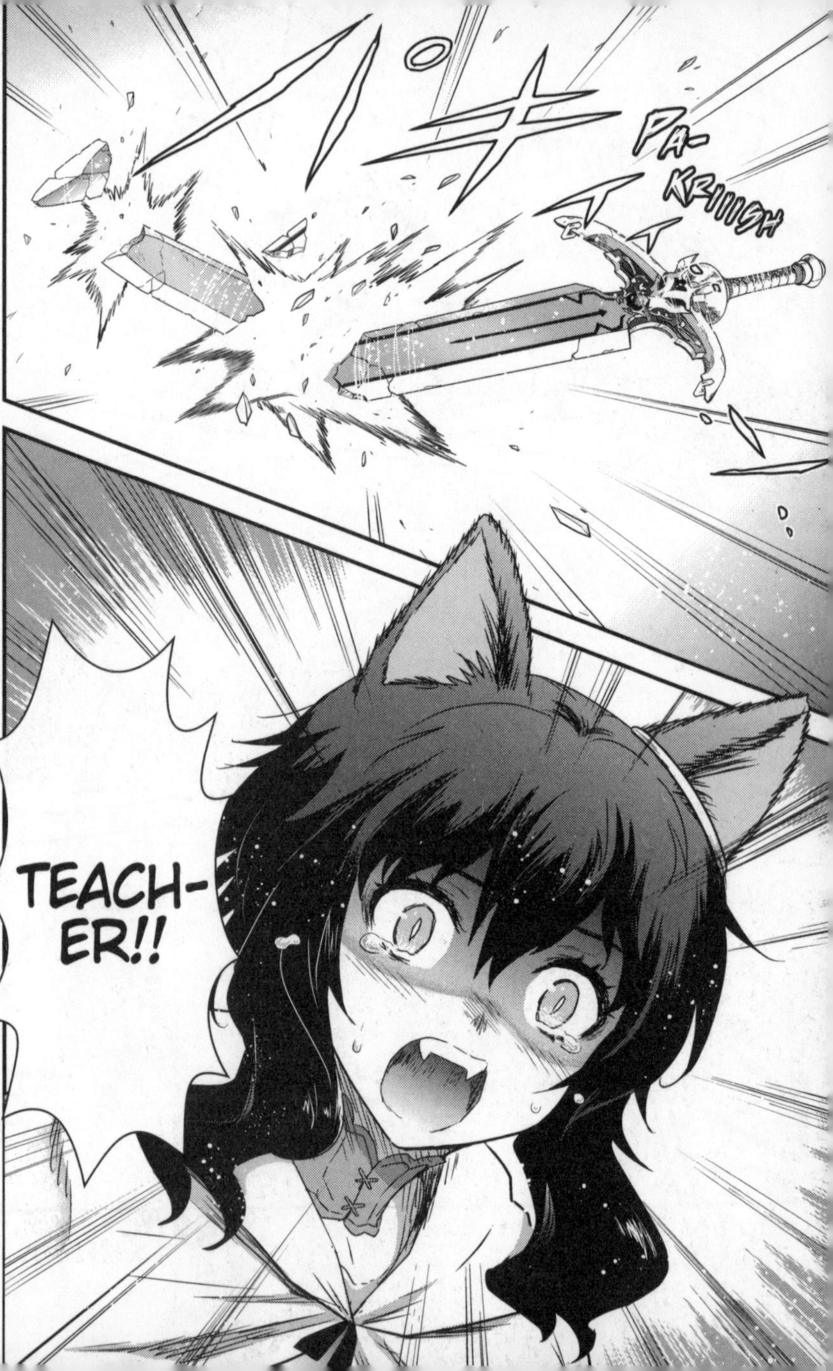
PA-KRIIIISH
TEACH-ER!!

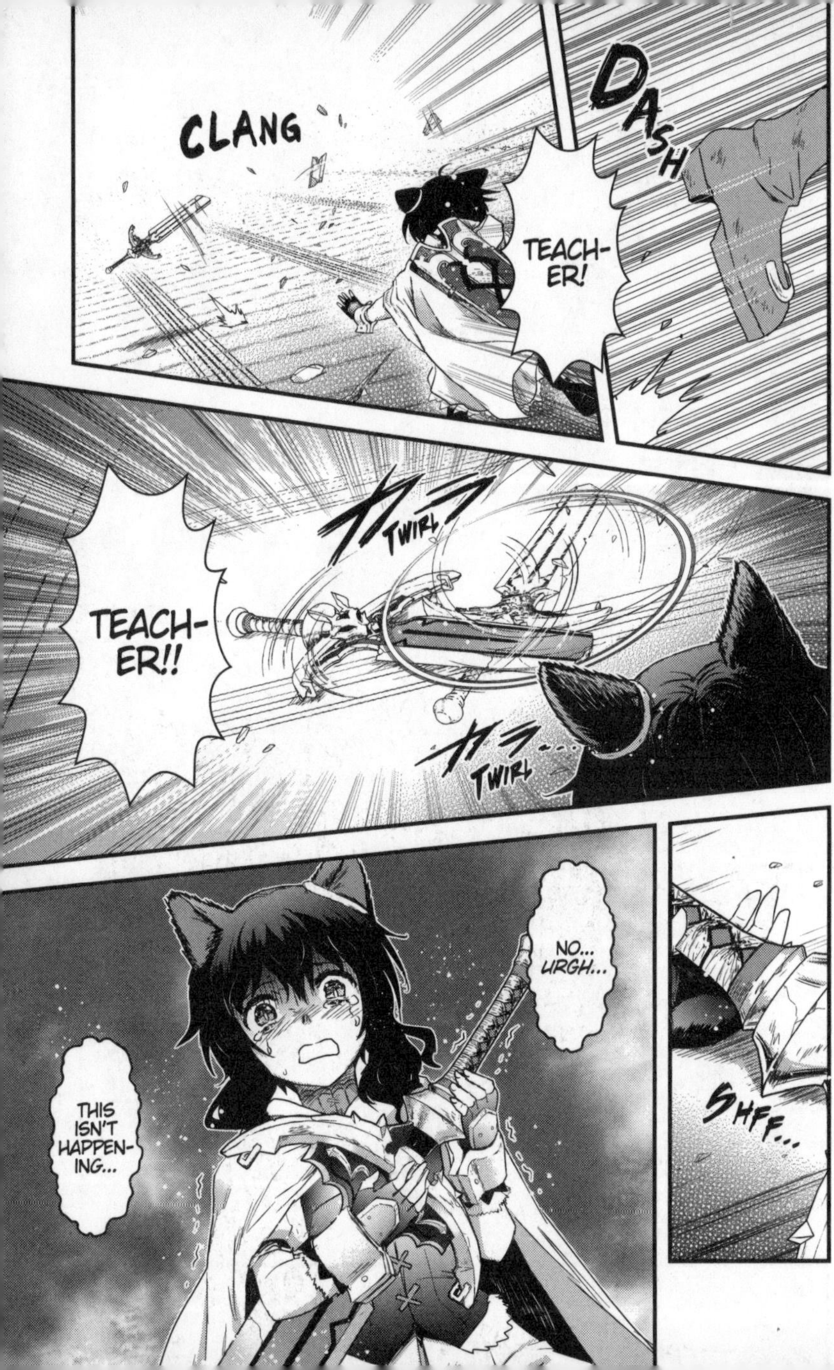
DASH
TEACH-ER!
CLANG
TWIRL
TEACH-ER!!
TWIRL
SHFF...
NO... URGH...
THIS ISN'T HAPPEN-ING...

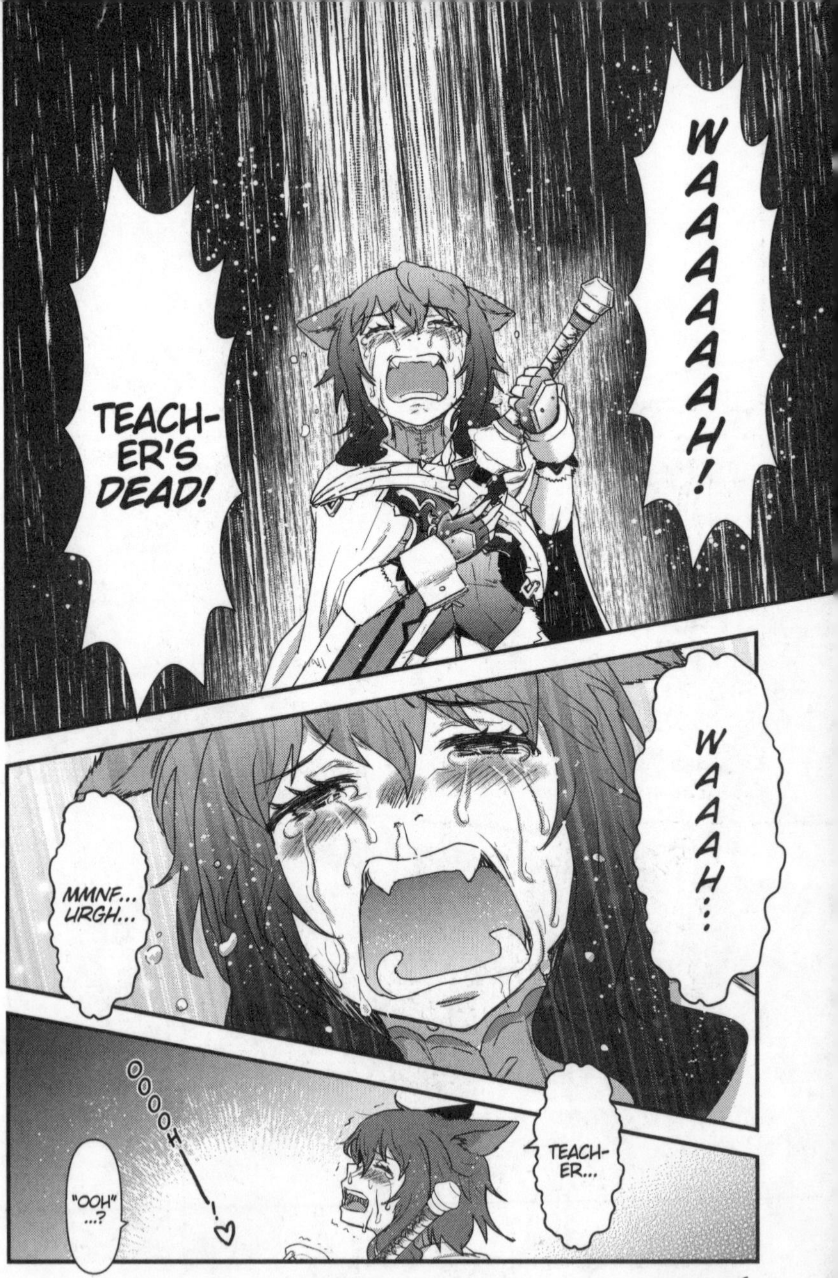
WAAAAAAH!
TEACH-ER'S DEAD!
WAAAH...
MMNF... URGH...
TEACH-ER...
OOOOOH—!♡
"OOH" ...?

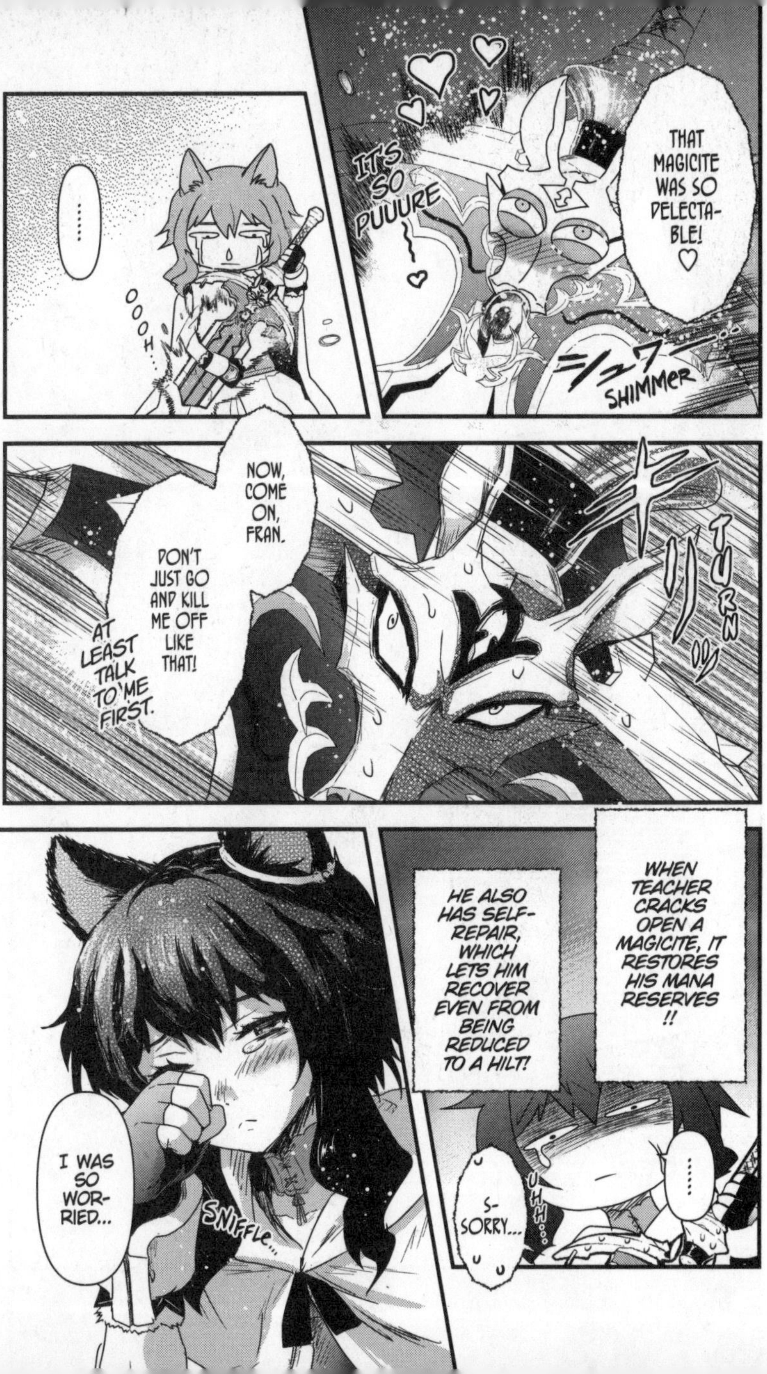
THAT MAGICITE WAS SO DELECTABLE! ♡
IT'S SO PUUURE~ ♡
SHIMMER
......
OOOH...
TURN
NOW, COME ON, FRAN.
DON'T JUST GO AND KILL ME OFF LIKE THAT!
AT LEAST TALK TO ME FIRST.
WHEN TEACHER CRACKS OPEN A MAGICITE, IT RESTORES HIS MANA RESERVES!!
HE ALSO HAS SELF-REPAIR, WHICH LETS HIM RECOVER EVEN FROM BEING REDUCED TO A HILT!
......
UHHH...
S-SORRY...
I WAS SO WORRIED...
SNIFFLE...

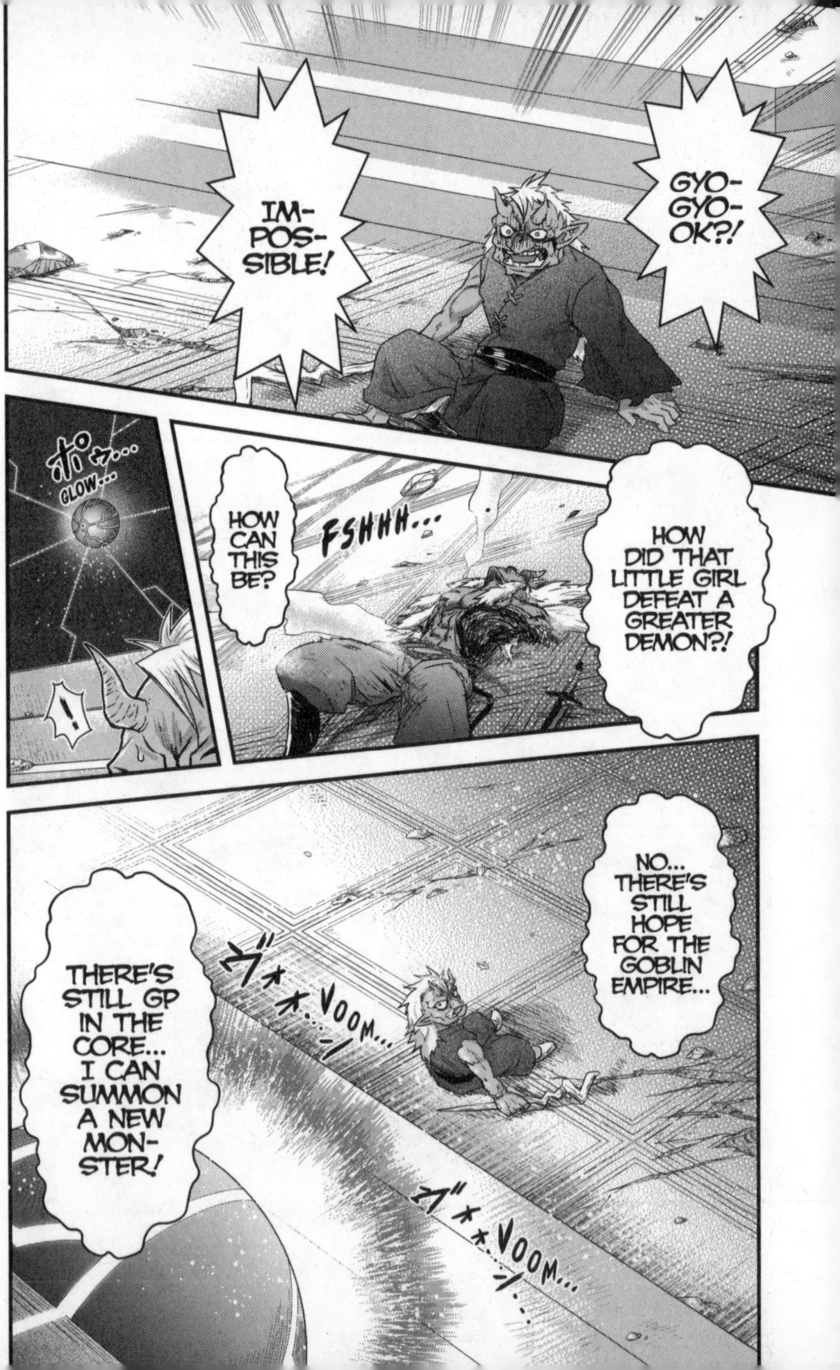
GYO-GYO-OK?!
IM-POS-SIBLE!
HOW DID THAT LITTLE GIRL DEFEAT A GREATER DEMON?!
FSHHH...
HOW CAN THIS BE?
GLOW...
!
NO... THERE'S STILL HOPE FOR THE GOBLIN EMPIRE...
VOOM...
THERE'S STILL GP IN THE CORE... I CAN SUMMON A NEW MON-STER!
VOOM...

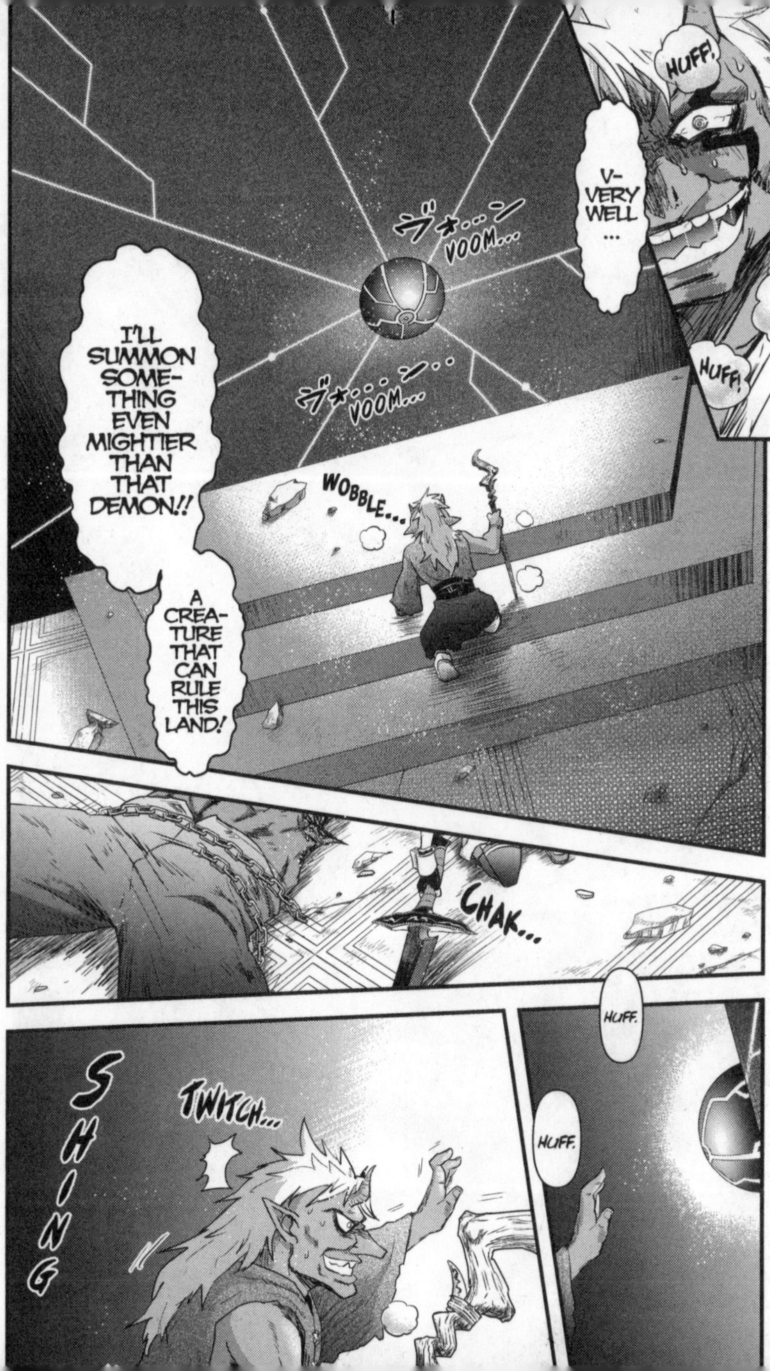
HUFF!
V-VERY WELL...
HUFF!
ヴォ…ン
VOOM...
ヴォ…ン…
VOOM...
I'LL SUMMON SOMETHING EVEN MIGHTIER THAN THAT DEMON!!
A CREATURE THAT CAN RULE THIS LAND!
WOBBLE...
CHAK...
HUFF.
HUFF.
TWITCH...
!
SHING

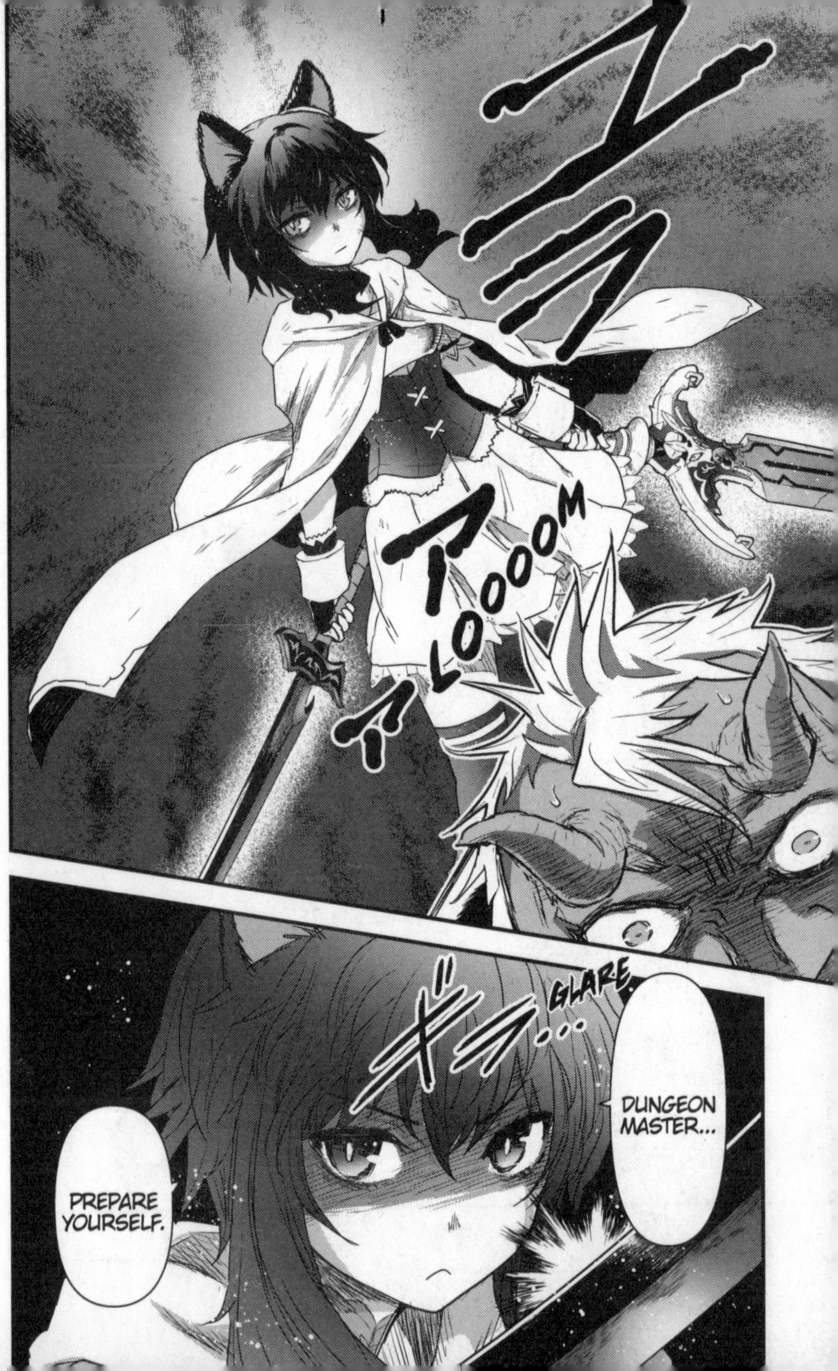
ZOOOOM
GLARE...
DUNGEON MASTER...
PREPARE YOURSELF.

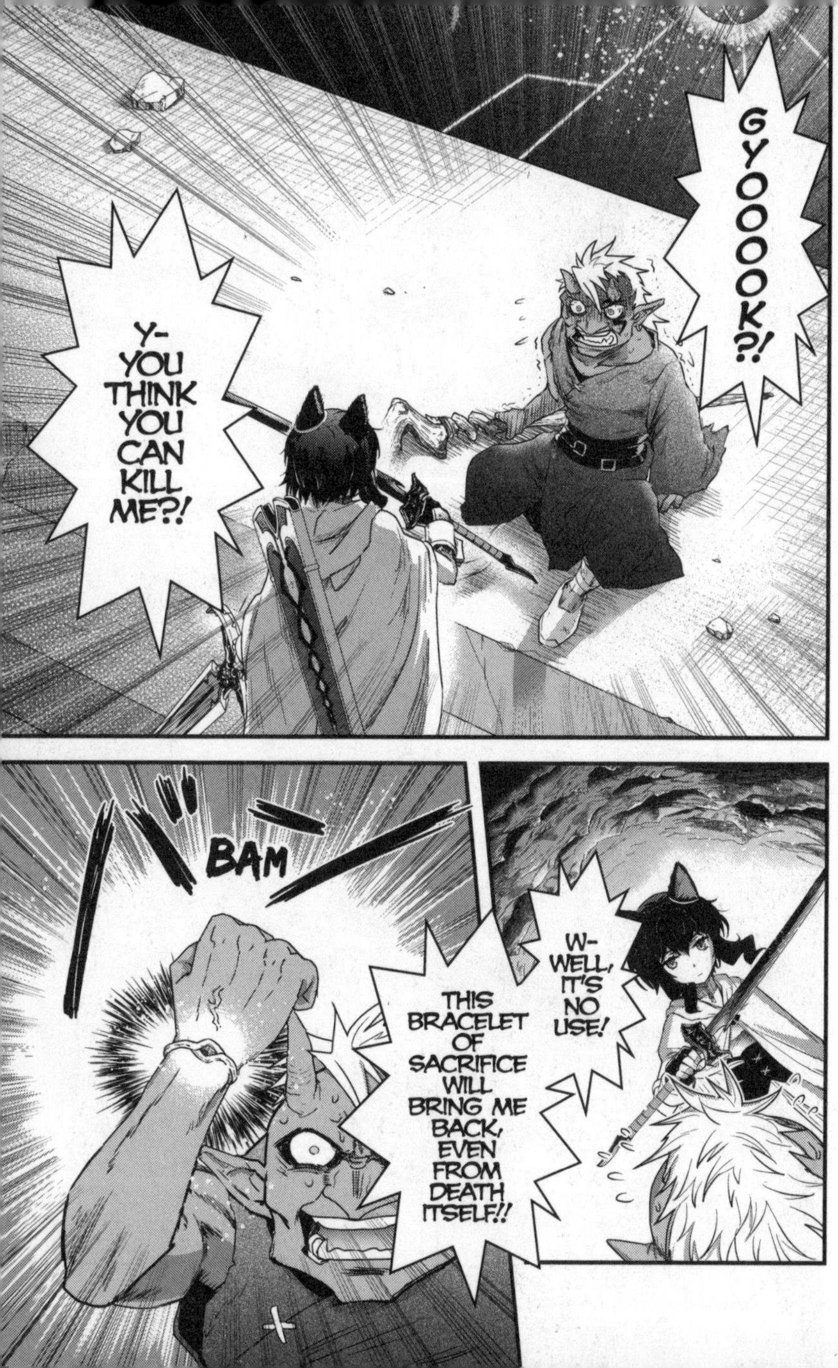
GYOOOOK?!
Y-YOU THINK YOU CAN KILL ME?!
W-WELL, IT'S NO USE!
BAM
THIS BRACELET OF SACRIFICE WILL BRING ME BACK, EVEN FROM DEATH ITSELF!!

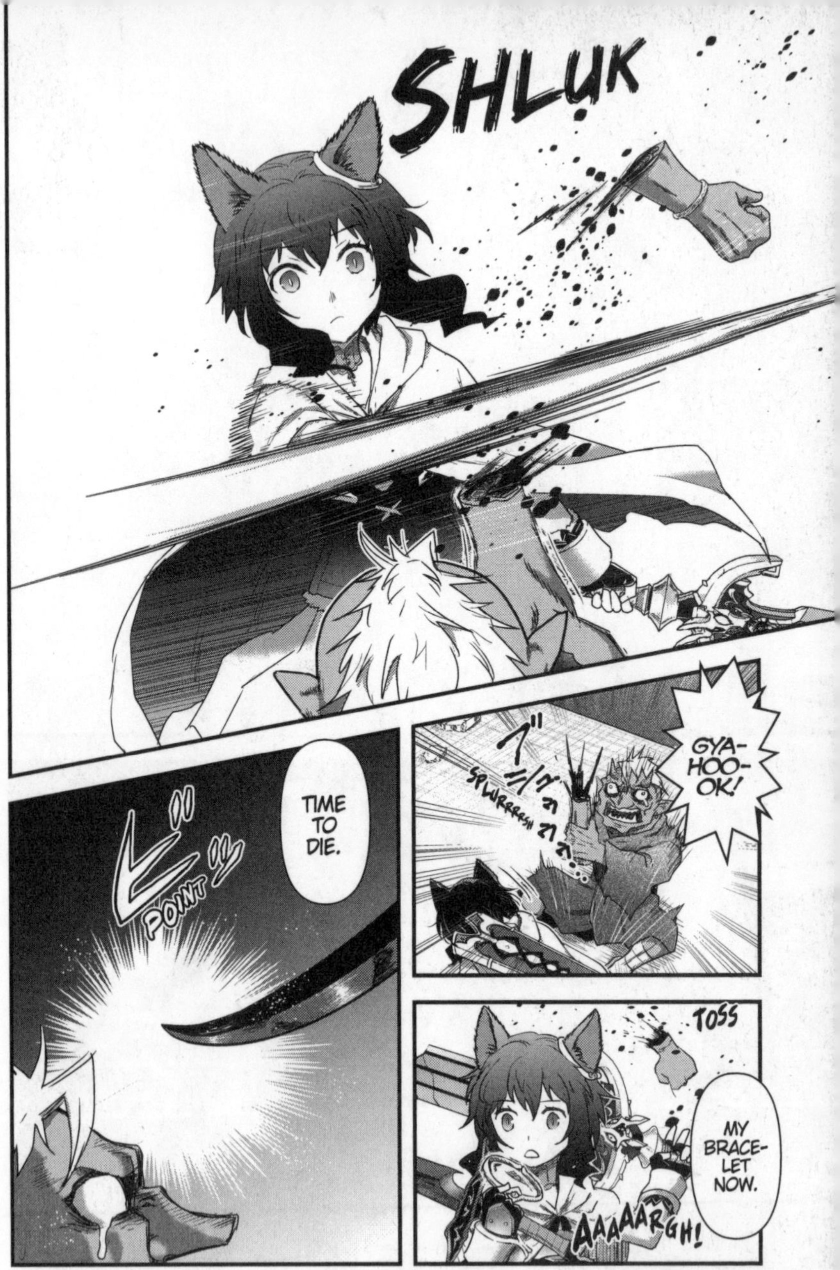
SHLUK
GYA-HOO-OK!
SPLURRRSH
TOSS
MY BRACE-LET NOW.
AAAARGH!
TIME TO DIE.
POINT

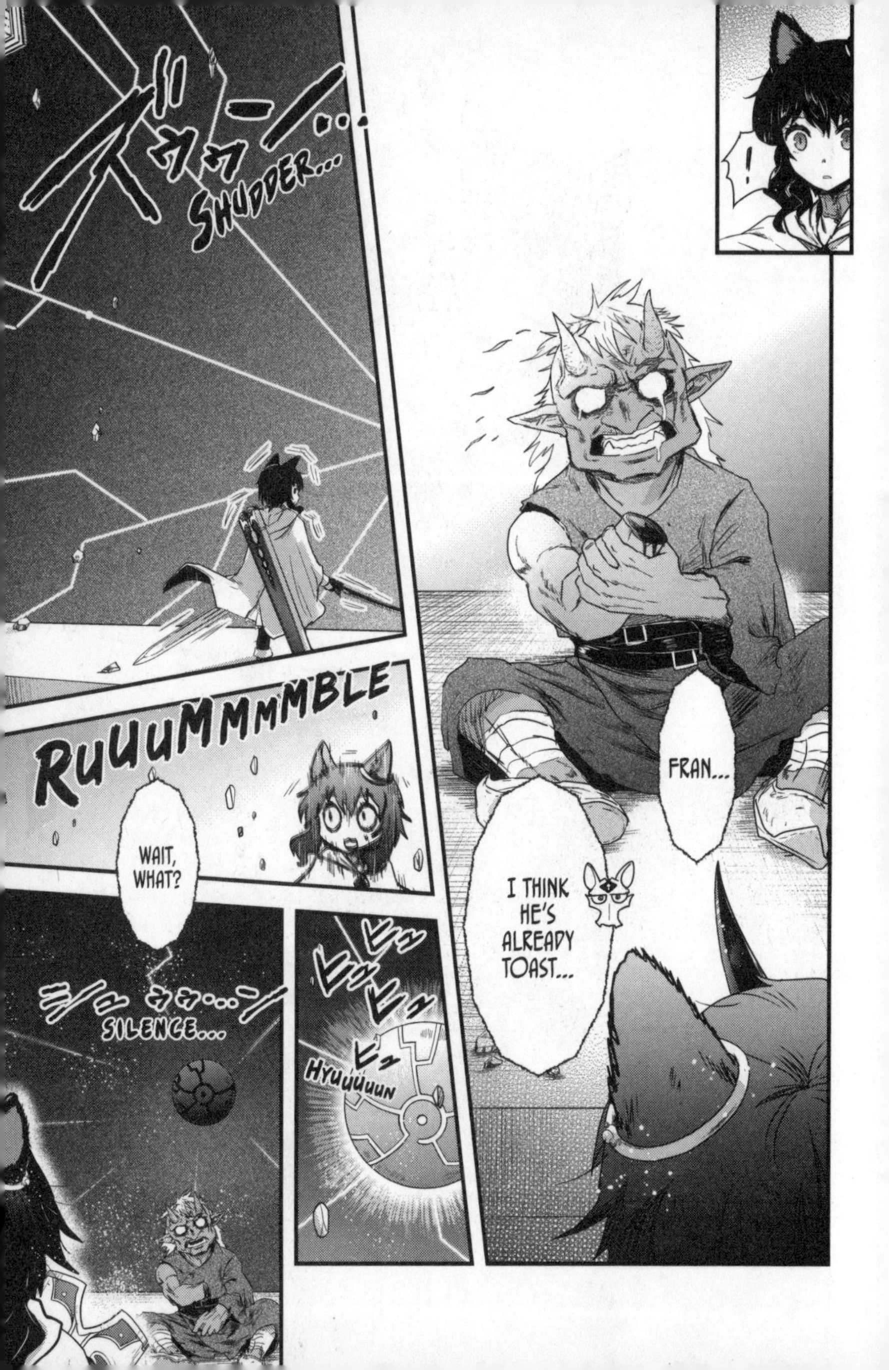
!
FRAN...
I THINK HE'S ALREADY TOAST...
SHUDDER...
RUUUMMMMMBLE
WAIT, WHAT?
HYUUUUUN
SILENCE...

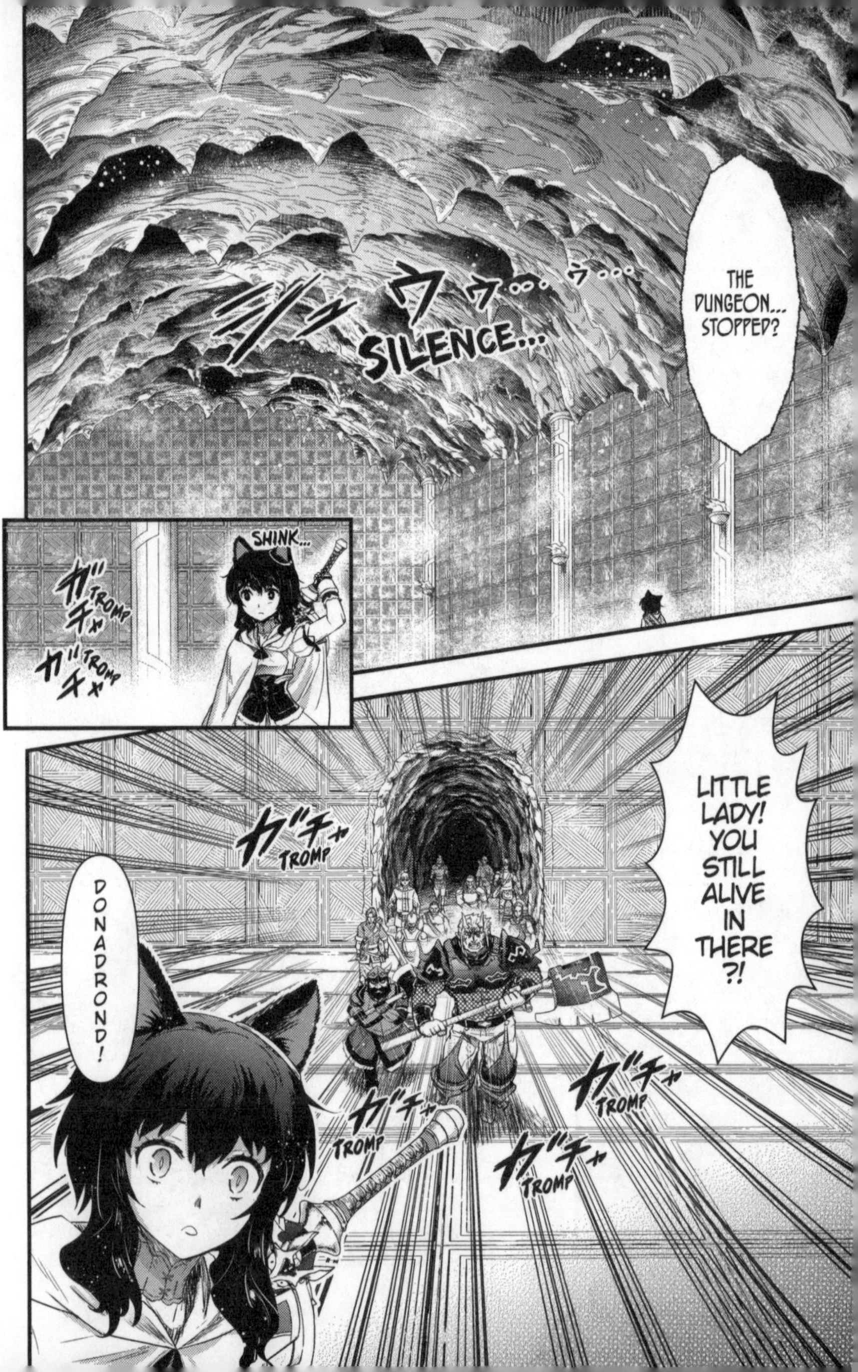
THE DUNGEON... STOPPED?
SILENCE...
SHINK...
TROMP
TROMP
LITTLE LADY! YOU STILL ALIVE IN THERE?!
TROMP
DONADROND!
TROMP
TROMP
TROMP

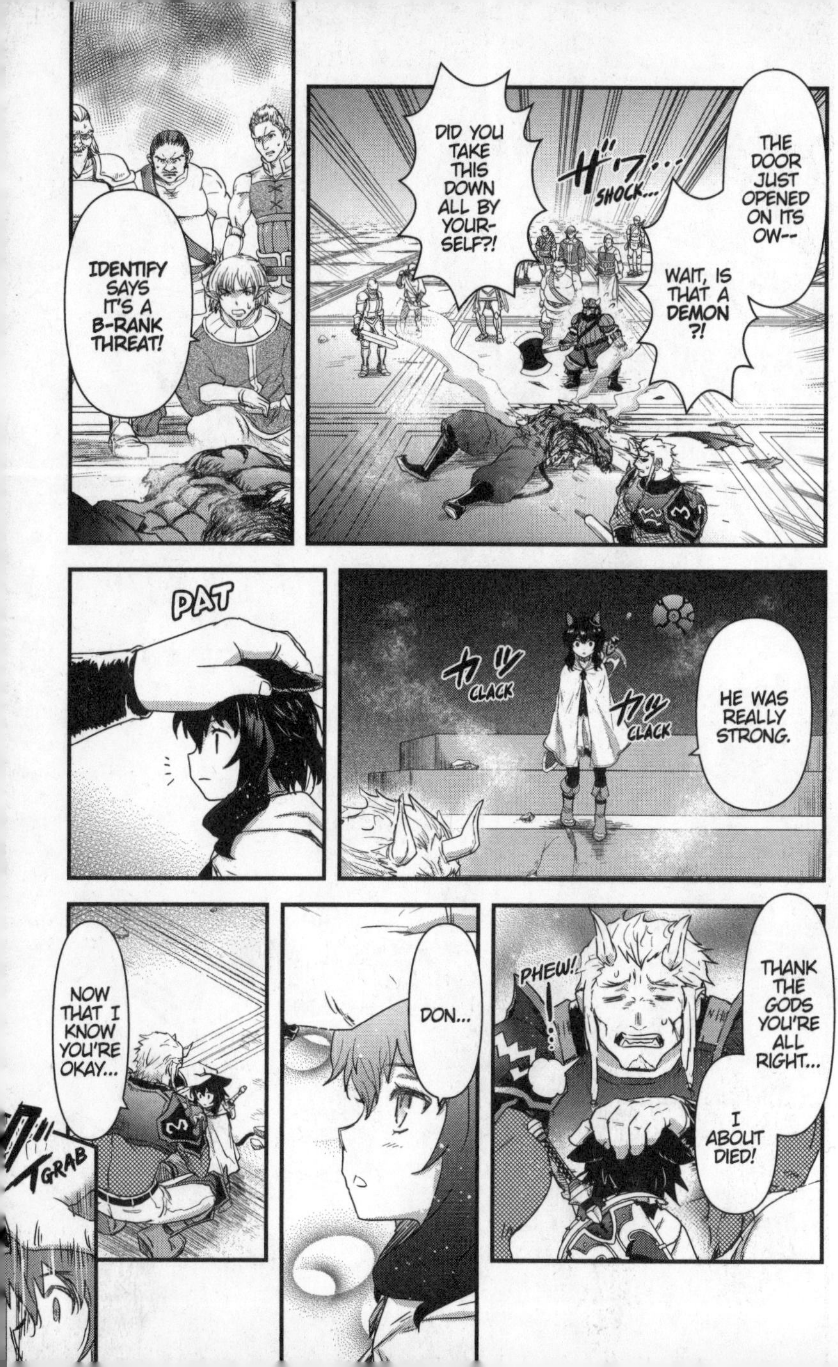
THE DOOR JUST OPENED ON ITS OW--
WAIT, IS THAT A DEMON?!
ザワ… SHOCK...
DID YOU TAKE THIS DOWN ALL BY YOURSELF?!
IDENTIFY SAYS IT'S A B-RANK THREAT!
HE WAS REALLY STRONG.
カツ CLACK
カツ CLACK
PAT
THANK THE GODS YOU'RE ALL RIGHT...
I ABOUT DIED!
PHEW!
DON...
NOW THAT I KNOW YOU'RE OKAY...
GRAB

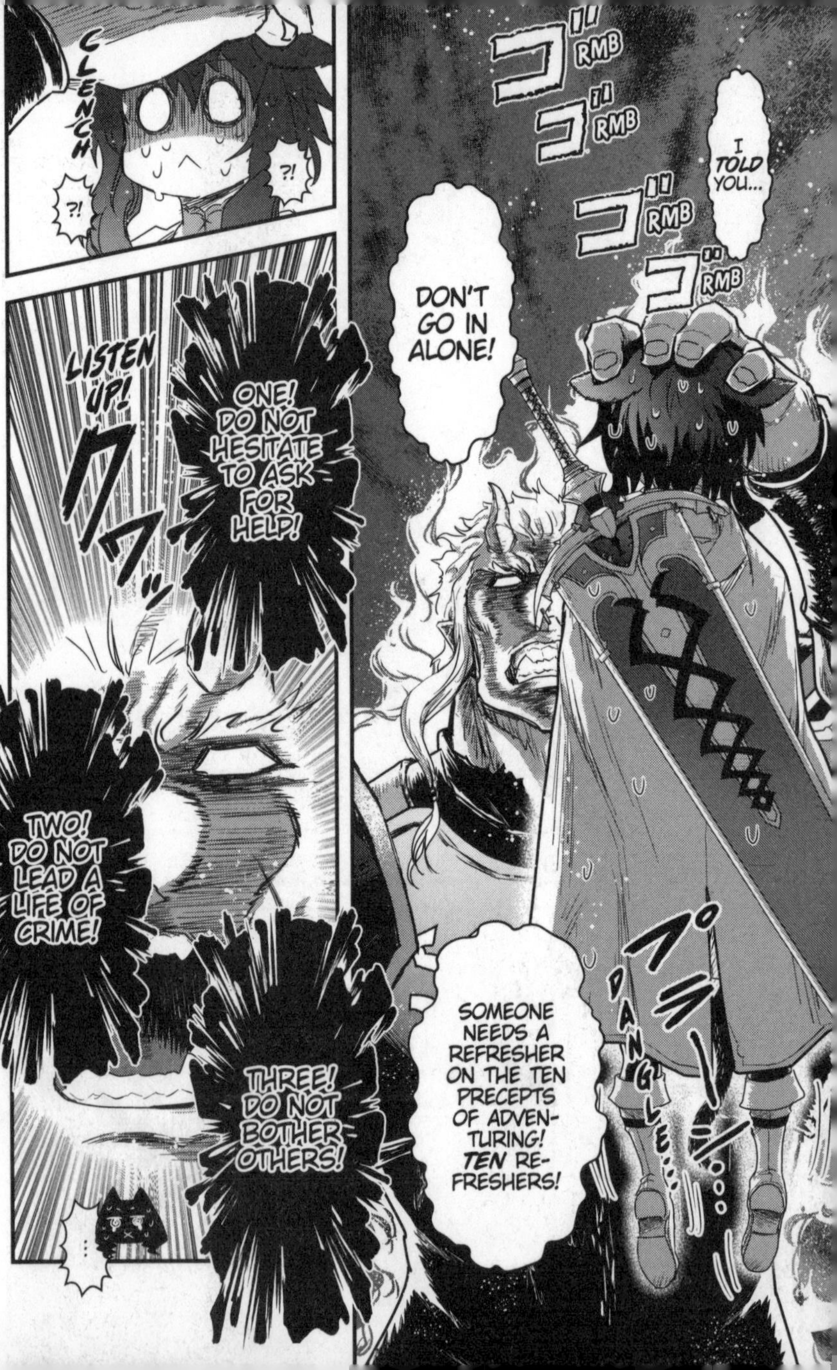
RMB
RMB
RMB
RMB
I TOLD YOU...
DON'T GO IN ALONE!
SOMEONE NEEDS A REFRESHER ON THE TEN PRECEPTS OF ADVENTURING! *TEN* REFRESHERS!
DANGLE...
CLENCH
?!
?!
LISTEN UP!
ONE! DO NOT HESITATE TO ASK FOR HELP!
TWO! DO NOT LEAD A LIFE OF CRIME!
THREE! DO NOT BOTHER OTHERS!
...
?!

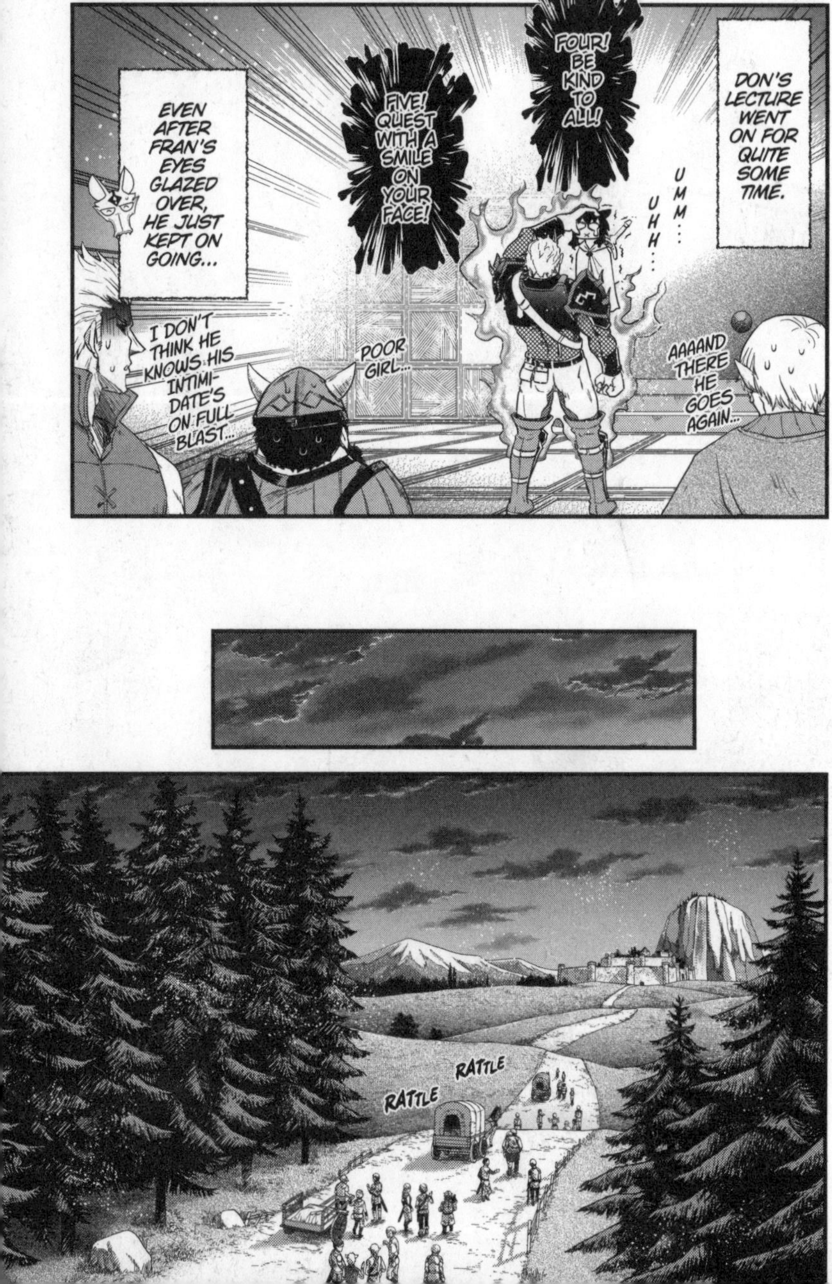
DON'S LECTURE WENT ON FOR QUITE SOME TIME.
UMM...
UHH...
FOUR! BE KIND TO ALL!
FIVE! QUEST WITH A SMILE ON YOUR FACE!
EVEN AFTER FRAN'S EYES GLAZED OVER, HE JUST KEPT ON GOING...
AAAAND THERE HE GOES AGAIN...
POOR GIRL...
I DON'T THINK HE KNOWS HIS INTIMIDATE'S ON FULL BLAST...
RATTLE
RATTLE

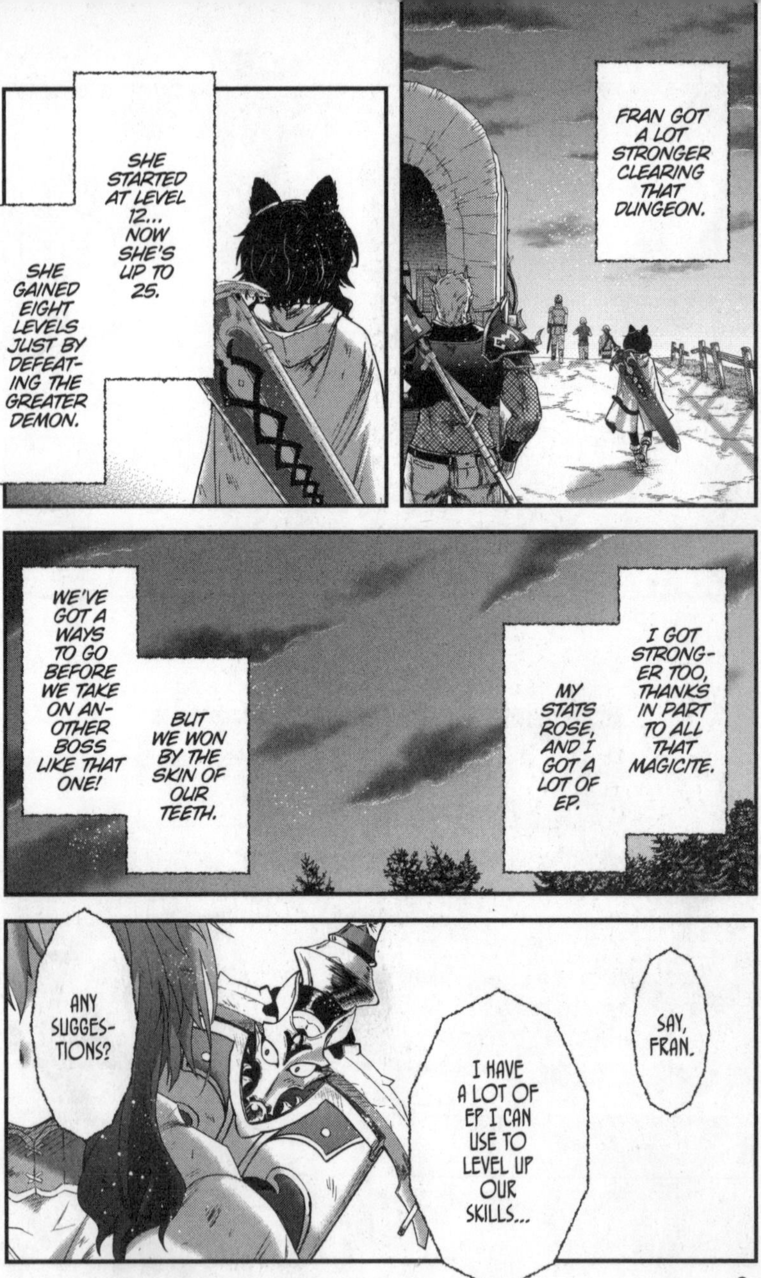
FRAN GOT A LOT STRONGER CLEARING THAT DUNGEON.
SHE STARTED AT LEVEL 12... NOW SHE'S UP TO 25.
SHE GAINED EIGHT LEVELS JUST BY DEFEATING THE GREATER DEMON.
I GOT STRONGER TOO, THANKS IN PART TO ALL THAT MAGICITE.
MY STATS ROSE, AND I GOT A LOT OF EP.
BUT WE WON BY THE SKIN OF OUR TEETH.
WE'VE GOT A WAYS TO GO BEFORE WE TAKE ON ANOTHER BOSS LIKE THAT ONE!
SAY, FRAN.
I HAVE A LOT OF EP I CAN USE TO LEVEL UP OUR SKILLS...
ANY SUGGESTIONS?

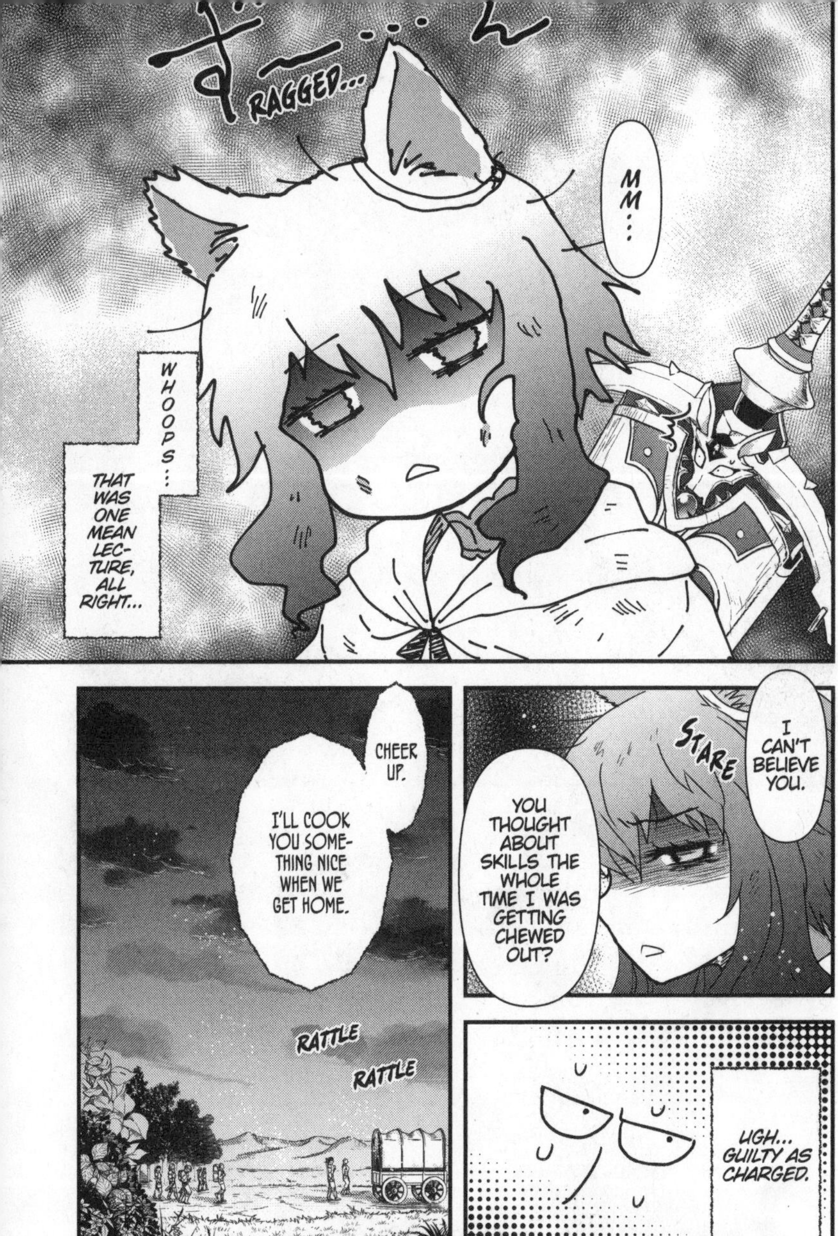
ず～…ん
RAGGED...
MM...
WHOOPS... THAT WAS ONE MEAN LECTURE, ALL RIGHT...
I CAN'T BELIEVE YOU.
STARE
YOU THOUGHT ABOUT SKILLS THE WHOLE TIME I WAS GETTING CHEWED OUT?
UGH... GUILTY AS CHARGED.
CHEER UP.
I'LL COOK YOU SOMETHING NICE WHEN WE GET HOME.
RATTLE
RATTLE

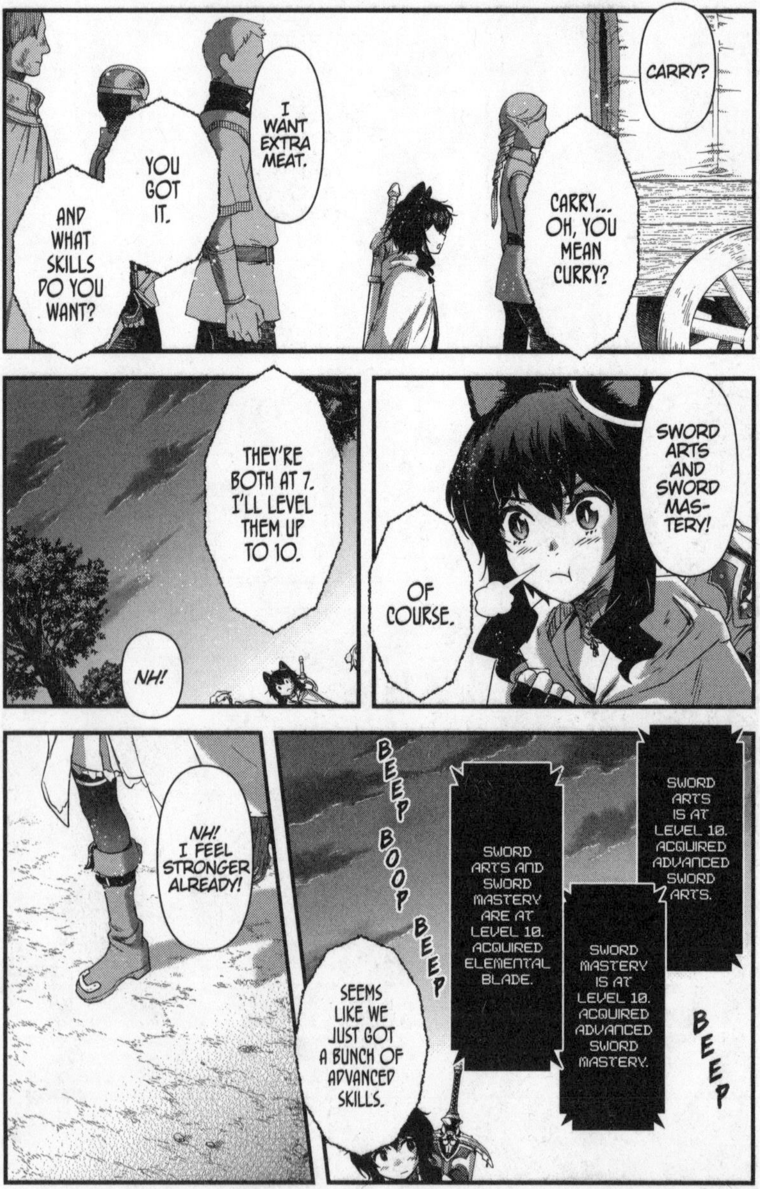
CARRY?
CARRY... OH, YOU MEAN CURRY?
I WANT EXTRA MEAT.
YOU GOT IT.
AND WHAT SKILLS DO YOU WANT?
SWORD ARTS AND SWORD MAS-TERY!
OF COURSE.
THEY'RE BOTH AT 7. I'LL LEVEL THEM UP TO 10.
NH!
SWORD ARTS IS AT LEVEL 10. ACQUIRED ADVANCED SWORD ARTS.
BEEP
SWORD MASTERY IS AT LEVEL 10. ACQUIRED ADVANCED SWORD MASTERY.
BEEP BOOP BEEP
SWORD ARTS AND SWORD MASTERY ARE AT LEVEL 10. ACQUIRED ELEMENTAL BLADE.
SEEMS LIKE WE JUST GOT A BUNCH OF ADVANCED SKILLS.
NH! I FEEL STRONGER ALREADY!

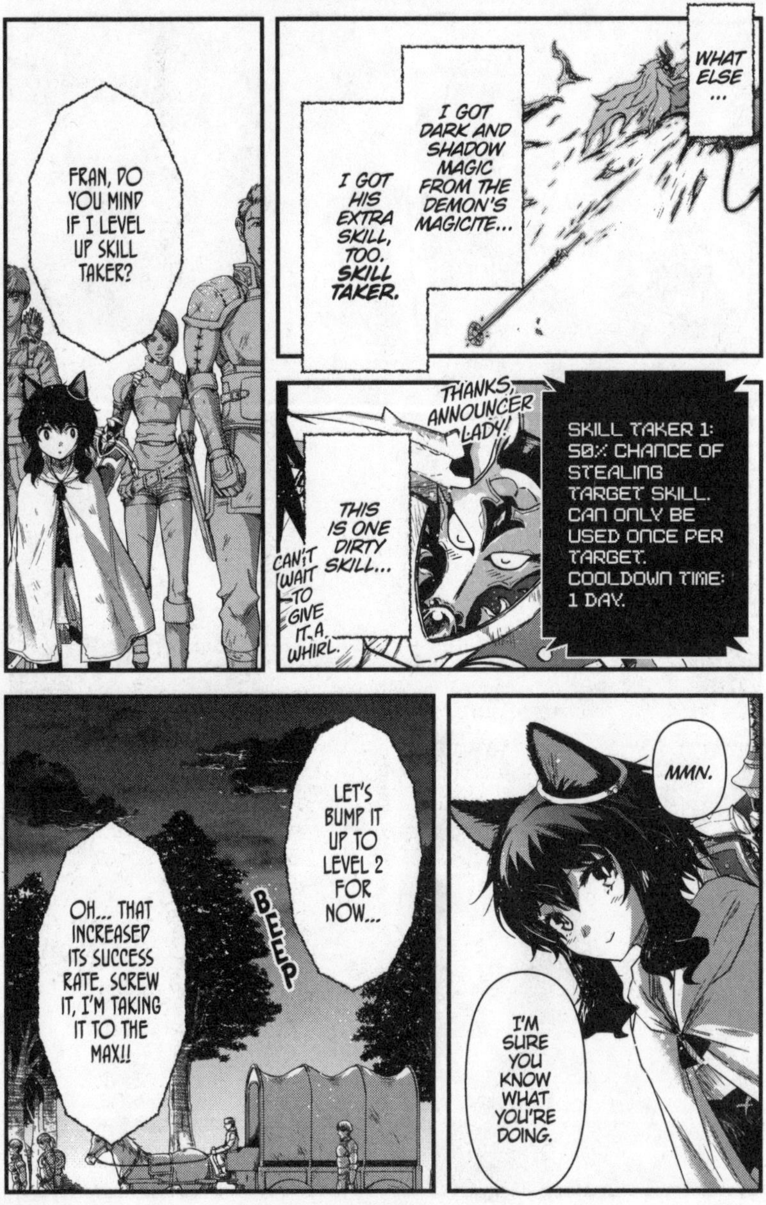
WHAT ELSE ...
I GOT DARK AND SHADOW MAGIC FROM THE DEMON'S MAGICITE...
I GOT HIS EXTRA SKILL, TOO. SKILL TAKER.
SKILL TAKER 1: 50% CHANCE OF STEALING TARGET SKILL. CAN ONLY BE USED ONCE PER TARGET. COOLDOWN TIME: 1 DAY.
THANKS, ANNOUNCER LADY!
THIS IS ONE DIRTY SKILL...
CAN'T WAIT TO GIVE IT A WHIRL.
FRAN, DO YOU MIND IF I LEVEL UP SKILL TAKER?
MMN.
I'M SURE YOU KNOW WHAT YOU'RE DOING.
LET'S BUMP IT UP TO LEVEL 2 FOR NOW...
BEEP
OH... THAT INCREASED ITS SUCCESS RATE. SCREW IT, I'M TAKING IT TO THE MAX!!

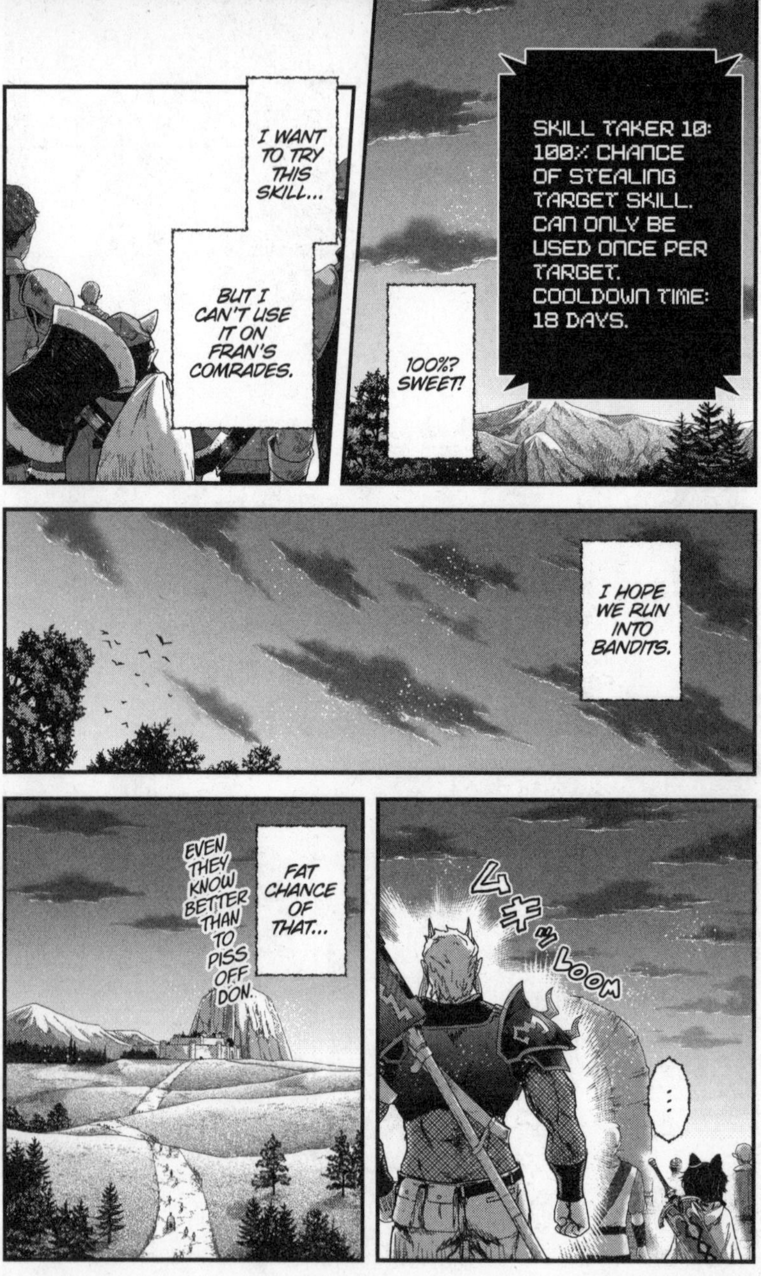

SKILL TAKER 10: 100% CHANCE OF STEALING TARGET SKILL. CAN ONLY BE USED ONCE PER TARGET. COOLDOWN TIME: 18 DAYS.
100%? SWEET!
I WANT TO TRY THIS SKILL...
BUT I CAN'T USE IT ON FRAN'S COMRADES.
I HOPE WE RUN INTO BANDITS.
ムキッ
BOOM
...
FAT CHANCE OF THAT...
EVEN THEY KNOW BETTER THAN TO PISS OFF DON.

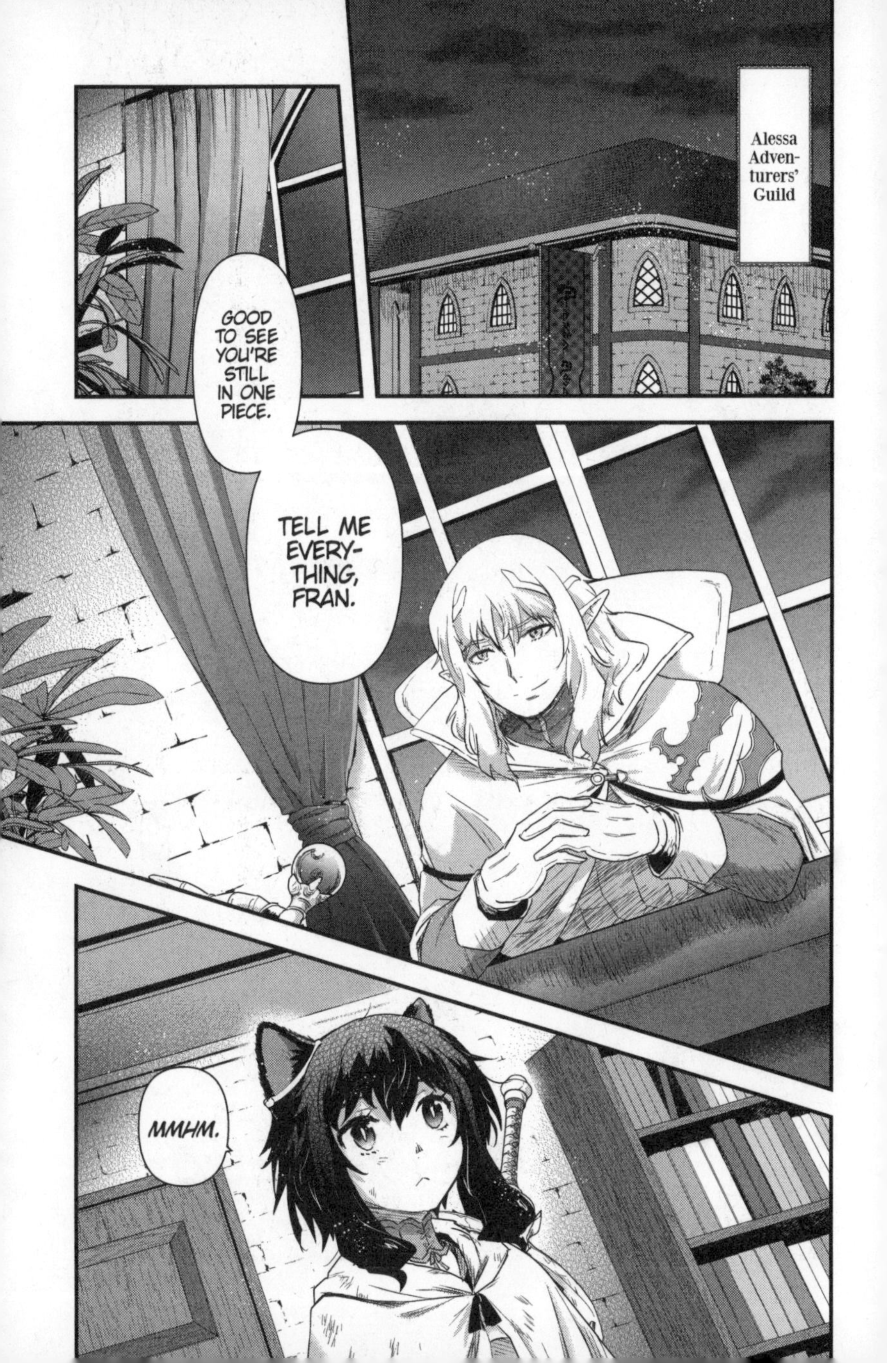

Alessa Adventurers' Guild
GOOD TO SEE YOU'RE STILL IN ONE PIECE.
TELL ME EVERYTHING, FRAN.
MMHM.

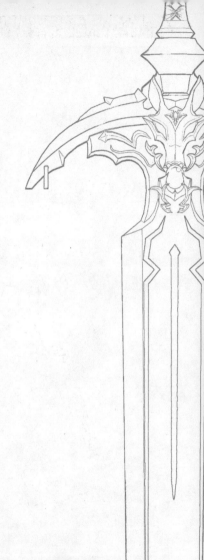

Reincarnated
as a sword

Chapter 14: Essence of Falsehood

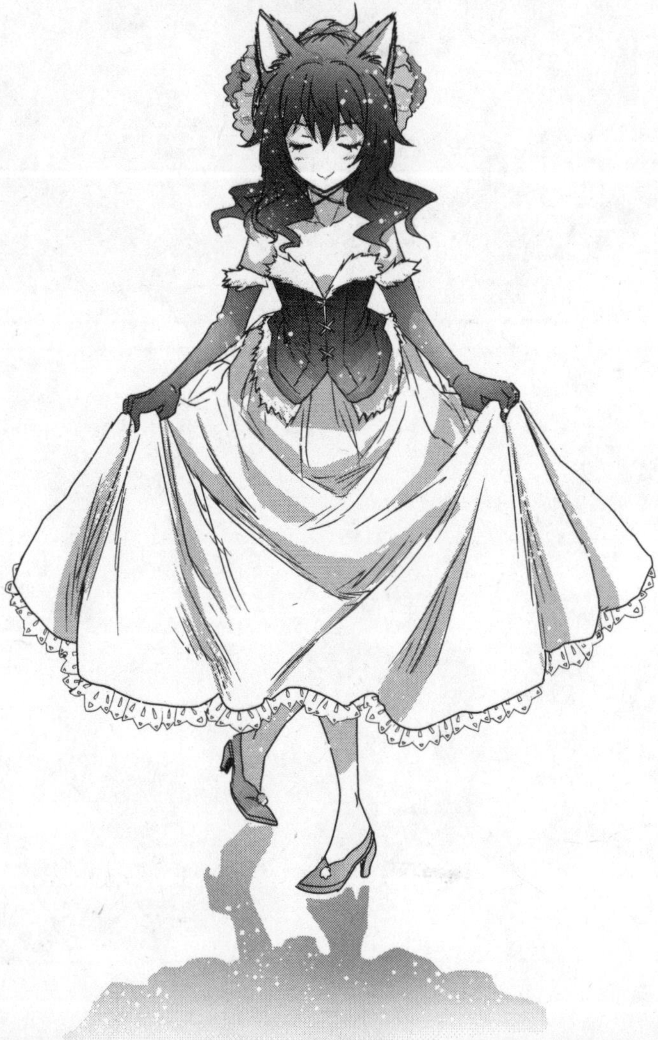

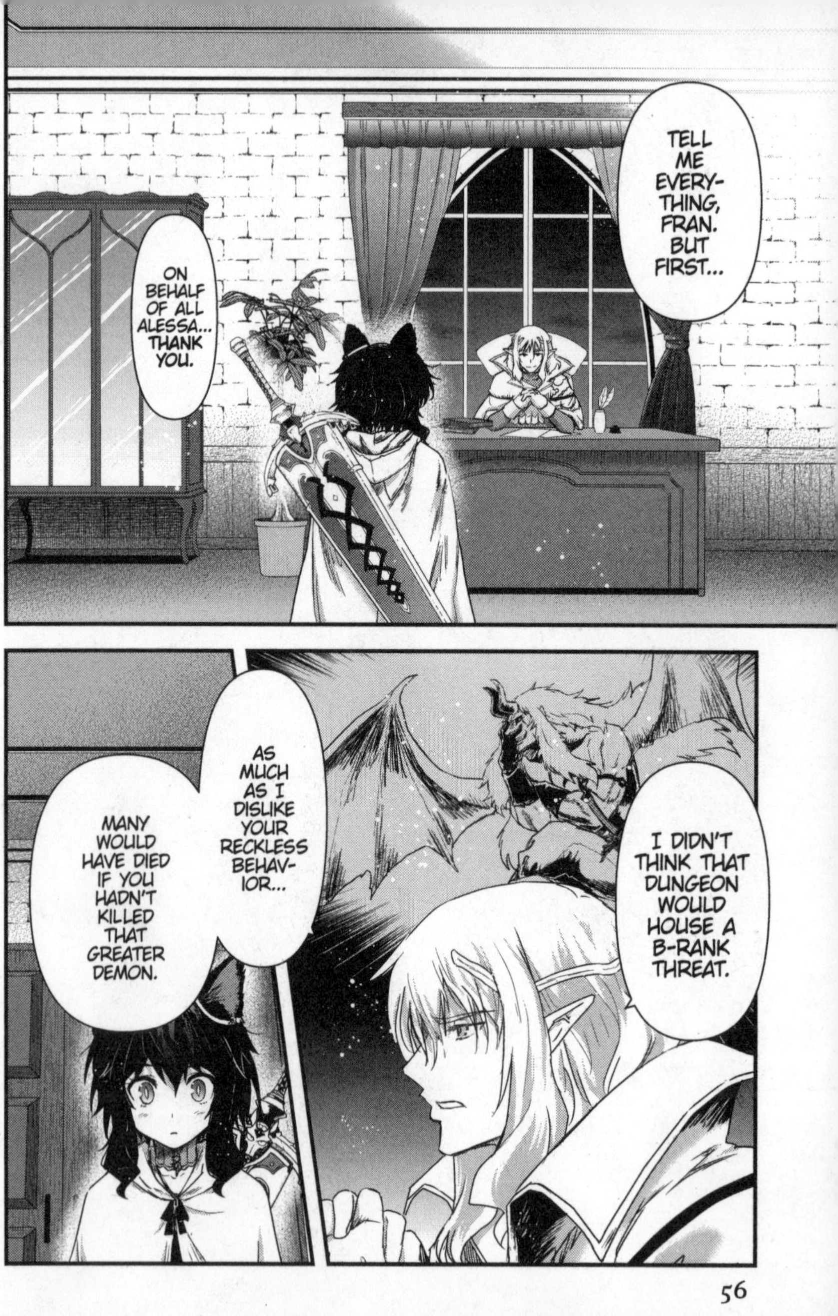
TELL ME EVERYTHING, FRAN. BUT FIRST...
ON BEHALF OF ALL ALESSA... THANK YOU.
I DIDN'T THINK THAT DUNGEON WOULD HOUSE A B-RANK THREAT.
AS MUCH AS I DISLIKE YOUR RECKLESS BEHAVIOR...
MANY WOULD HAVE DIED IF YOU HADN'T KILLED THAT GREATER DEMON.

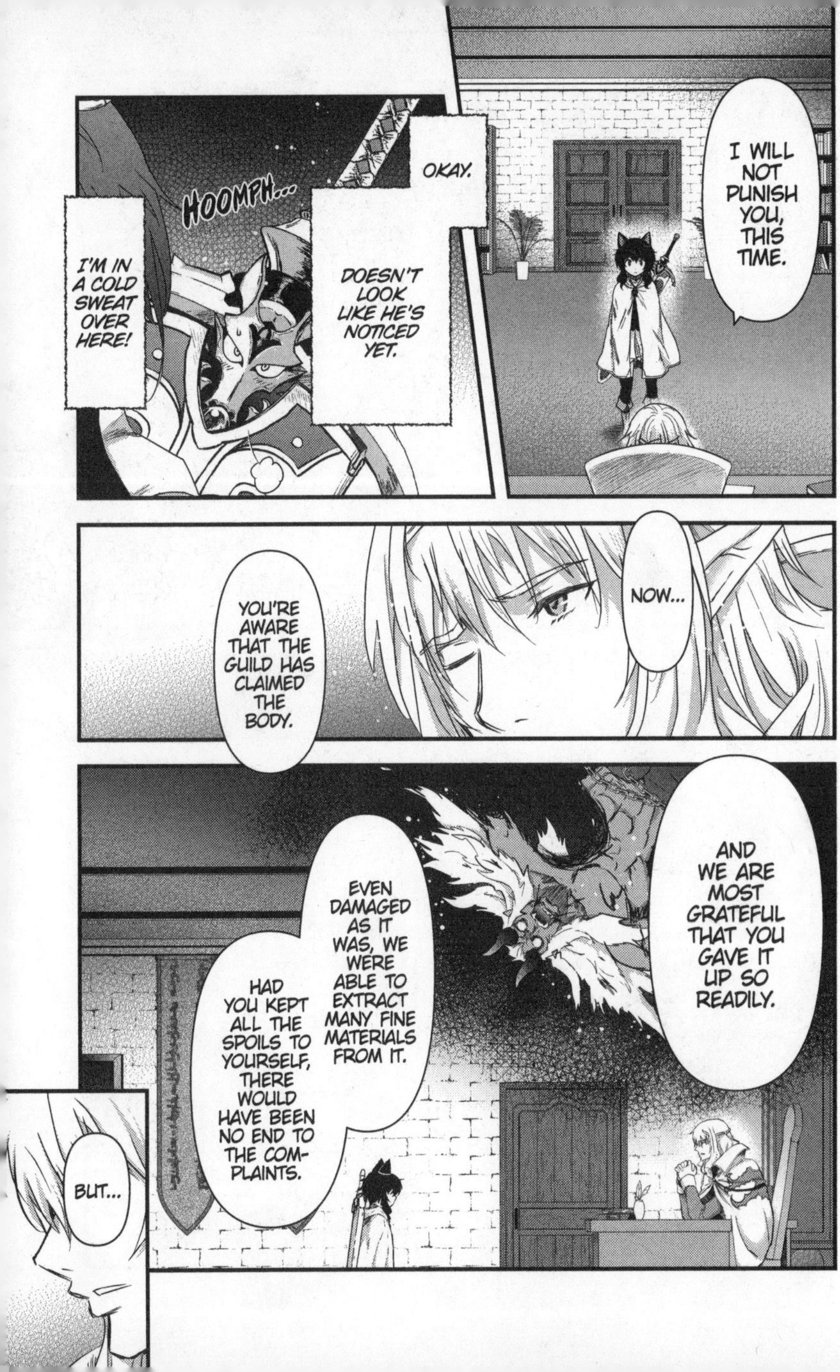
I WILL NOT PUNISH YOU, THIS TIME.
OKAY.
DOESN'T LOOK LIKE HE'S NOTICED YET.
HOOMPH...
I'M IN A COLD SWEAT OVER HERE!
NOW...
YOU'RE AWARE THAT THE GUILD HAS CLAIMED THE BODY.
AND WE ARE MOST GRATEFUL THAT YOU GAVE IT UP SO READILY.
EVEN DAMAGED AS IT WAS, WE WERE ABLE TO EXTRACT MANY FINE MATERIALS FROM IT.
HAD YOU KEPT ALL THE SPOILS TO YOURSELF, THERE WOULD HAVE BEEN NO END TO THE COM-PLAINTS.
BUT...

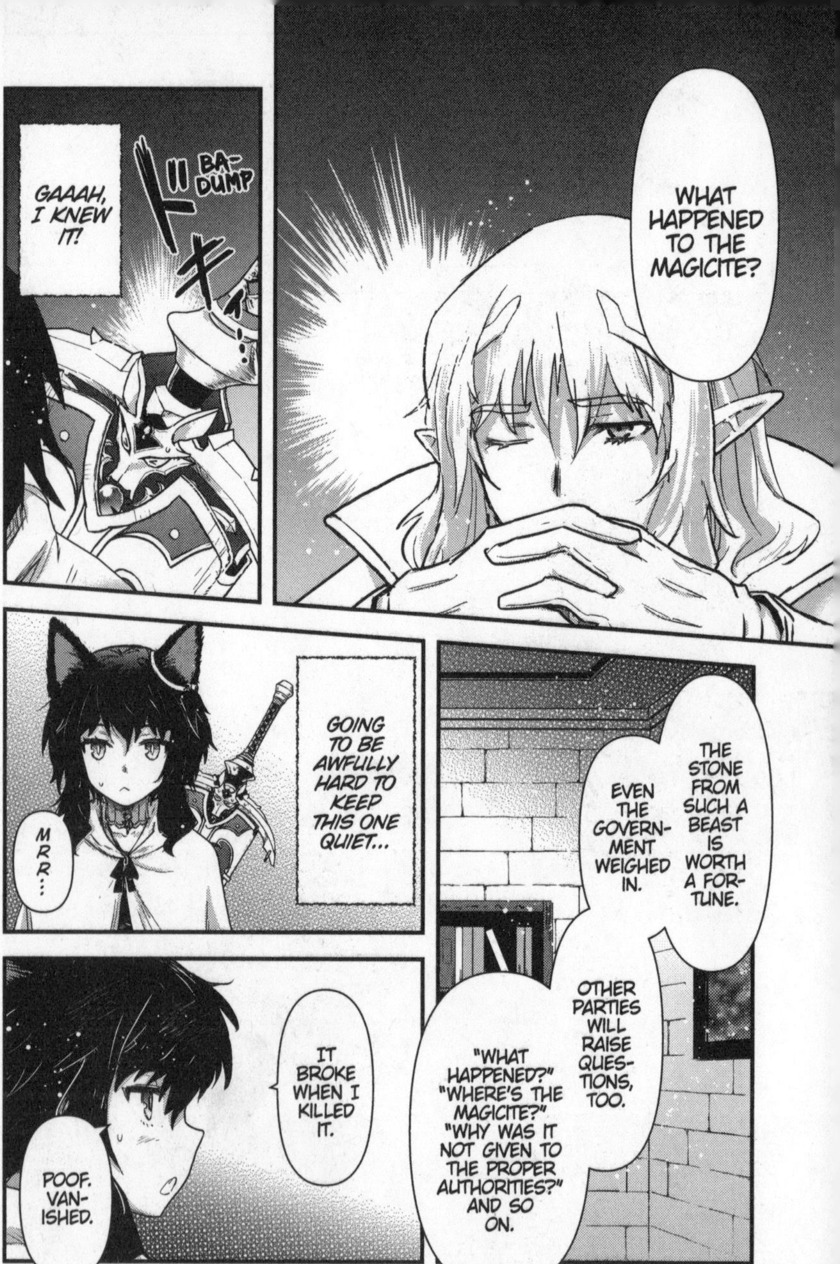
WHAT HAPPENED TO THE MAGICITE?
BA-DUMP
GAAAH, I KNEW IT!
THE STONE FROM SUCH A BEAST IS WORTH A FORTUNE.
EVEN THE GOVERNMENT WEIGHED IN.
OTHER PARTIES WILL RAISE QUESTIONS, TOO.
"WHAT HAPPENED?" "WHERE'S THE MAGICITE?" "WHY WAS IT NOT GIVEN TO THE PROPER AUTHORITIES?" AND SO ON.
GOING TO BE AWFULLY HARD TO KEEP THIS ONE QUIET...
MRR...
IT BROKE WHEN I KILLED IT.
POOF. VANISHED.

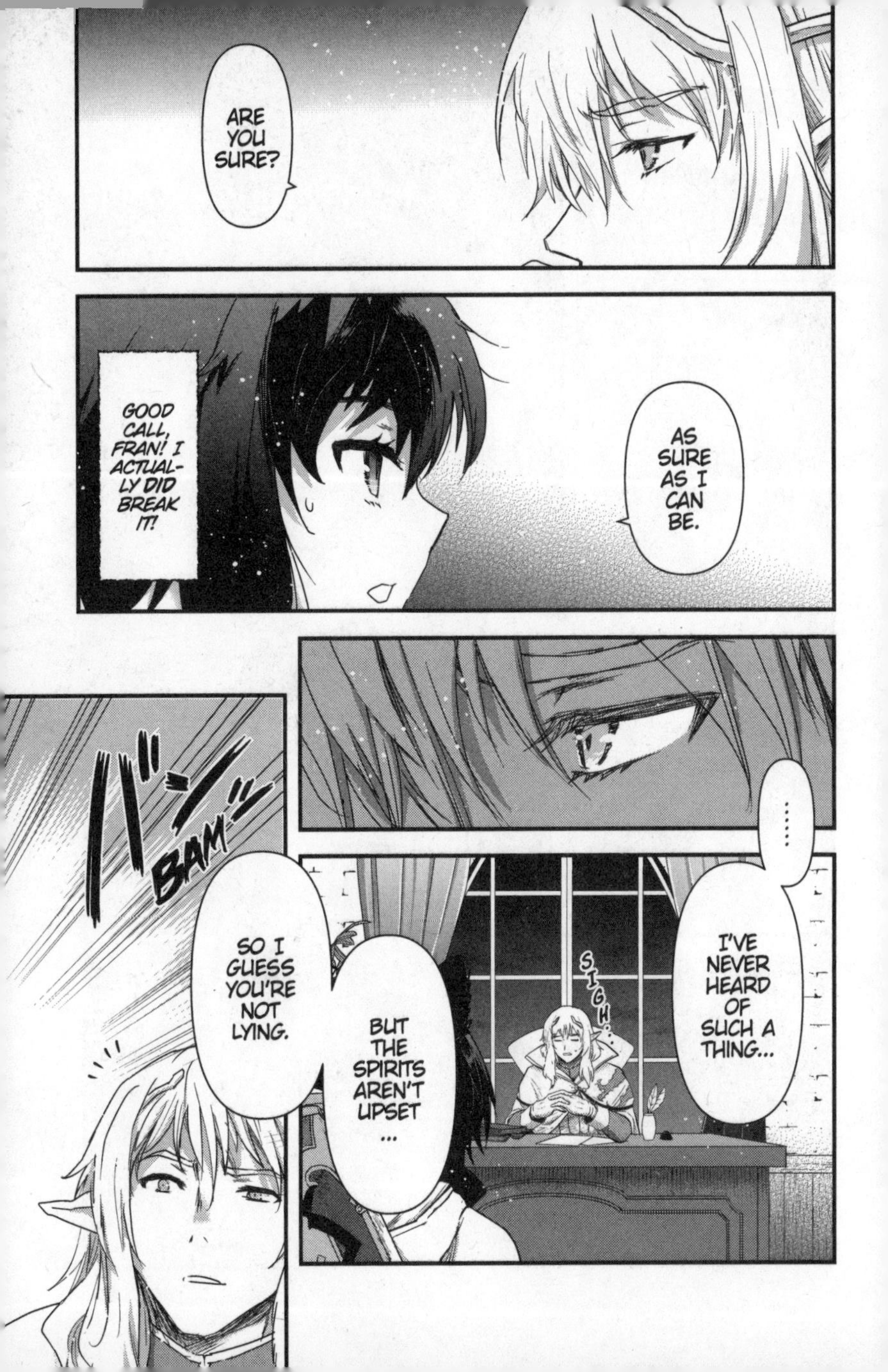
ARE YOU SURE?
AS SURE AS I CAN BE.
GOOD CALL, FRAN! I ACTUALLY DID BREAK IT!
......
I'VE NEVER HEARD OF SUCH A THING...
SIGH...
BUT THE SPIRITS AREN'T UPSET ...
SO I GUESS YOU'RE NOT LYING.
BAM

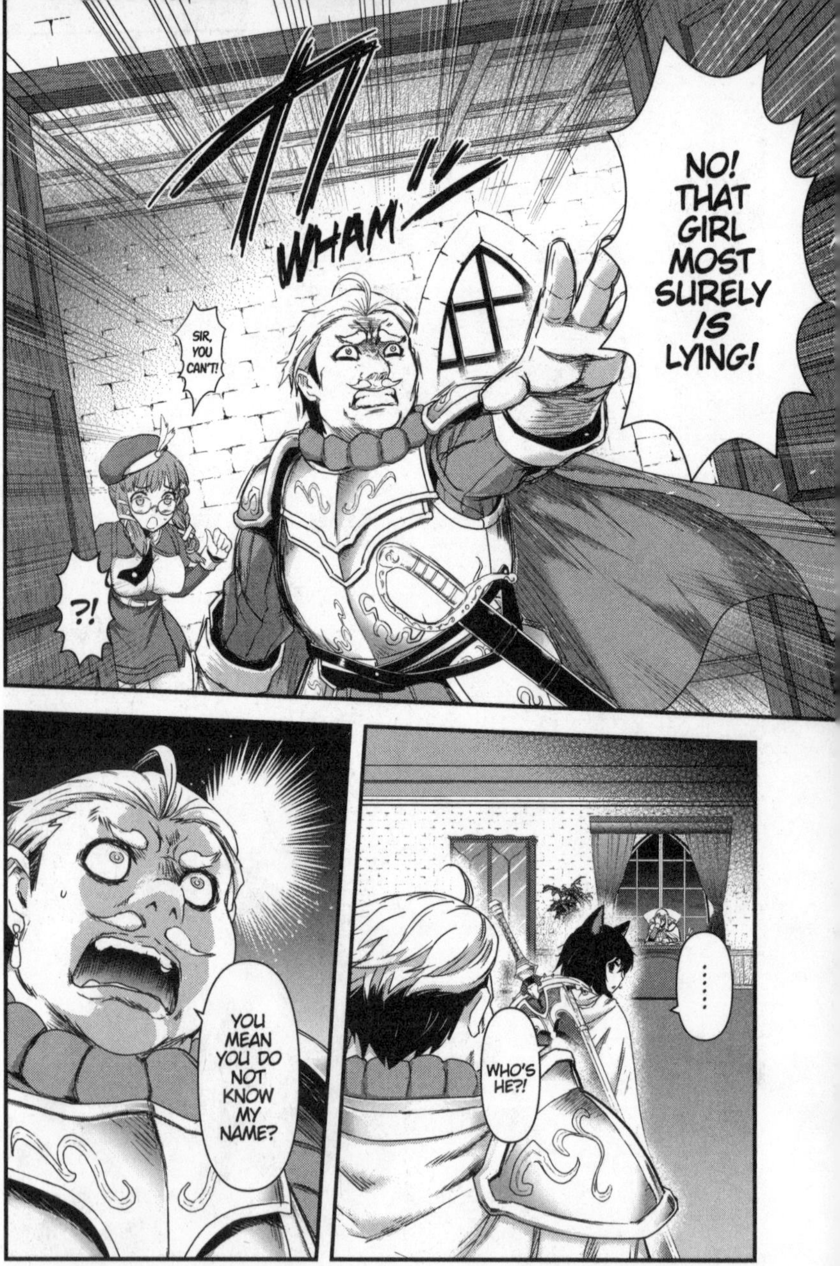
NO! THAT GIRL MOST SURELY IS LYING!
WHAM
SIR, YOU CAN'T!
?!
......
WHO'S HE?!
YOU MEAN YOU DO NOT KNOW MY NAME?

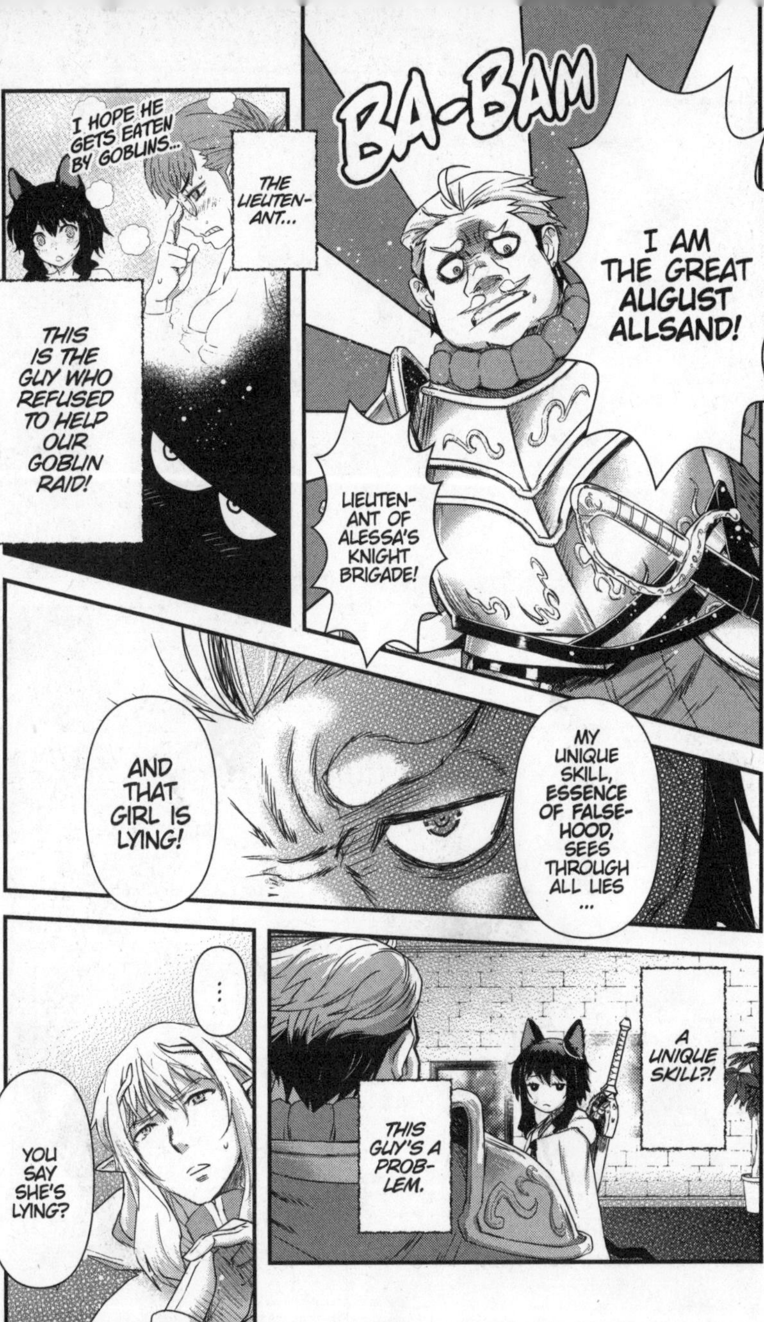
BA-BAM
I AM THE GREAT AUGUST ALLSAND!
LIEUTENANT OF ALESSA'S KNIGHT BRIGADE!
THE LIEUTENANT...
I HOPE HE GETS EATEN BY GOBLINS...
THIS IS THE GUY WHO REFUSED TO HELP OUR GOBLIN RAID!
MY UNIQUE SKILL, ESSENCE OF FALSEHOOD, SEES THROUGH ALL LIES ...
AND THAT GIRL IS LYING!
A UNIQUE SKILL?!
THIS GUY'S A PROBLEM.
...
YOU SAY SHE'S LYING?

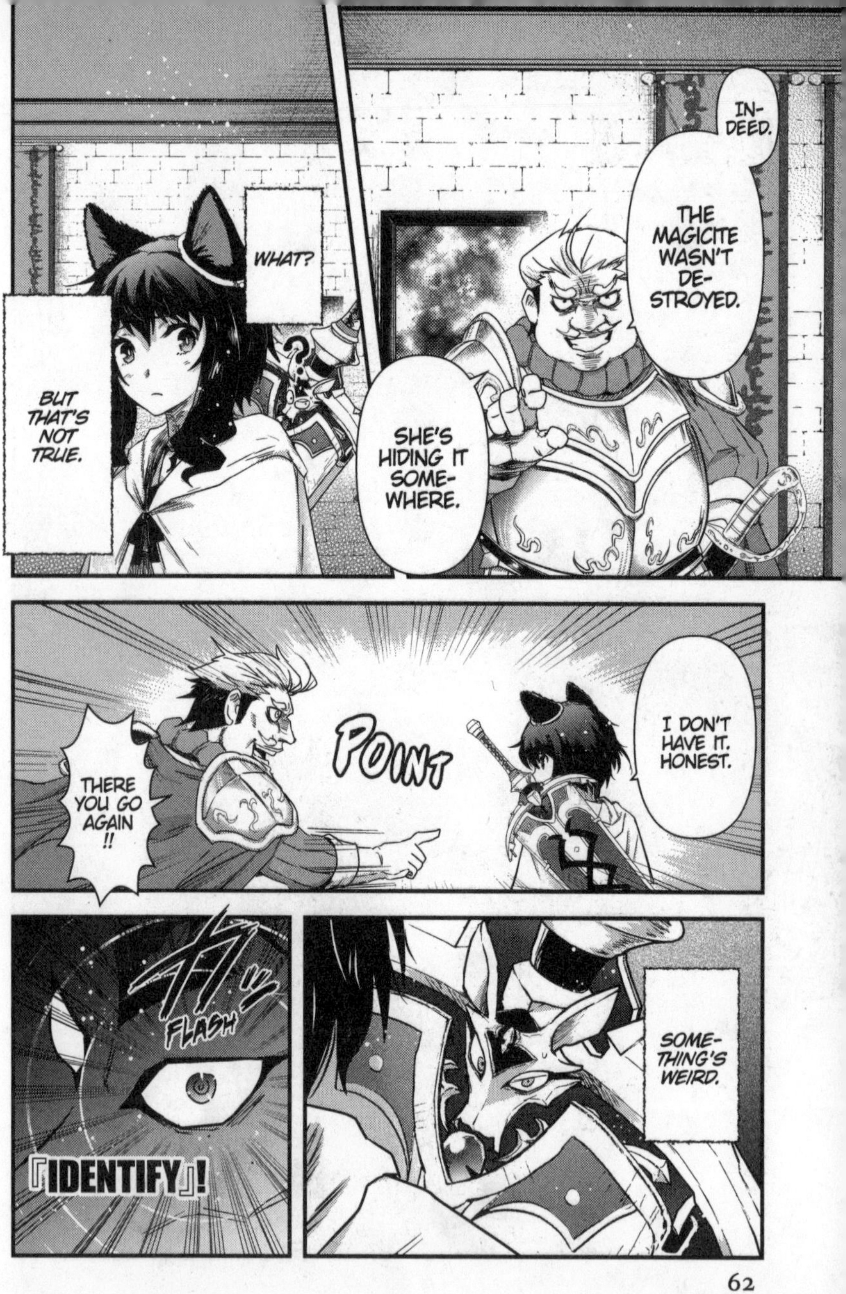
IN-DEED.
THE MAGICITE WASN'T DE-STROYED.
SHE'S HIDING IT SOME-WHERE.
WHAT?
BUT THAT'S NOT TRUE.
I DON'T HAVE IT. HONEST.
POINT
THERE YOU GO AGAIN!!
SOME-THING'S WEIRD.
FLASH
『IDENTIFY』!

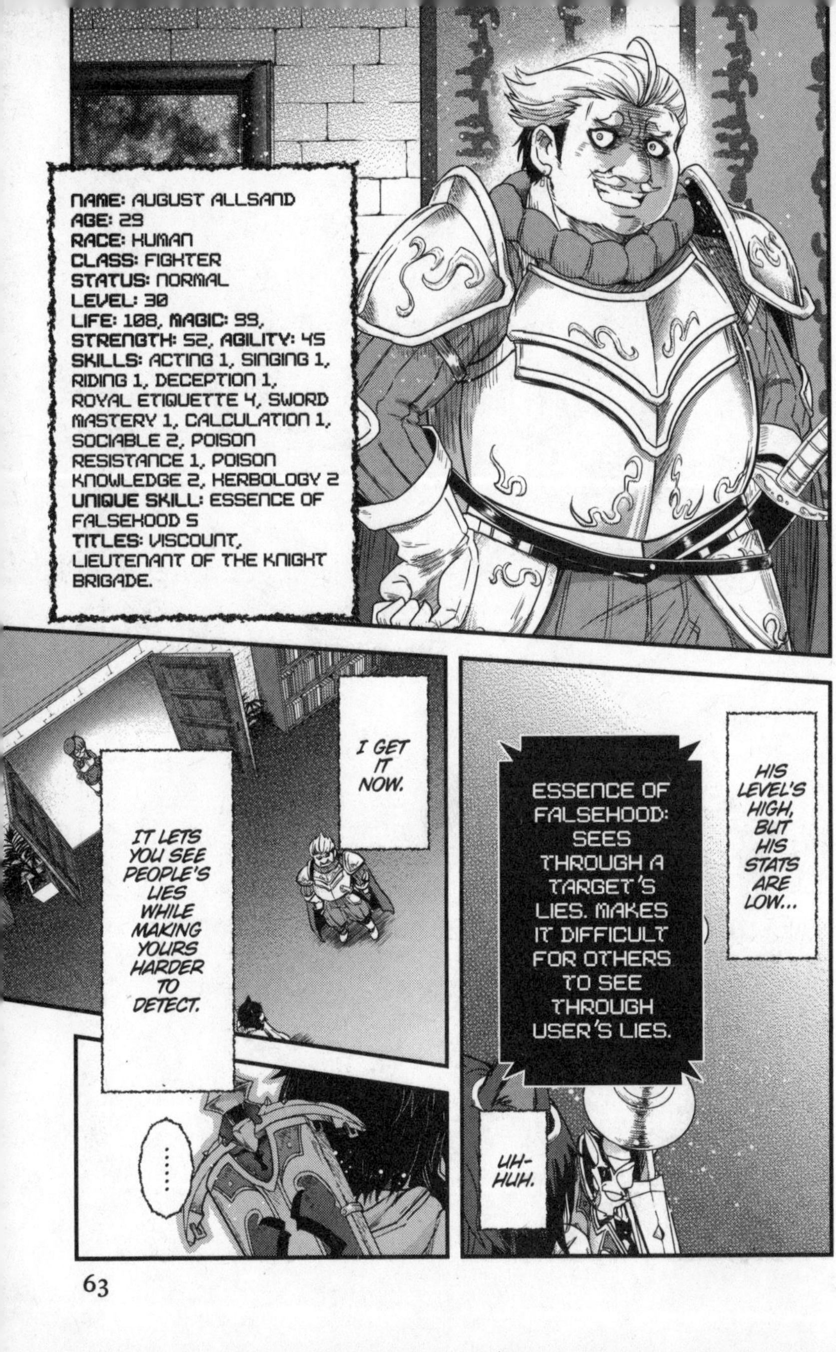
NAME: AUGUST ALLSAND
AGE: 29
RACE: HUMAN
CLASS: FIGHTER
STATUS: NORMAL
LEVEL: 30
LIFE: 108, MAGIC: 99,
STRENGTH: 52, ABILITY: 45
SKILLS: ACTING 1, SINGING 1, RIDING 1, DECEPTION 1, ROYAL ETIQUETTE 4, SWORD MASTERY 1, CALCULATION 1, SOCIABLE 2, POISON RESISTANCE 1, POISON KNOWLEDGE 2, HERBOLOGY 2
UNIQUE SKILL: ESSENCE OF FALSEHOOD 5
TITLES: VISCOUNT, LIEUTENANT OF THE KNIGHT BRIGADE.
HIS LEVEL'S HIGH, BUT HIS STATS ARE LOW...
ESSENCE OF FALSEHOOD: SEES THROUGH A TARGET'S LIES. MAKES IT DIFFICULT FOR OTHERS TO SEE THROUGH USER'S LIES.
UH-HUH.
I GET IT NOW.
IT LETS YOU SEE PEOPLE'S LIES WHILE MAKING YOURS HARDER TO DETECT.
......

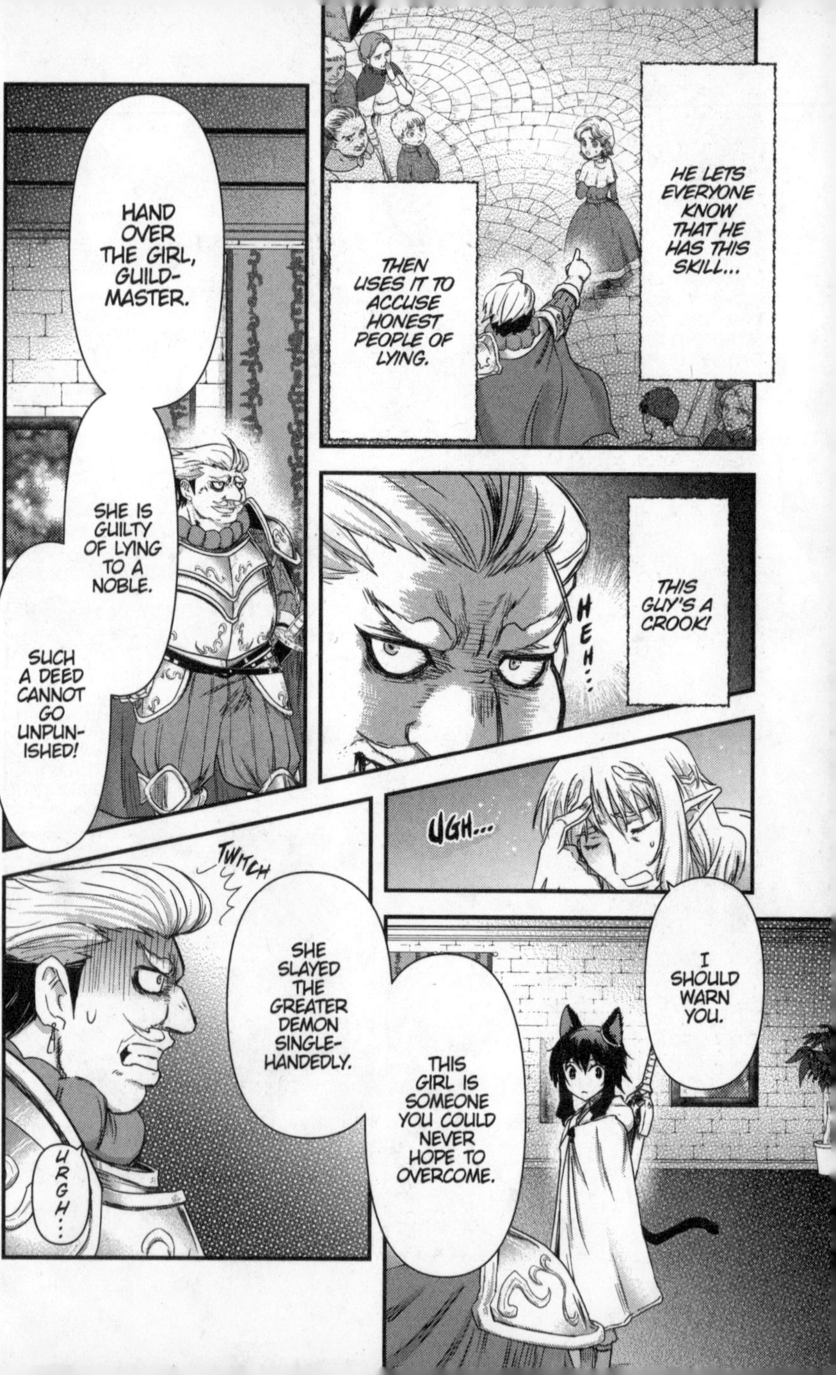
HE LETS EVERYONE KNOW THAT HE HAS THIS SKILL...
THEN USES IT TO ACCUSE HONEST PEOPLE OF LYING.
THIS GUY'S A CROOK!
HEH...
UGH...
HAND OVER THE GIRL, GUILD-MASTER.
SHE IS GUILTY OF LYING TO A NOBLE.
SUCH A DEED CANNOT GO UNPUN-ISHED!
I SHOULD WARN YOU.
THIS GIRL IS SOMEONE YOU COULD NEVER HOPE TO OVERCOME.
SHE SLAYED THE GREATER DEMON SINGLE-HANDEDLY.
TWITCH
URGH...

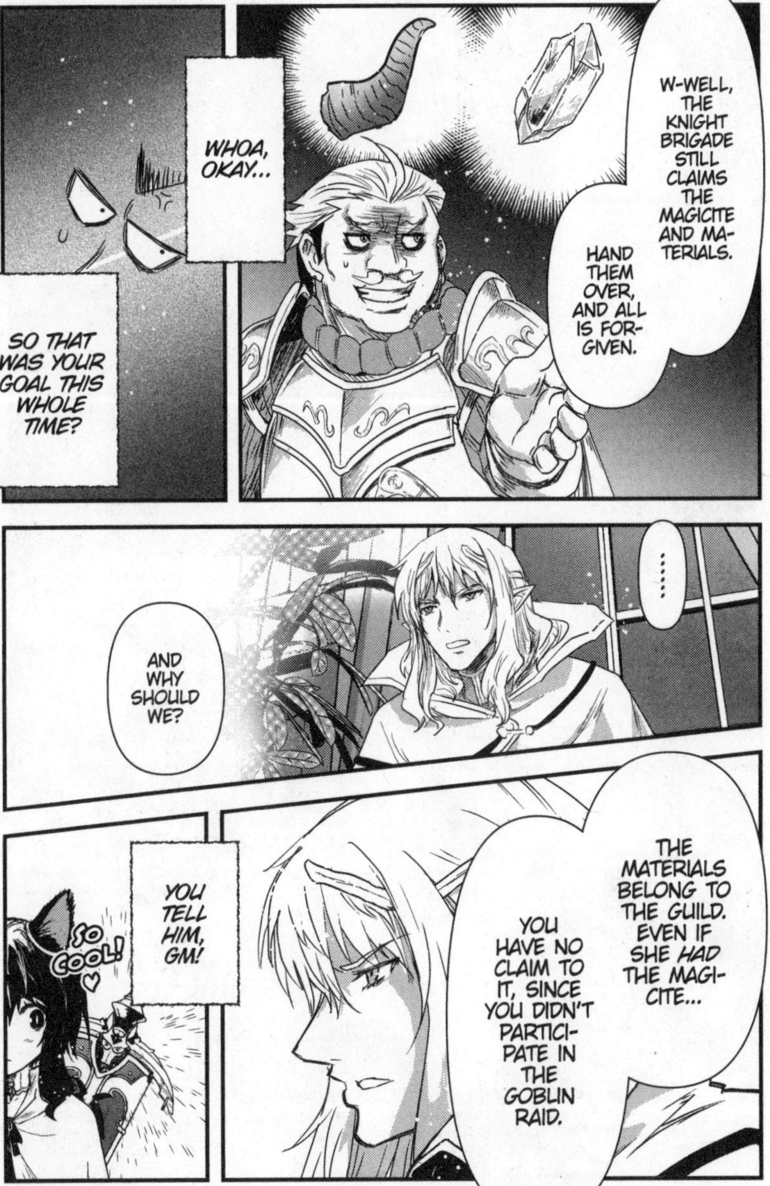
W-WELL, THE KNIGHT BRIGADE STILL CLAIMS THE MAGICITE AND MATERIALS.
HAND THEM OVER, AND ALL IS FORGIVEN.
WHOA, OKAY...
SO THAT WAS YOUR GOAL THIS WHOLE TIME?
......
AND WHY SHOULD WE?
THE MATERIALS BELONG TO THE GUILD. EVEN IF SHE *HAD* THE MAGICITE...
YOU HAVE NO CLAIM TO IT, SINCE YOU DIDN'T PARTICIPATE IN THE GOBLIN RAID.
YOU TELL HIM, GM!
SO COOL! ♥

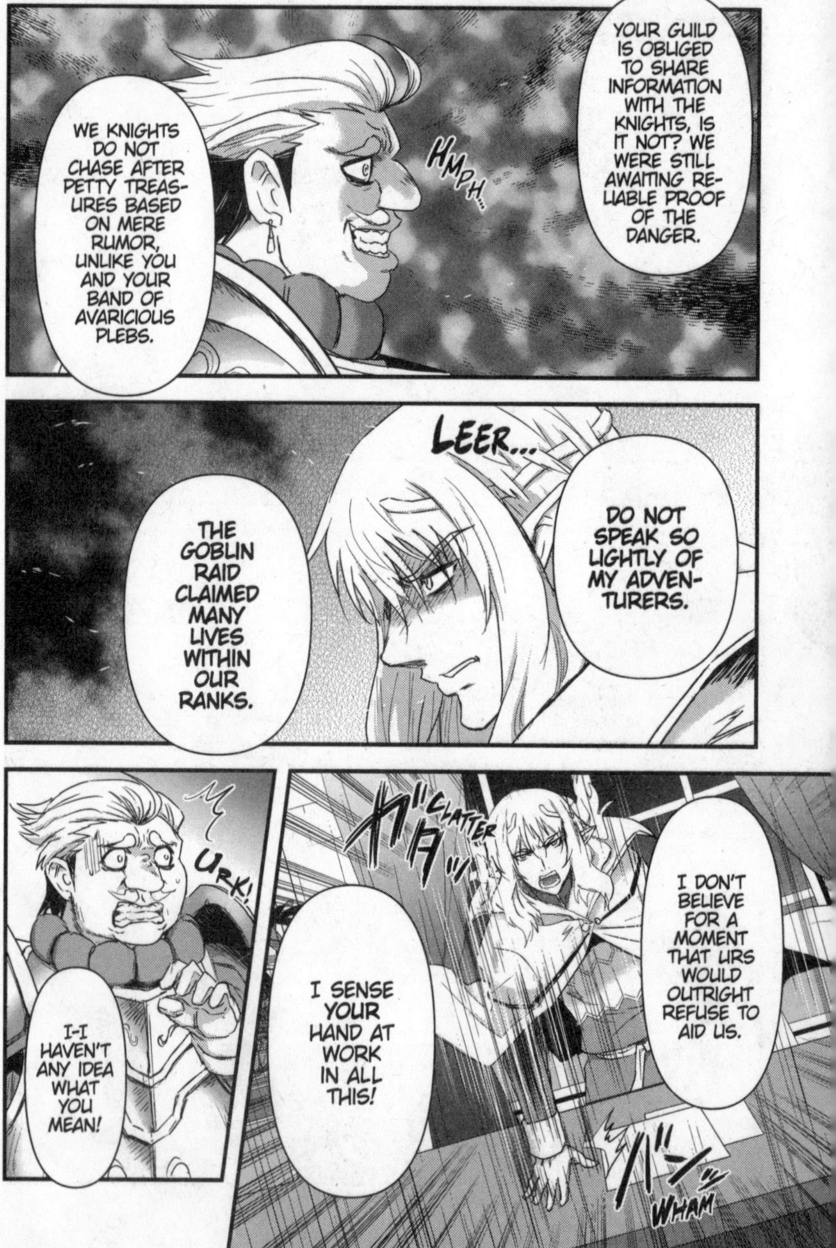
YOUR GUILD IS OBLIGED TO SHARE INFORMATION WITH THE KNIGHTS, IS IT NOT? WE WERE STILL AWAITING RE-LIABLE PROOF OF THE DANGER.
HMPH..
WE KNIGHTS DO NOT CHASE AFTER PETTY TREAS-URES BASED ON MERE RUMOR, UNLIKE YOU AND YOUR BAND OF AVARICIOUS PLEBS.
LEER...
DO NOT SPEAK SO LIGHTLY OF MY ADVEN-TURERS.
THE GOBLIN RAID CLAIMED MANY LIVES WITHIN OUR RANKS.
CLATTER
I DON'T BELIEVE FOR A MOMENT THAT URS WOULD OUTRIGHT REFUSE TO AID US.
I SENSE YOUR HAND AT WORK IN ALL THIS!
WHAM
M URK!
I-I HAVEN'T ANY IDEA WHAT YOU MEAN!

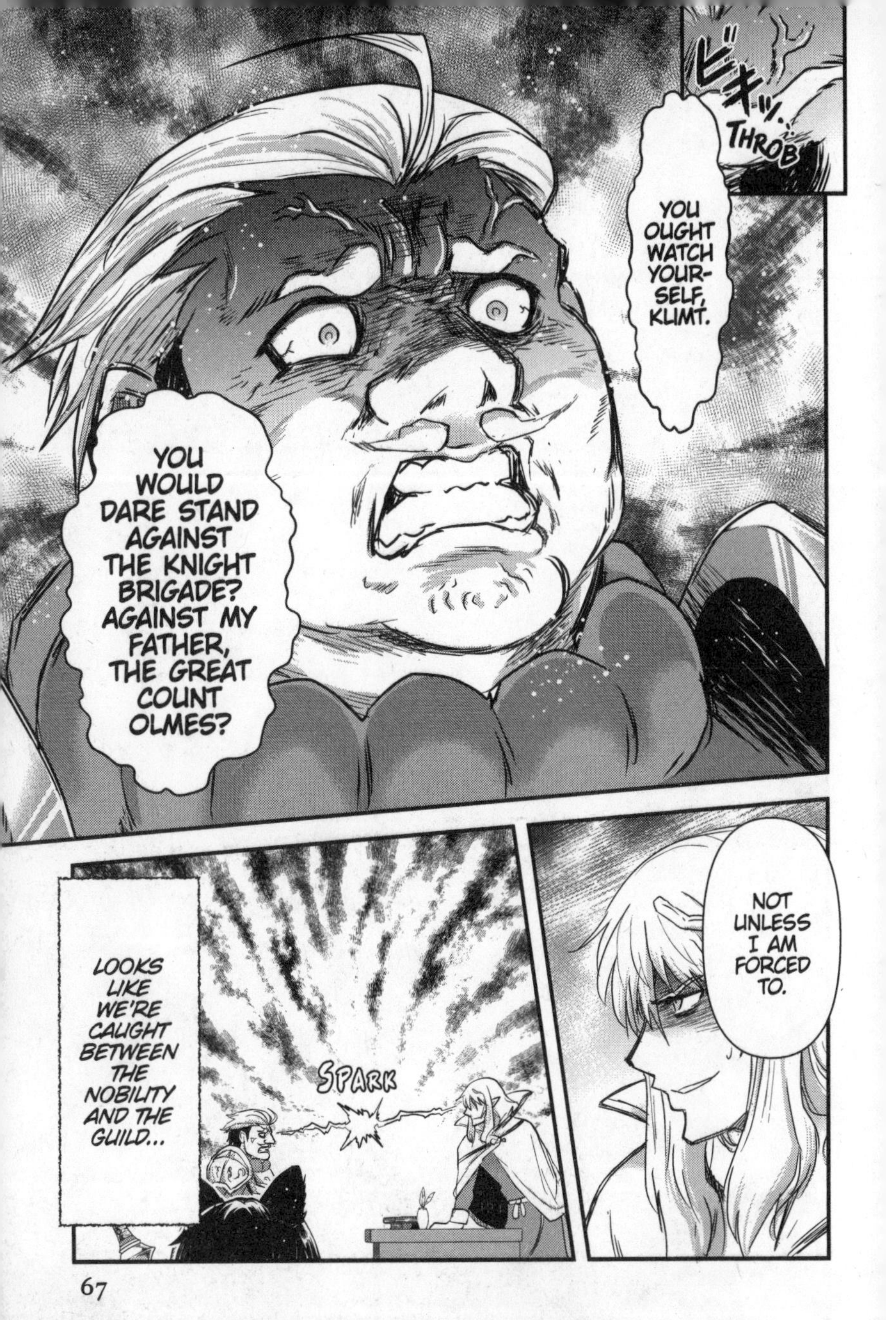
ビキッ
THROB
YOU OUGHT WATCH YOURSELF, KLIMT.
YOU WOULD DARE STAND AGAINST THE KNIGHT BRIGADE? AGAINST MY FATHER, THE GREAT COUNT OLMES?
NOT UNLESS I AM FORCED TO.
LOOKS LIKE WE'RE CAUGHT BETWEEN THE NOBILITY AND THE GUILD...
SPARK

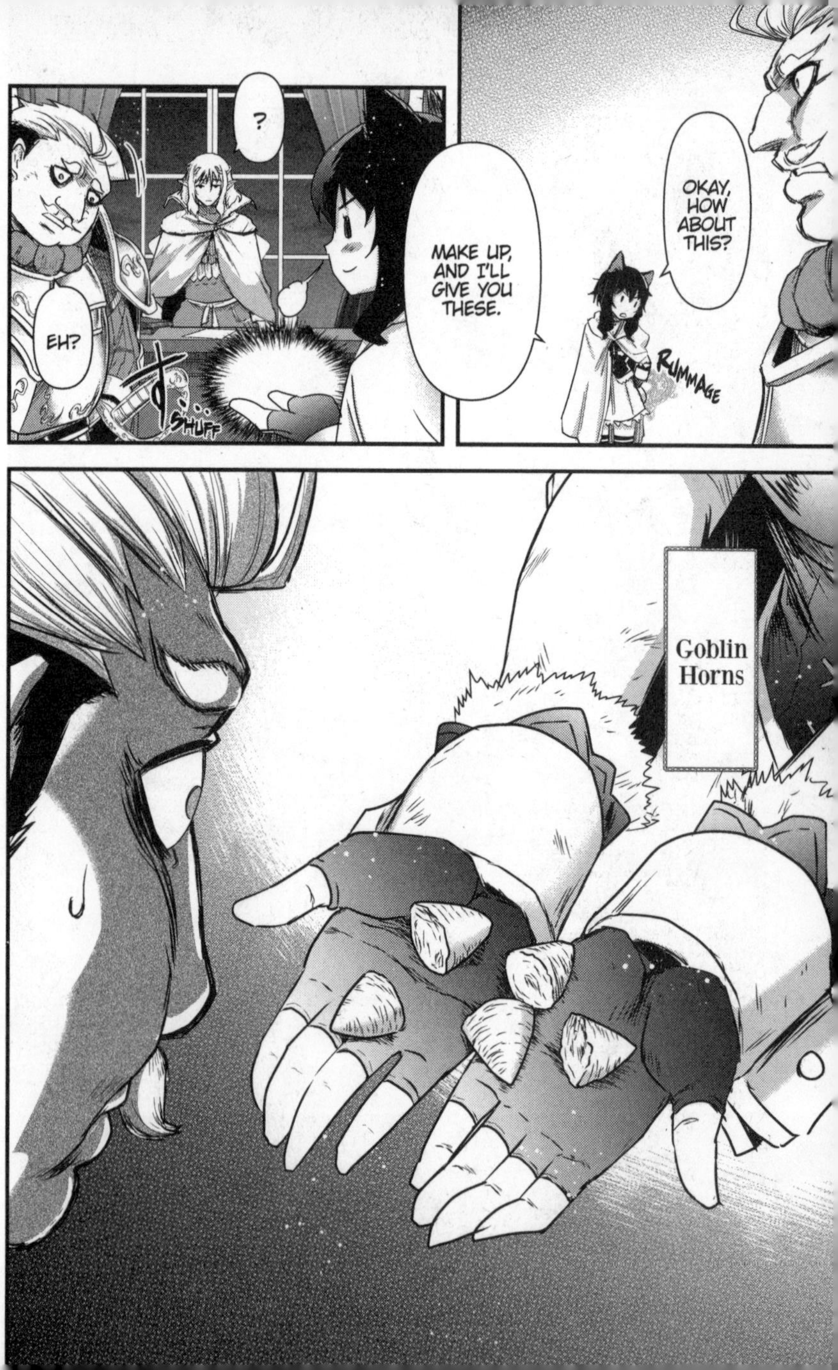
OKAY, HOW ABOUT THIS?
RUMMAGE
?
MAKE UP, AND I'LL GIVE YOU THESE.
EH?
SHUFF
Goblin Horns

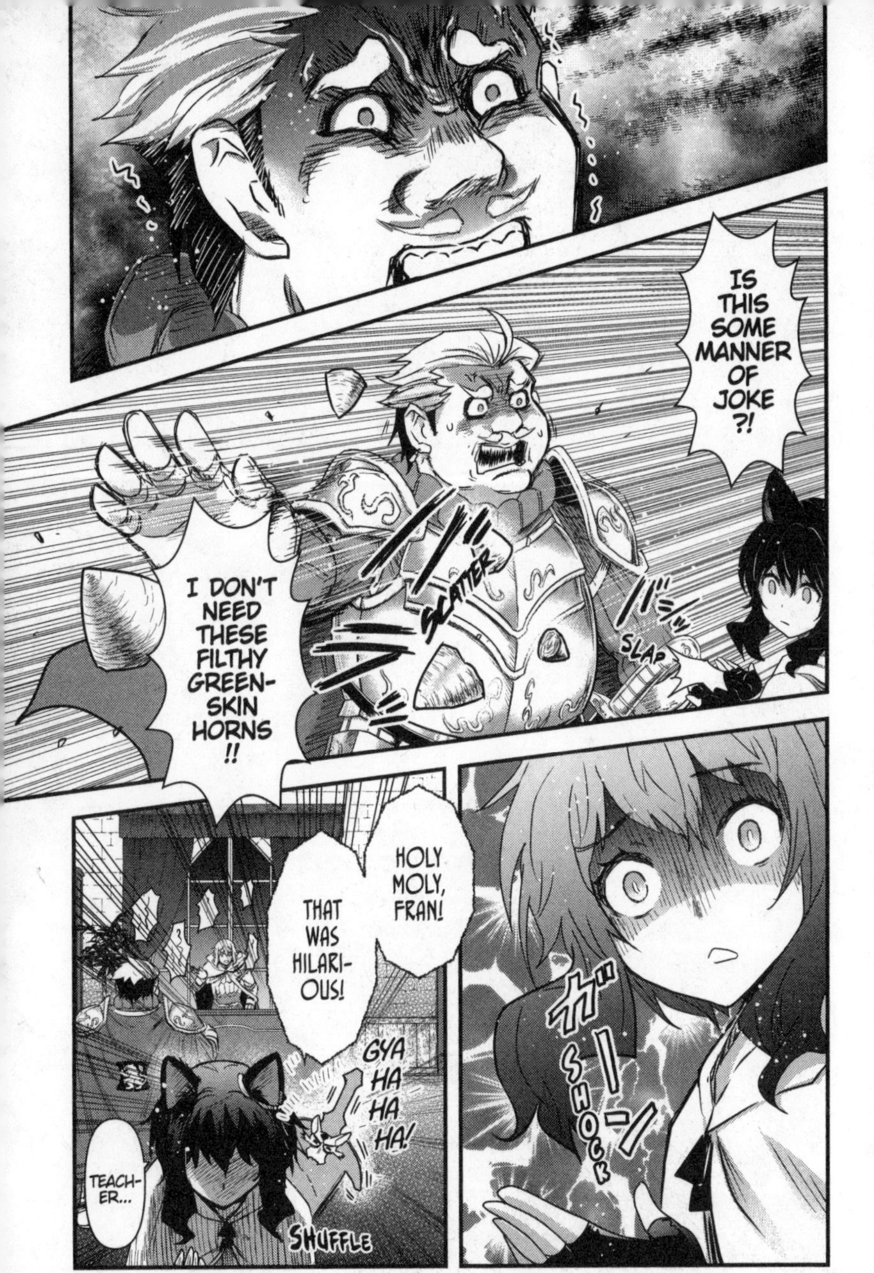
IS THIS SOME MANNER OF JOKE ?!
SCATTER
SLAP
I DON'T NEED THESE FILTHY GREEN-SKIN HORNS !!
SHOCK
HOLY MOLY, FRAN!
THAT WAS HILARI-OUS!
GYA HA HA HA!
TEACH-ER...
SHUFFLE

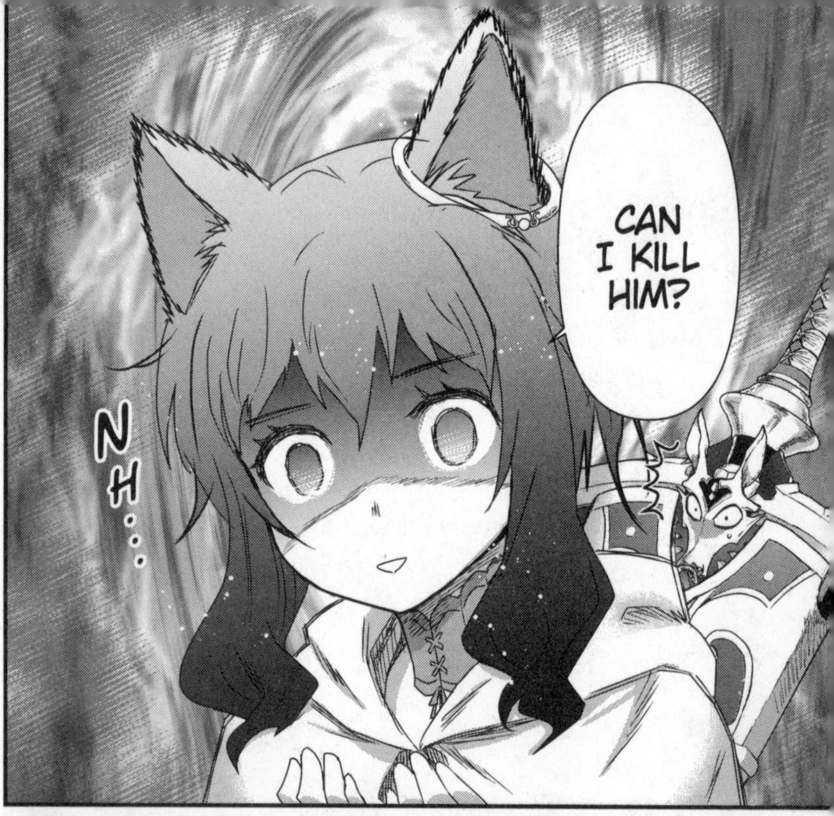
CAN I KILL HIM?
NH...
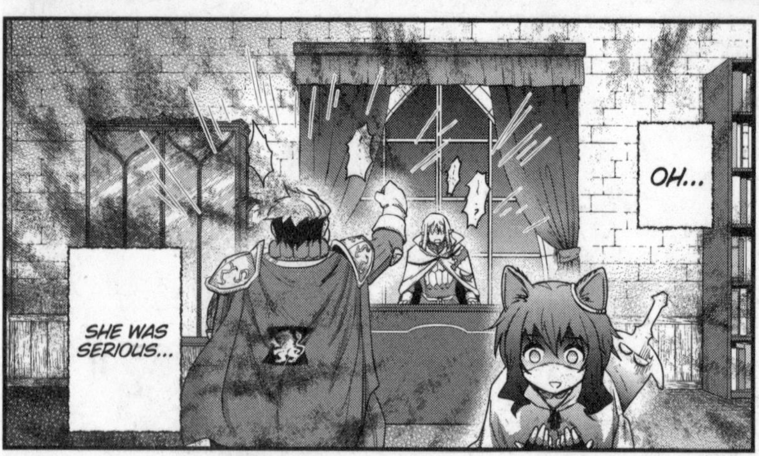
OH...
SHE WAS SERIOUS...

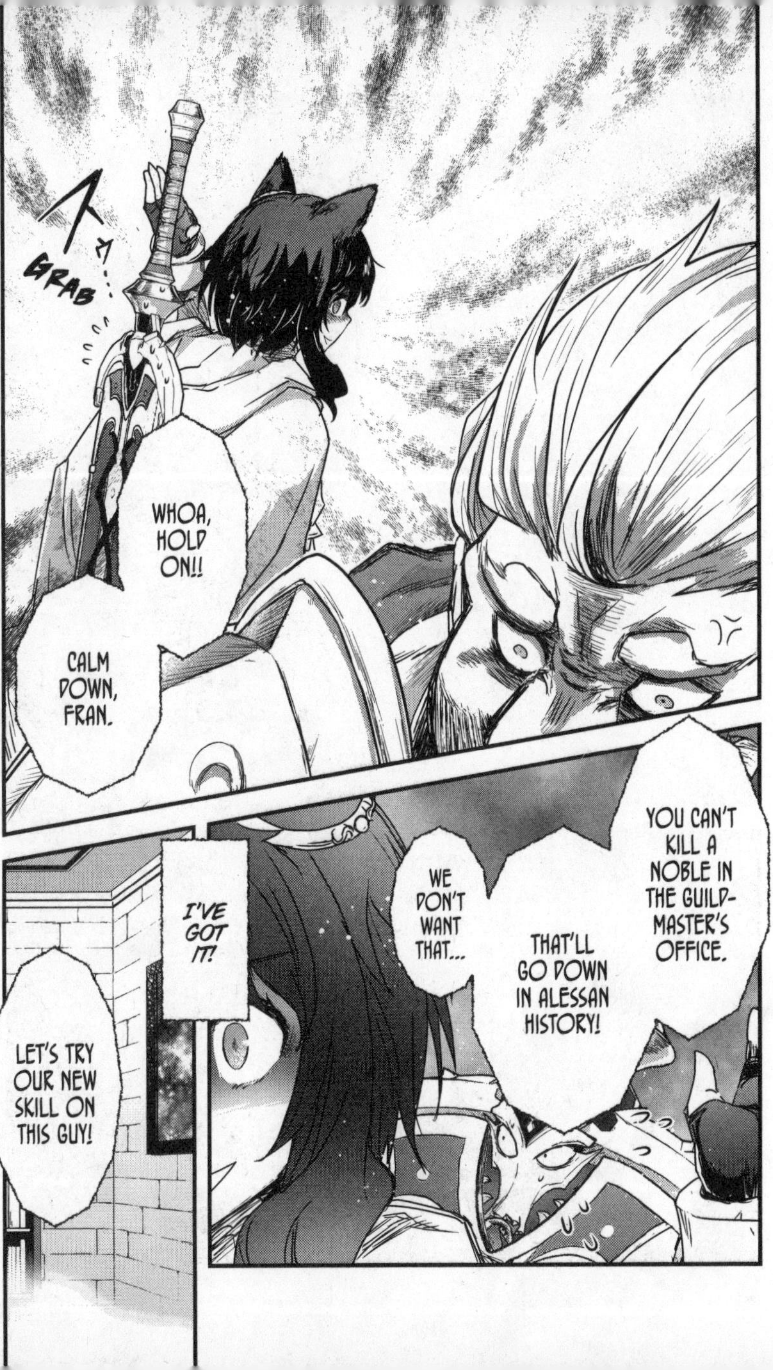
GRAB
WHOA, HOLD ON!!
CALM DOWN, FRAN.
YOU CAN'T KILL A NOBLE IN THE GUILD-MASTER'S OFFICE.
THAT'LL GO DOWN IN ALESSAN HISTORY!
WE DON'T WANT THAT...
I'VE GOT IT!
LET'S TRY OUR NEW SKILL ON THIS GUY!

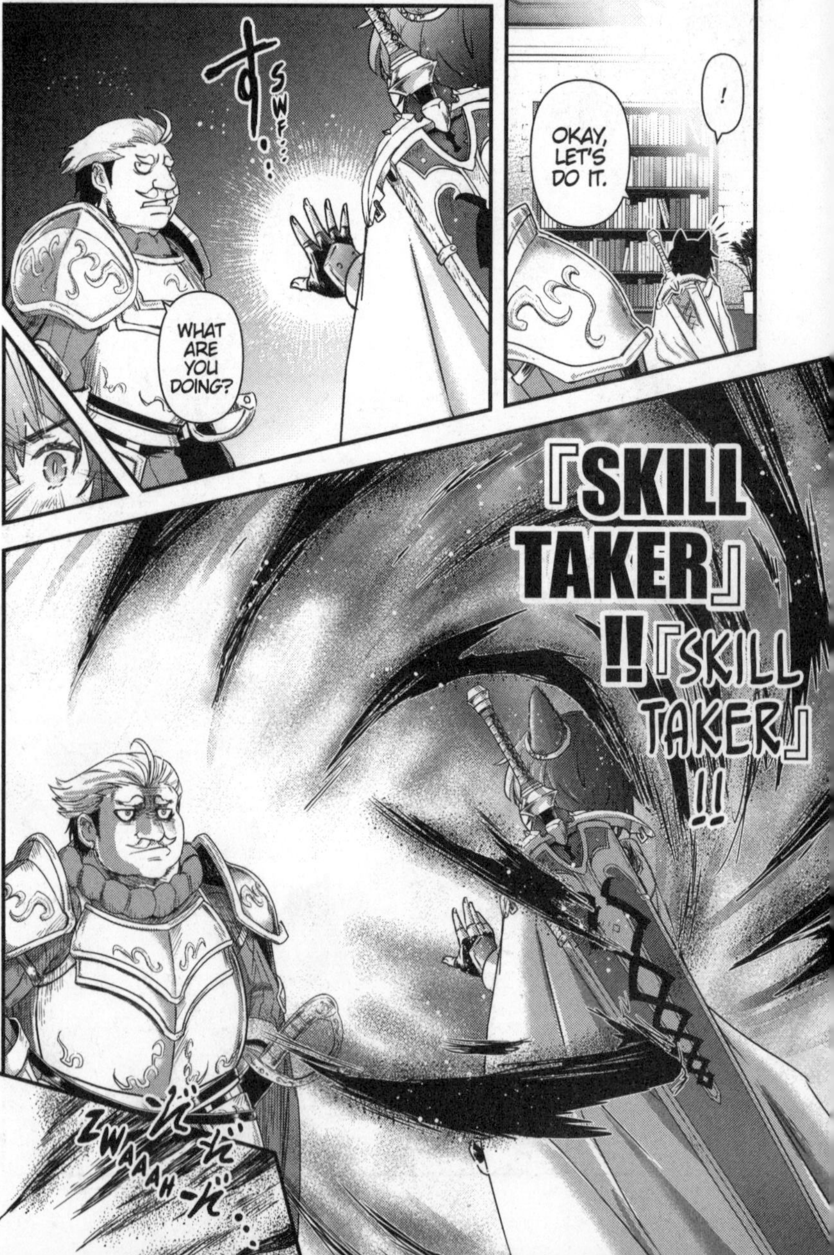
!
OKAY, LET'S DO IT.
す
SWF...!!
WHAT ARE YOU DOING?
『SKILL TAKER』!!
『SKILL TAKER』!!
ZWAAAH-...

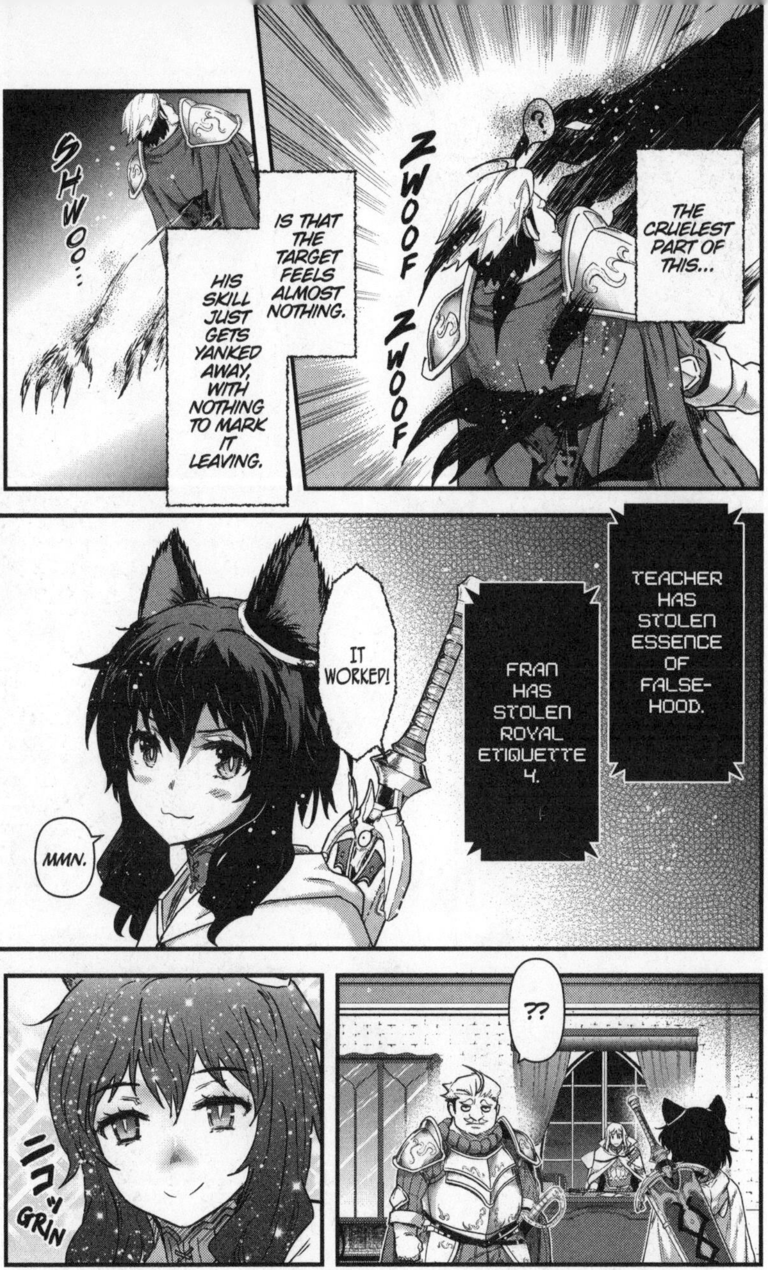
THE CRUELEST PART OF THIS...
ZWOOF ZWOOF
IS THAT THE TARGET FEELS ALMOST NOTHING.
HIS SKILL JUST GETS YANKED AWAY, WITH NOTHING TO MARK IT LEAVING.
SHWOO...
TEACHER HAS STOLEN ESSENCE OF FALSE-HOOD.
FRAN HAS STOLEN ROYAL ETIQUETTE 4.
IT WORKED!
MMN.
??
ニコッ
GRIN

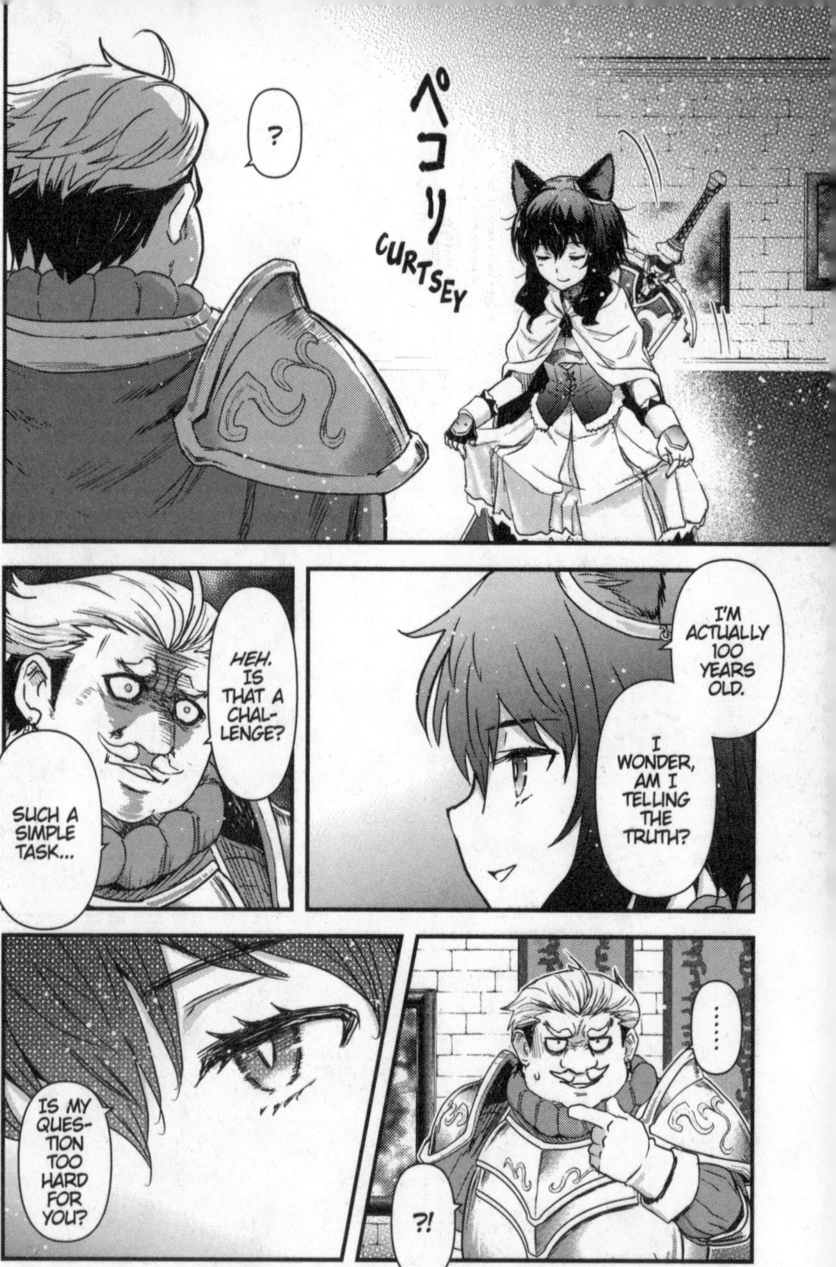
ペコリ
CURTSEY
?
I'M ACTUALLY 100 YEARS OLD.
I WONDER, AM I TELLING THE TRUTH?
HEH. IS THAT A CHAL-LENGE?
SUCH A SIMPLE TASK...
......
?!
IS MY QUES-TION TOO HARD FOR YOU?

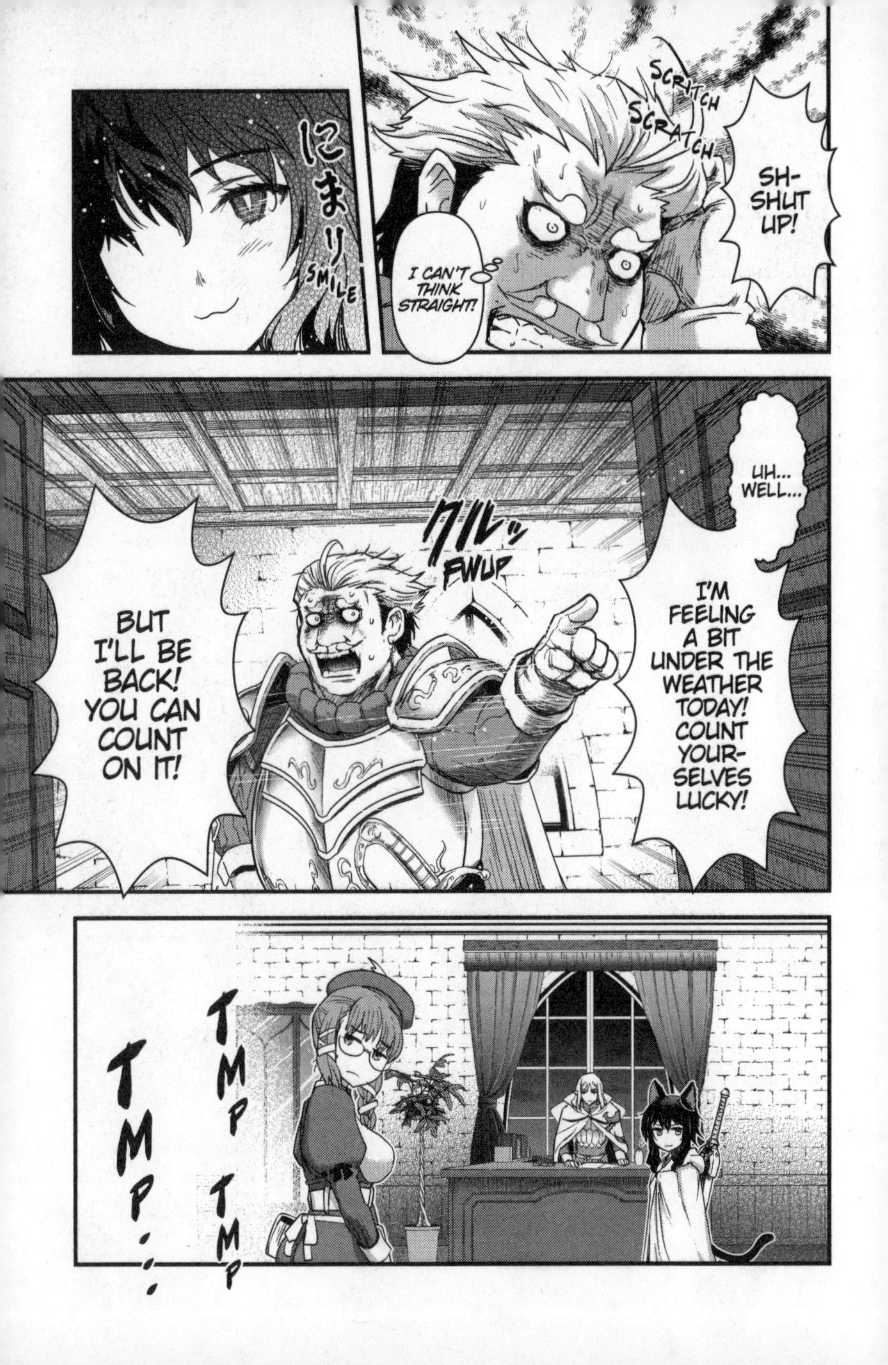
SCRITCH
SCRATCH
SH- SHUT UP!
I CAN'T THINK STRAIGHT!
にまり
SMILE
UH... WELL...
I'M FEELING A BIT UNDER THE WEATHER TODAY! COUNT YOUR-SELVES LUCKY!
クルッ
FWUP
BUT I'LL BE BACK! YOU CAN COUNT ON IT!
TMP
TMP
TMP...

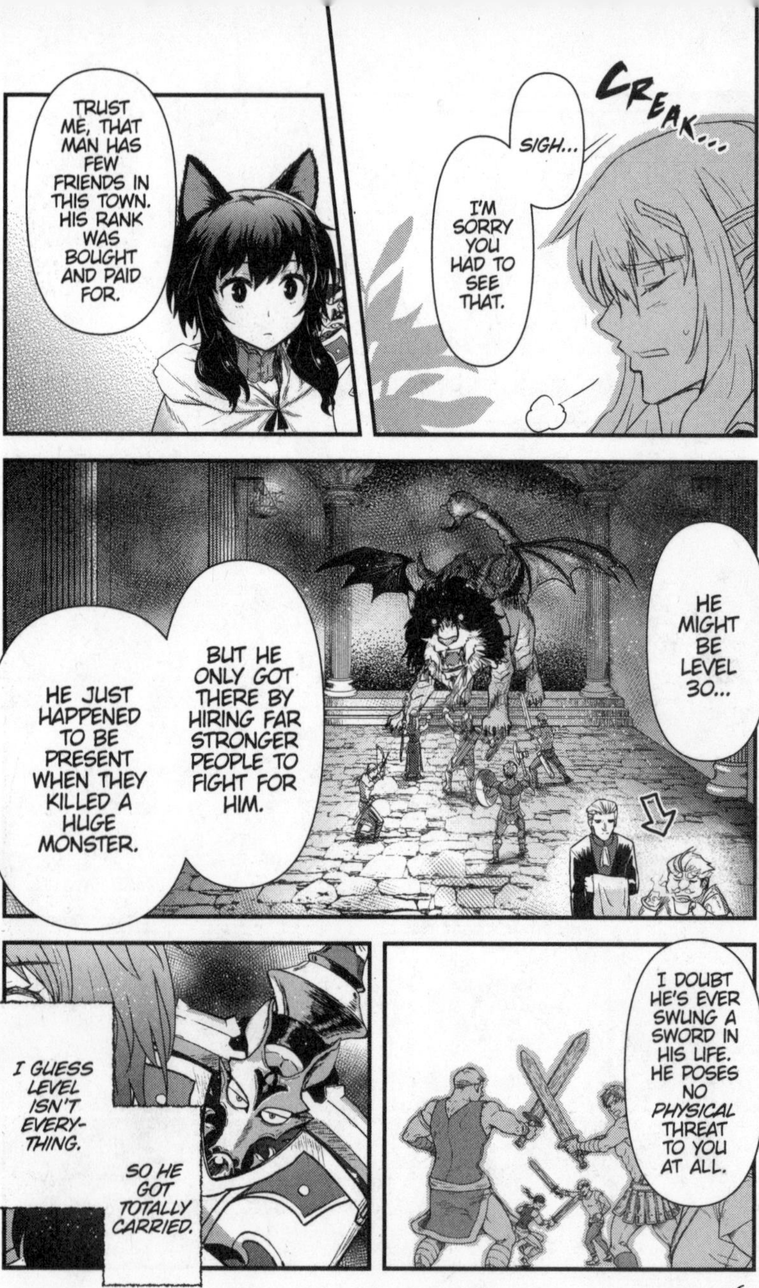
CREAK...
SIGH...
I'M SORRY YOU HAD TO SEE THAT.
TRUST ME, THAT MAN HAS FEW FRIENDS IN THIS TOWN. HIS RANK WAS BOUGHT AND PAID FOR.
HE MIGHT BE LEVEL 30...
BUT HE ONLY GOT THERE BY HIRING FAR STRONGER PEOPLE TO FIGHT FOR HIM.
HE JUST HAPPENED TO BE PRESENT WHEN THEY KILLED A HUGE MONSTER.
I DOUBT HE'S EVER SWUNG A SWORD IN HIS LIFE. HE POSES NO PHYSICAL THREAT TO YOU AT ALL.
I GUESS LEVEL ISN'T EVERY-THING.
SO HE GOT TOTALLY CARRIED.

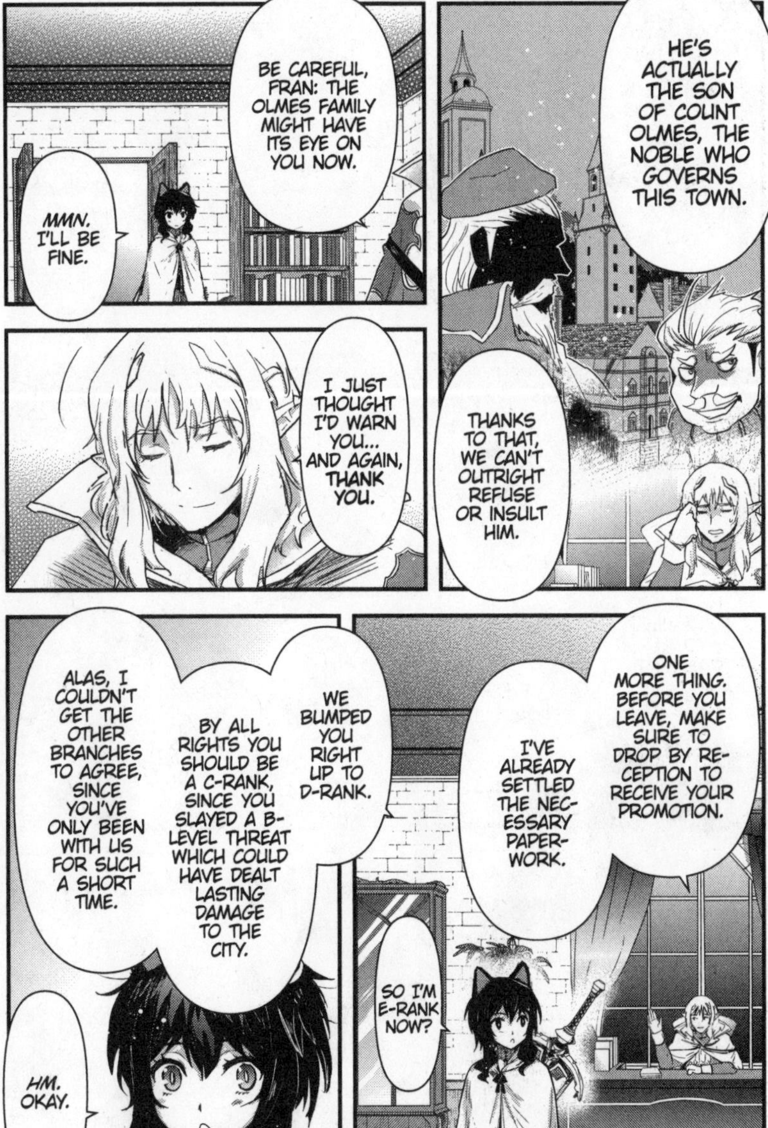
HE'S ACTUALLY THE SON OF COUNT OLMES, THE NOBLE WHO GOVERNS THIS TOWN.
THANKS TO THAT, WE CAN'T OUTRIGHT REFUSE OR INSULT HIM.
BE CAREFUL, FRAN: THE OLMES FAMILY MIGHT HAVE ITS EYE ON YOU NOW.
MMN. I'LL BE FINE.
I JUST THOUGHT I'D WARN YOU... AND AGAIN, THANK YOU.
ONE MORE THING. BEFORE YOU LEAVE, MAKE SURE TO DROP BY RE-CEPTION TO RECEIVE YOUR PROMOTION.
I'VE ALREADY SETTLED THE NEC-ESSARY PAPER-WORK.
SO I'M E-RANK NOW?
WE BUMPED YOU RIGHT UP TO D-RANK.
BY ALL RIGHTS YOU SHOULD BE A C-RANK, SINCE YOU SLAYED A B-LEVEL THREAT WHICH COULD HAVE DEALT LASTING DAMAGE TO THE CITY.
ALAS, I COULDN'T GET THE OTHER BRANCHES TO AGREE, SINCE YOU'VE ONLY BEEN WITH US FOR SUCH A SHORT TIME.
HM. OKAY.

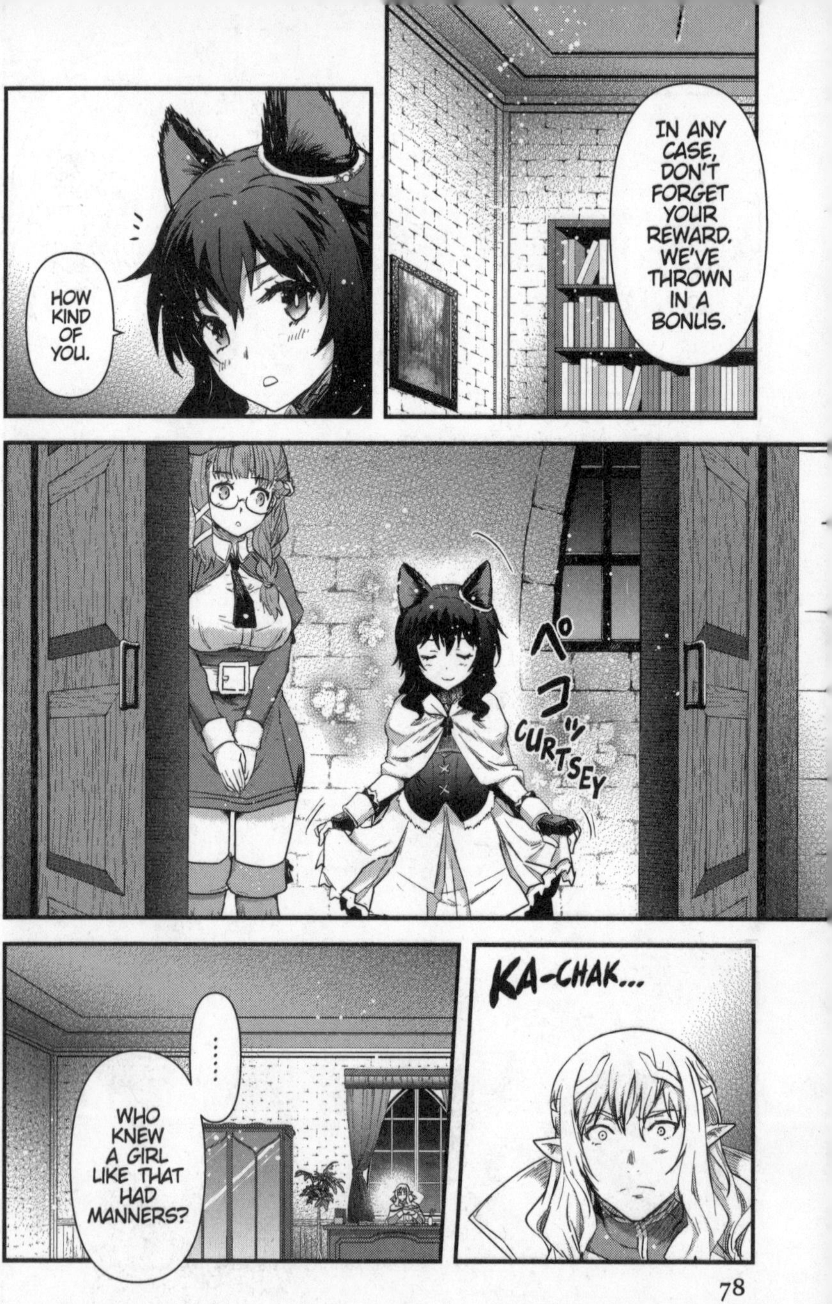
IN ANY CASE, DON'T FORGET YOUR REWARD. WE'VE THROWN IN A BONUS.
HOW KIND OF YOU.
ペコッ
CURTSEY
KA-CHAK...
......
WHO KNEW A GIRL LIKE THAT HAD MANNERS?

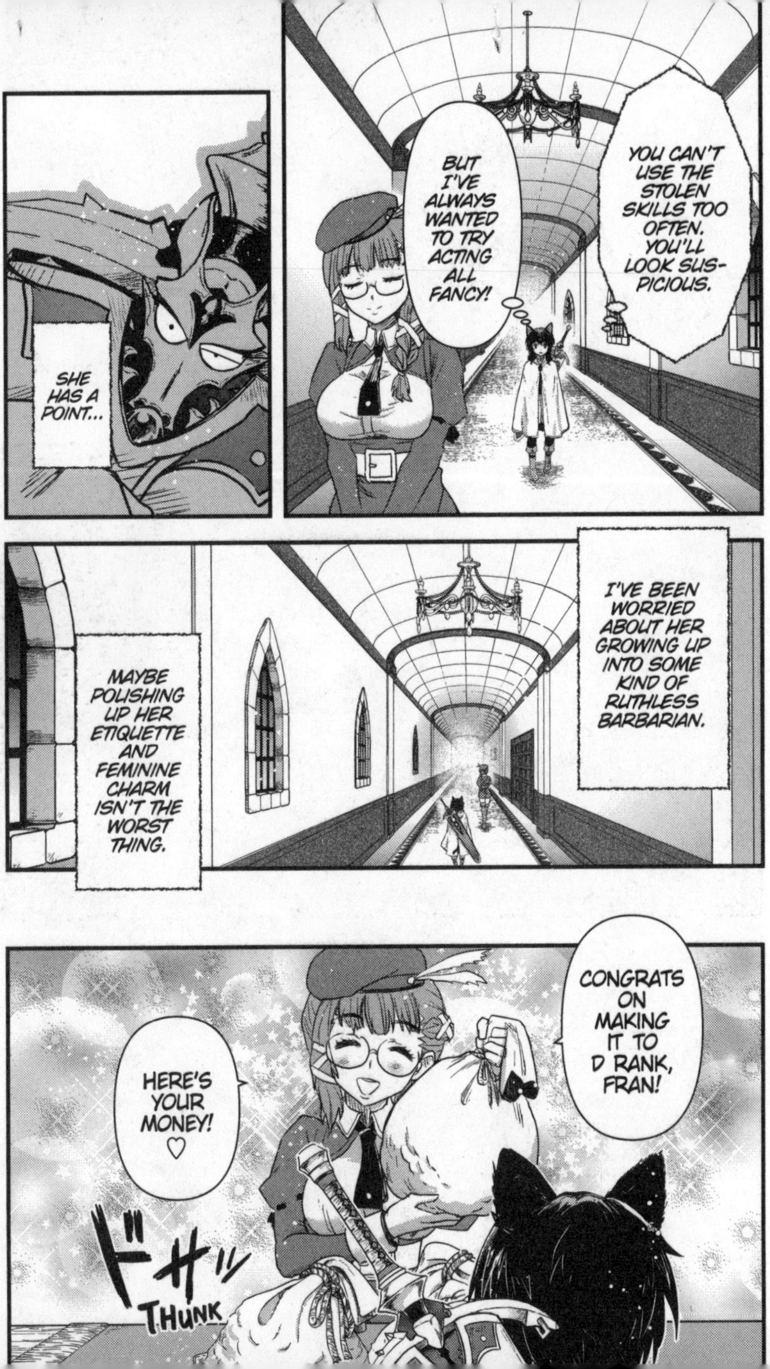
YOU CAN'T USE THE STOLEN SKILLS TOO OFTEN. YOU'LL LOOK SUS-PICIOUS.
BUT I'VE ALWAYS WANTED TO TRY ACTING ALL FANCY!
SHE HAS A POINT...
I'VE BEEN WORRIED ABOUT HER GROWING UP INTO SOME KIND OF RUTHLESS BARBARIAN.
MAYBE POLISHING UP HER ETIQUETTE AND FEMININE CHARM ISN'T THE WORST THING.
CONGRATS ON MAKING IT TO D RANK, FRAN!
HERE'S YOUR MONEY! ♡
ドサッ
THUNK

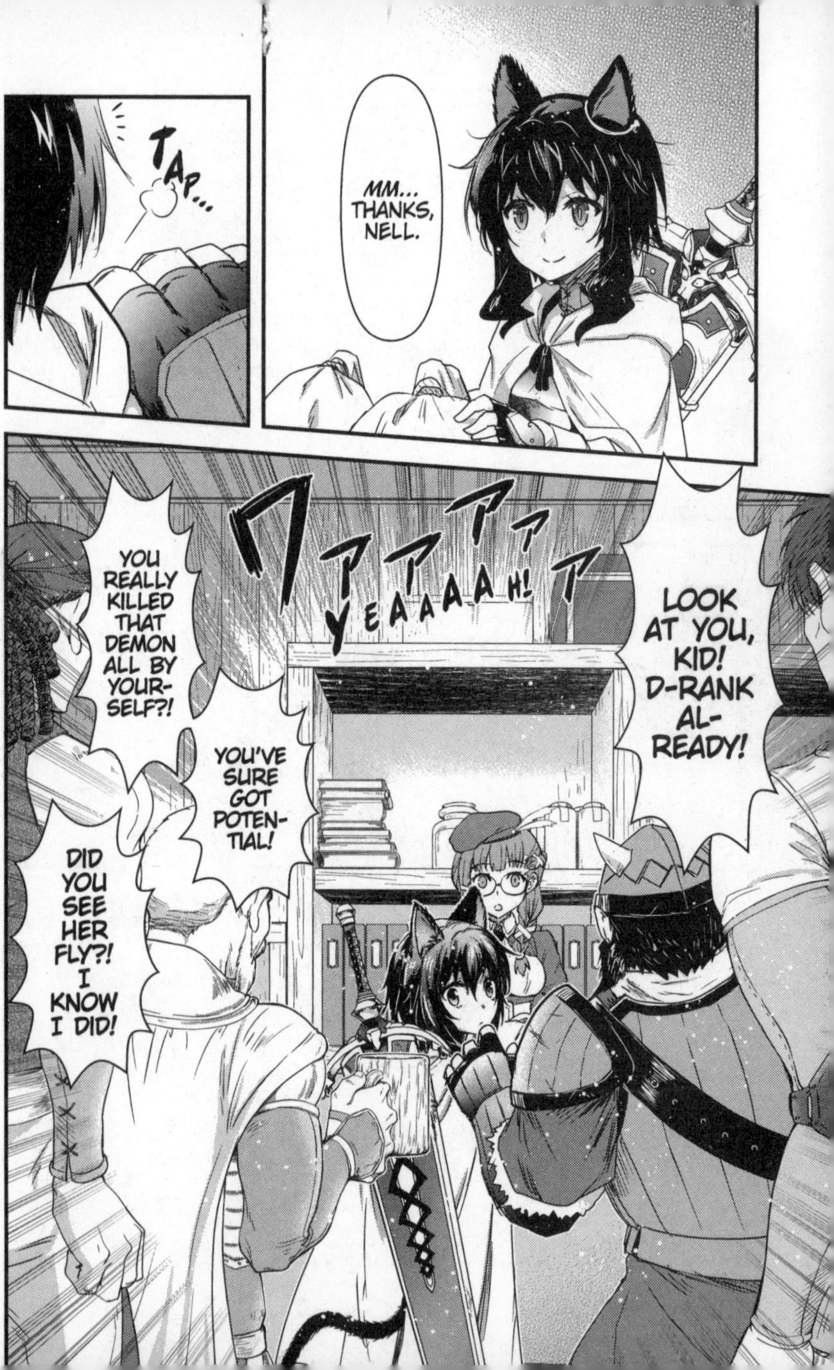
MM... THANKS, NELL.
TAP...
LOOK AT YOU, KID! D-RANK AL-READY!
YEAAAAH!
YOU REALLY KILLED THAT DEMON ALL BY YOUR-SELF?!
YOU'VE SURE GOT POTEN-TIAL!
DID YOU SEE HER FLY?! I KNOW I DID!

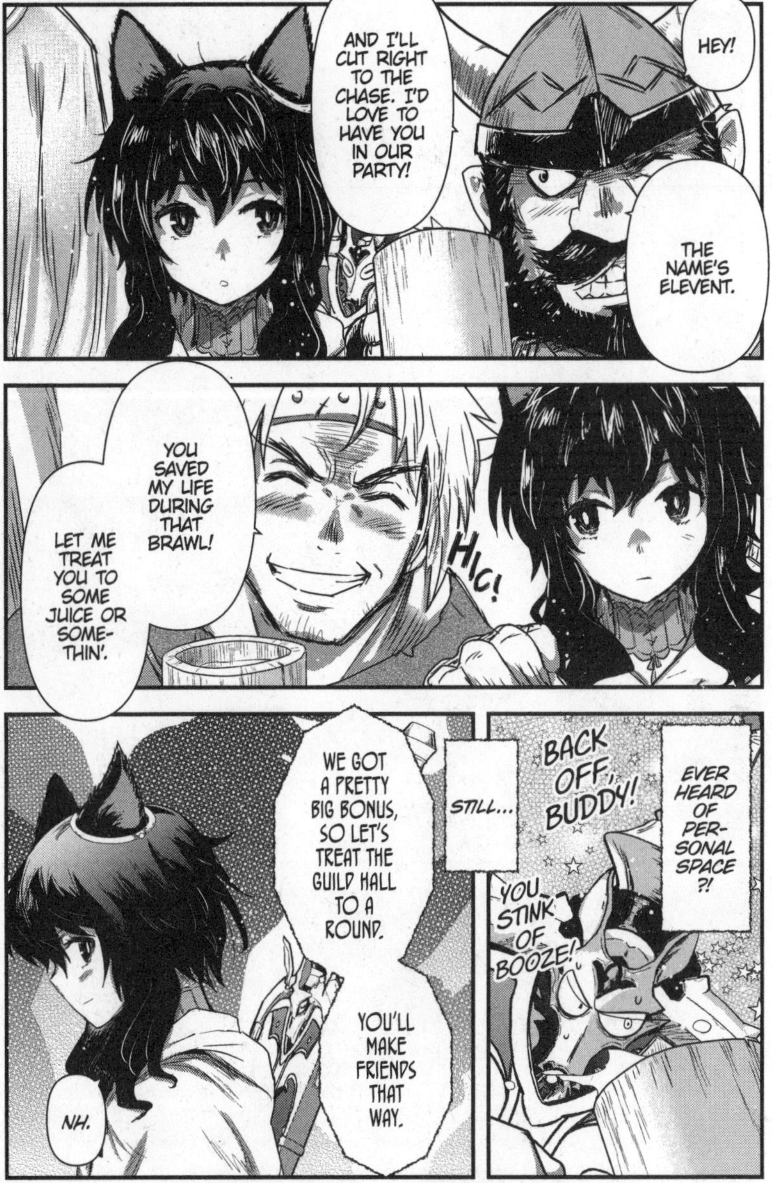
HEY!
THE NAME'S ELEVENT.
AND I'LL CUT RIGHT TO THE CHASE. I'D LOVE TO HAVE YOU IN OUR PARTY!
HIC!
YOU SAVED MY LIFE DURING THAT BRAWL!
LET ME TREAT YOU TO SOME JUICE OR SOME-THIN'.
EVER HEARD OF PER-SONAL SPACE?!
BACK OFF, BUDDY!
YOU STINK OF BOOZE!
STILL...
WE GOT A PRETTY BIG BONUS, SO LET'S TREAT THE GUILD HALL TO A ROUND.
YOU'LL MAKE FRIENDS THAT WAY.
NH.

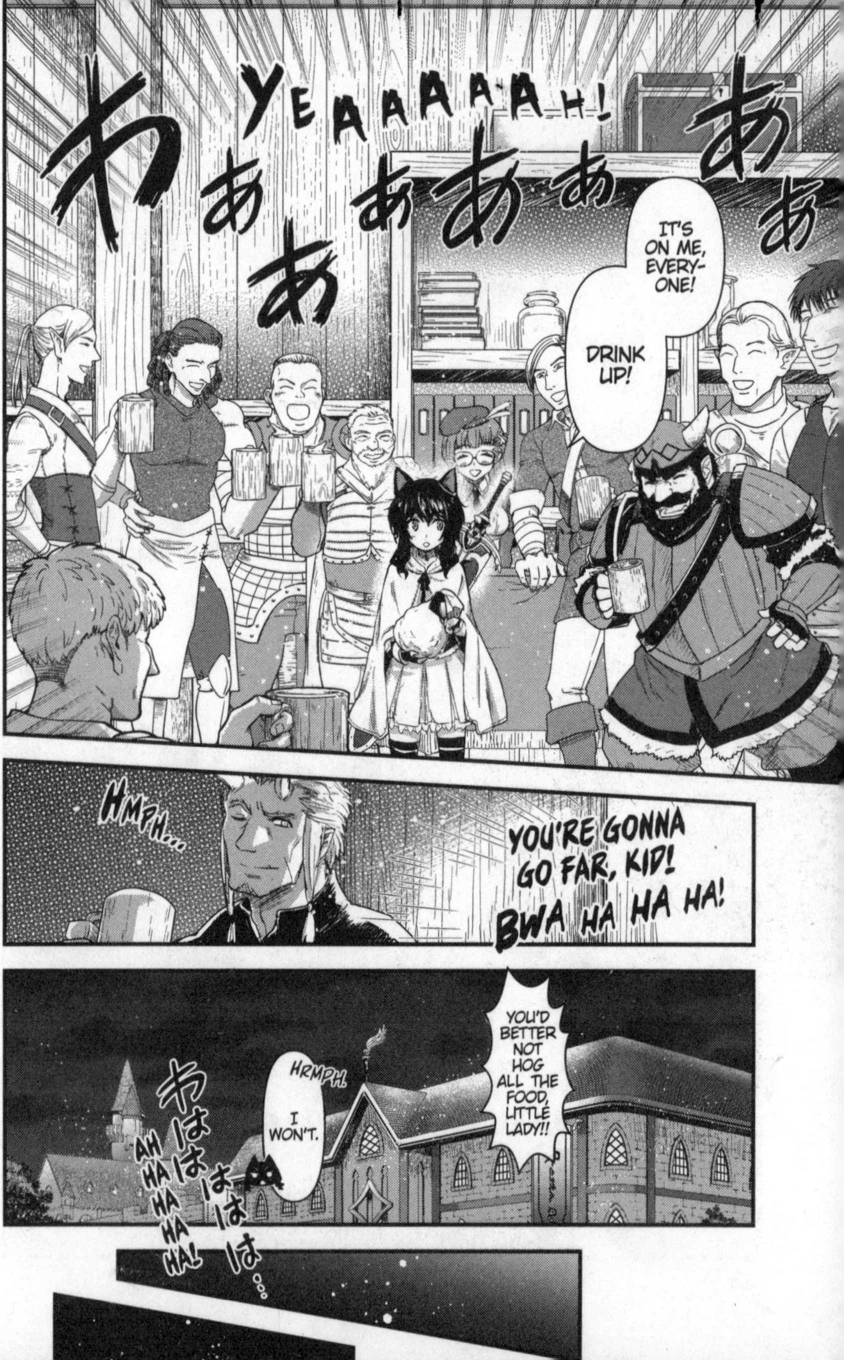

YEAAAAAH!
わあああああああ
IT'S ON ME, EVERYONE!
DRINK UP!
YOU'RE GONNA GO FAR, KID!
BWA HA HA HA!
HMPH...
YOU'D BETTER NOT HOG ALL THE FOOD, LITTLE LADY!!
HRMPH.
I WON'T.
やははははは…
AH HA HA HA HA!

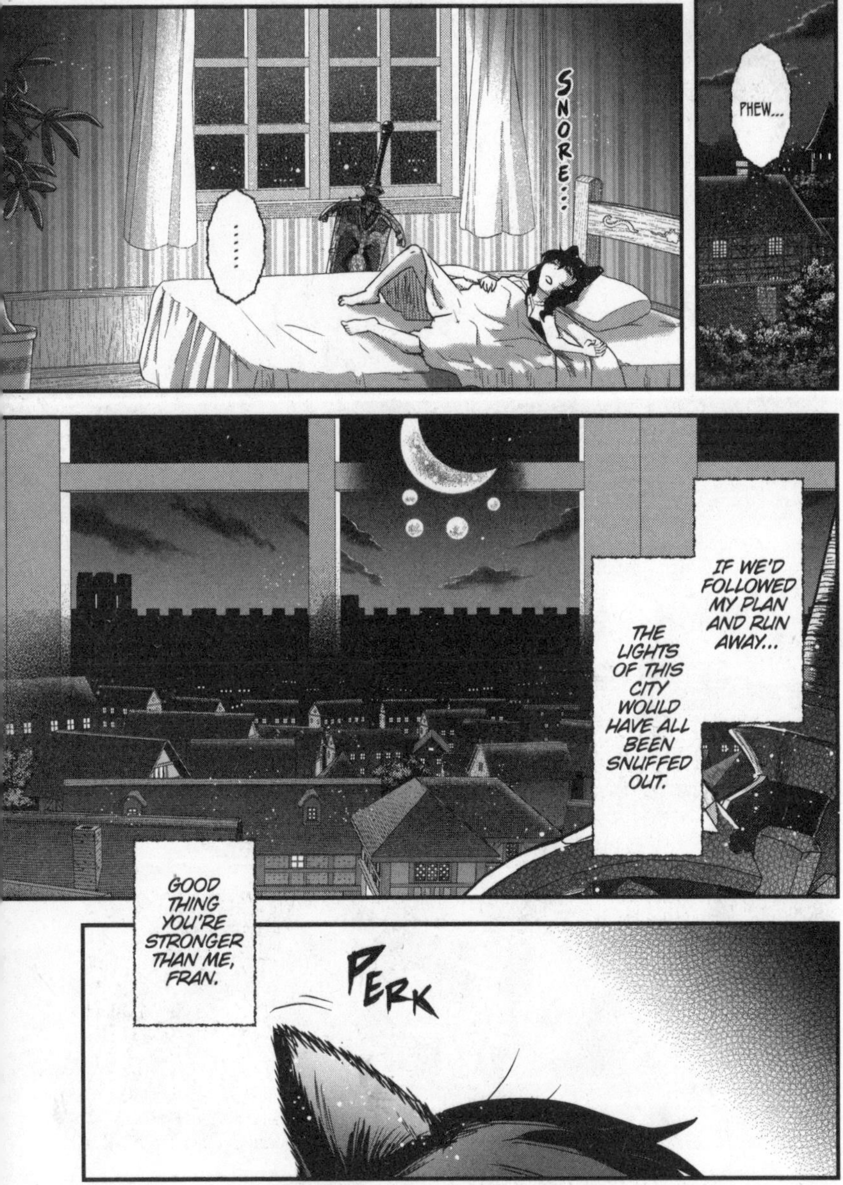
PHEW...
SNORE...
......
IF WE'D FOLLOWED MY PLAN AND RUN AWAY...
THE LIGHTS OF THIS CITY WOULD HAVE ALL BEEN SNUFFED OUT.
GOOD THING YOU'RE STRONGER THAN ME, FRAN.
PERK

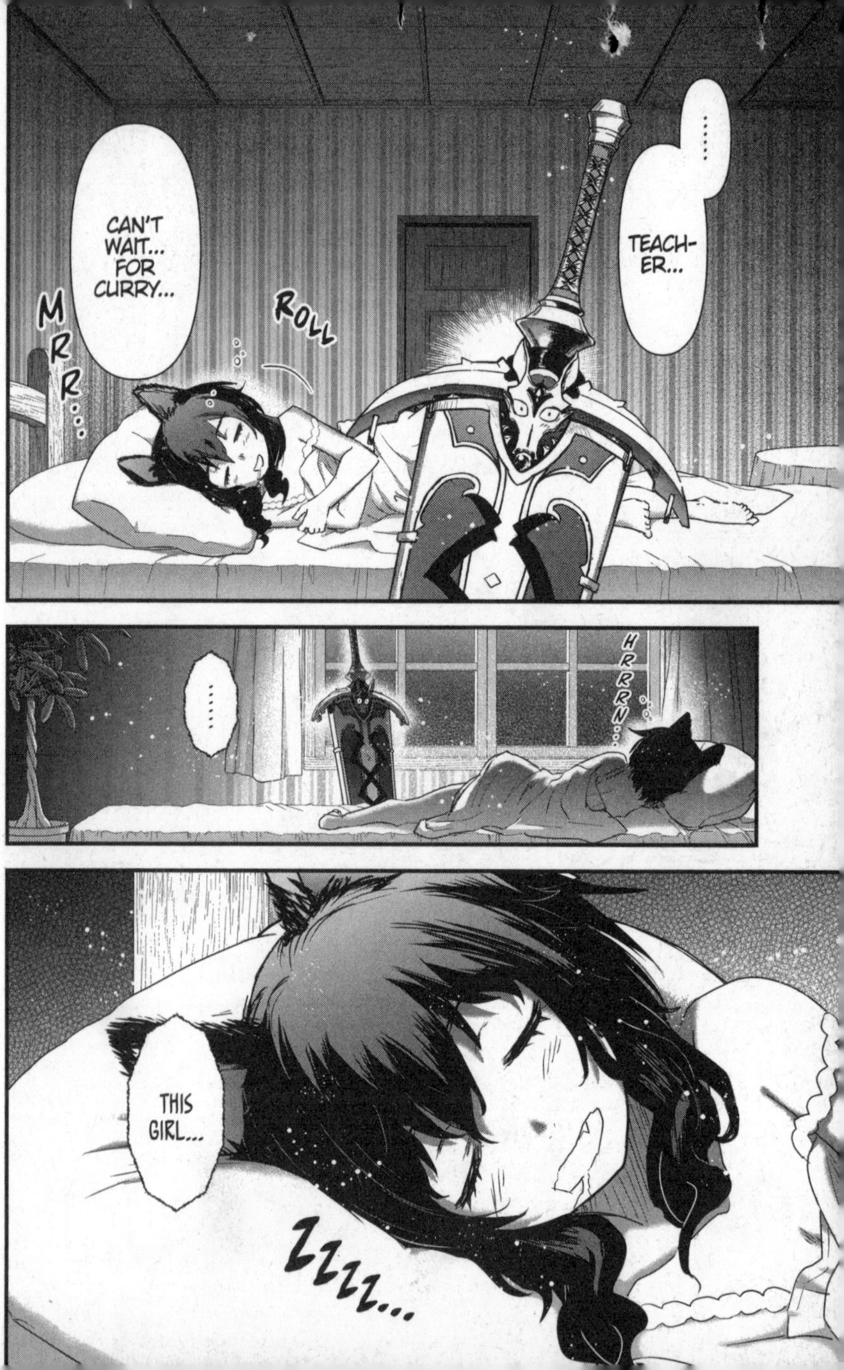
......
TEACHER...
CAN'T WAIT... FOR CURRY...
ROLL
MRR...
HRRRN...
......
THIS GIRL...
ZZZZ...

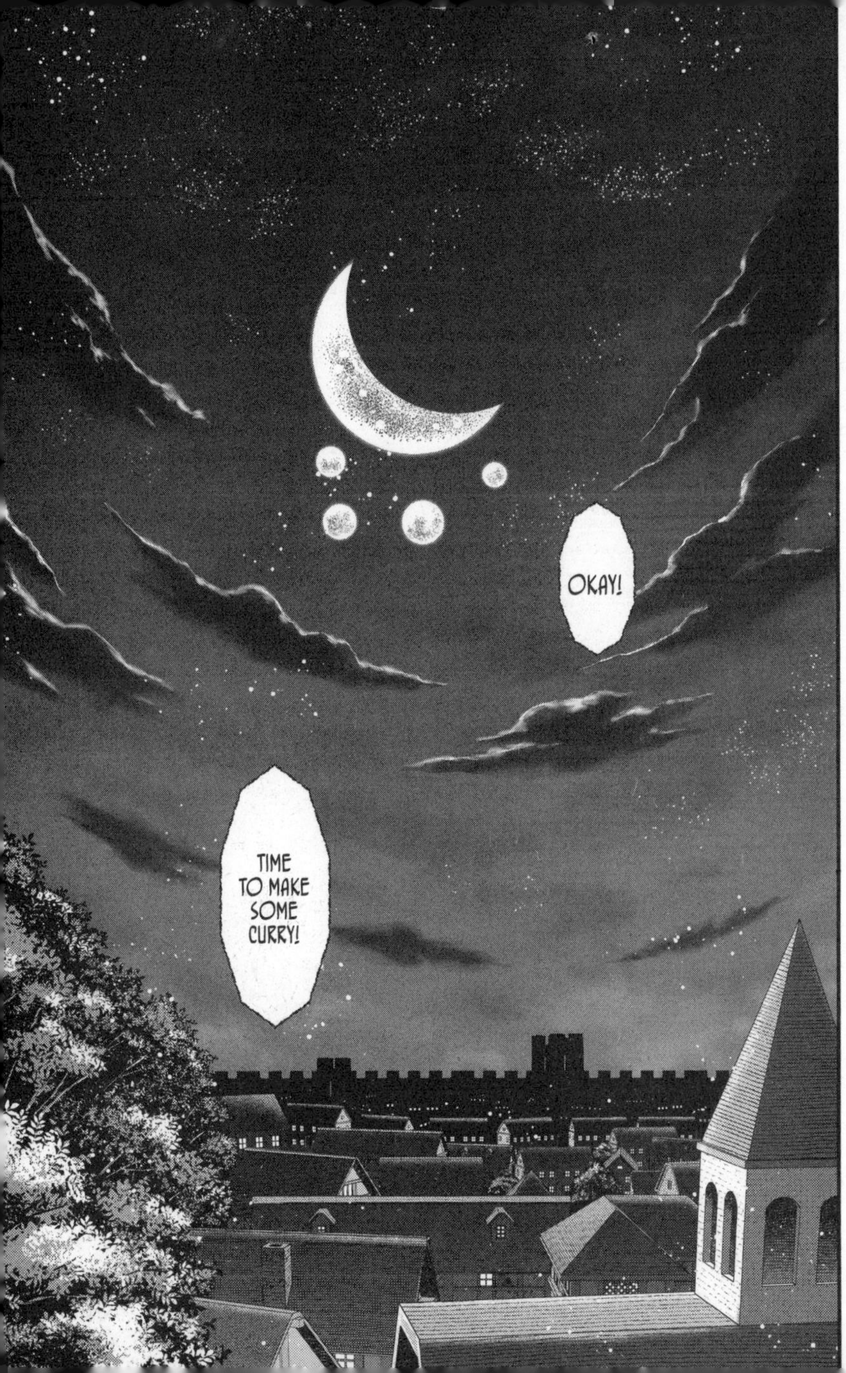
OKAY!
TIME TO MAKE SOME CURRY!

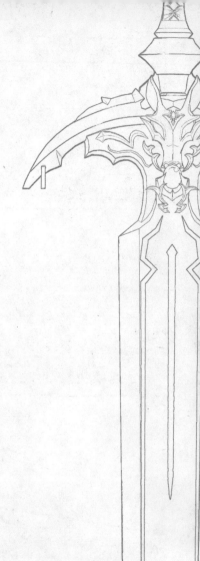

Reincarnated
as a sword

WHAT?

Chapter 15: Blue Cat Blood Feud

I DON'T UNDER-STAND ...

WHO ARE YOU ...?

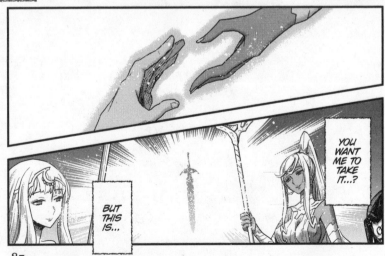

YOU WANT ME TO TAKE IT...?

BUT THIS IS...

87

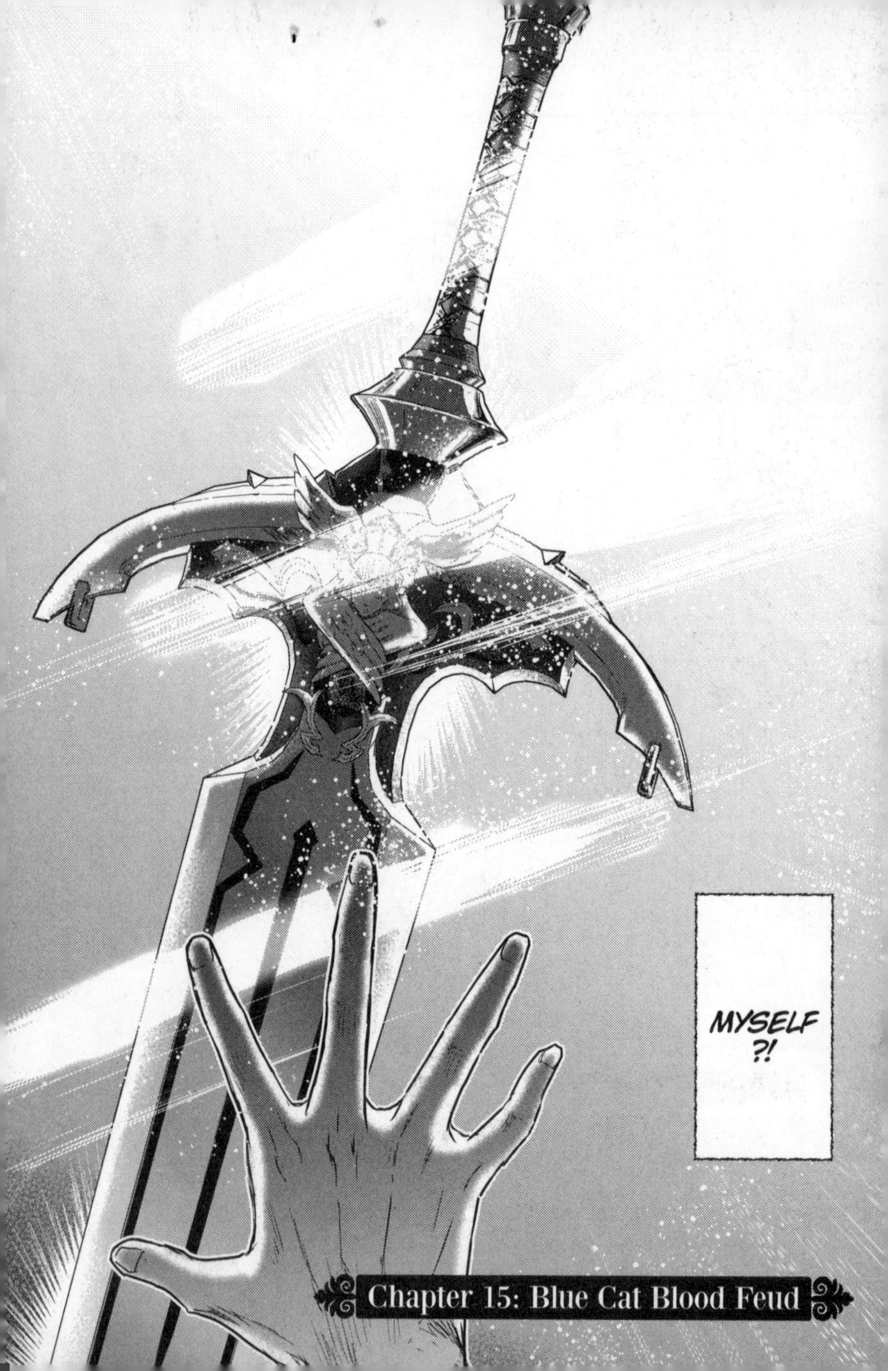
MYSELF
?!

Chapter 15: Blue Cat Blood Feud

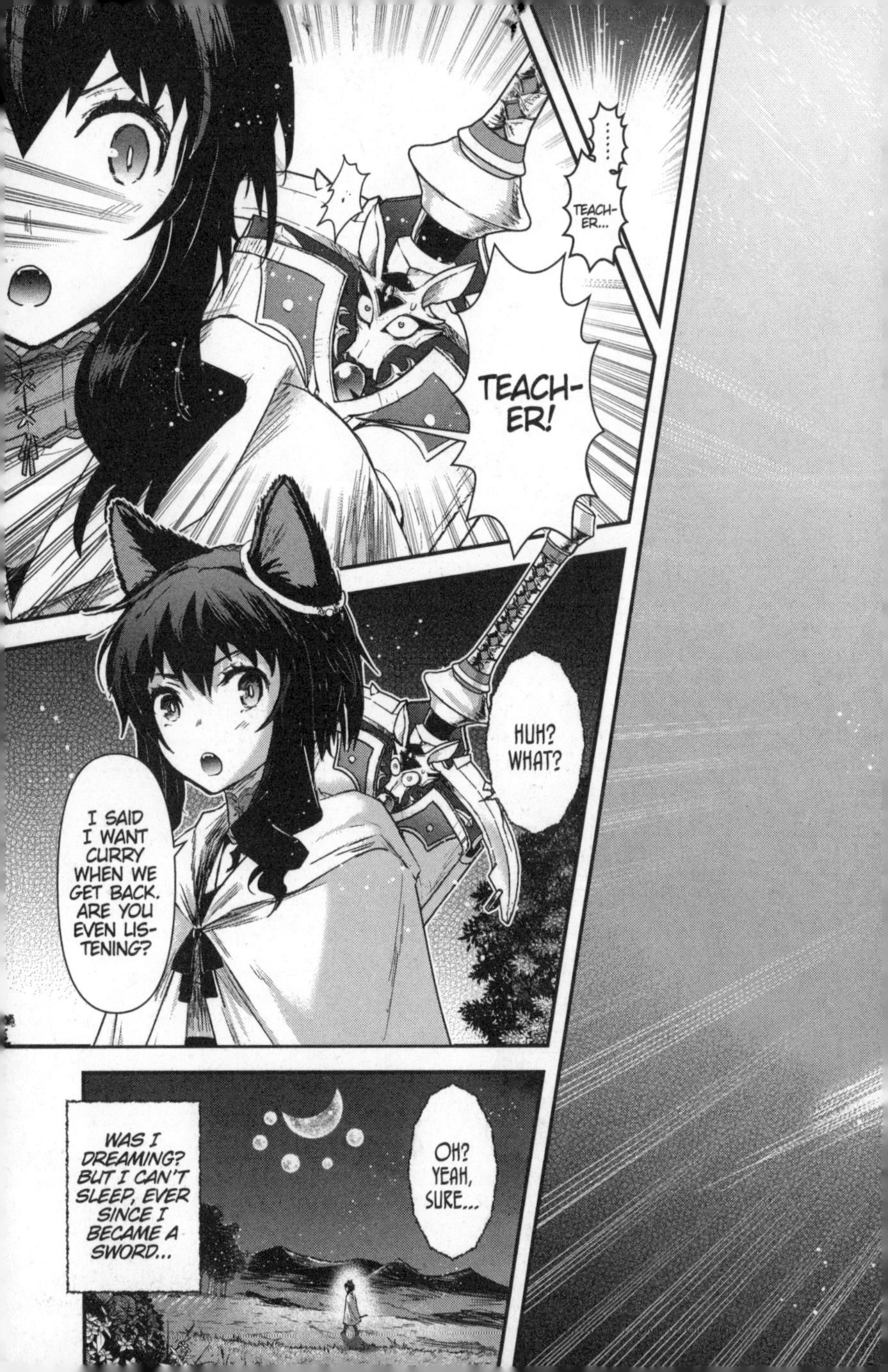
......
TEACH-ER...
TEACH-ER!
HUH? WHAT?
I SAID I WANT CURRY WHEN WE GET BACK. ARE YOU EVEN LIS-TENING?
OH? YEAH, SURE...
WAS I DREAMING? BUT I CAN'T SLEEP, EVER SINCE I BECAME A SWORD...

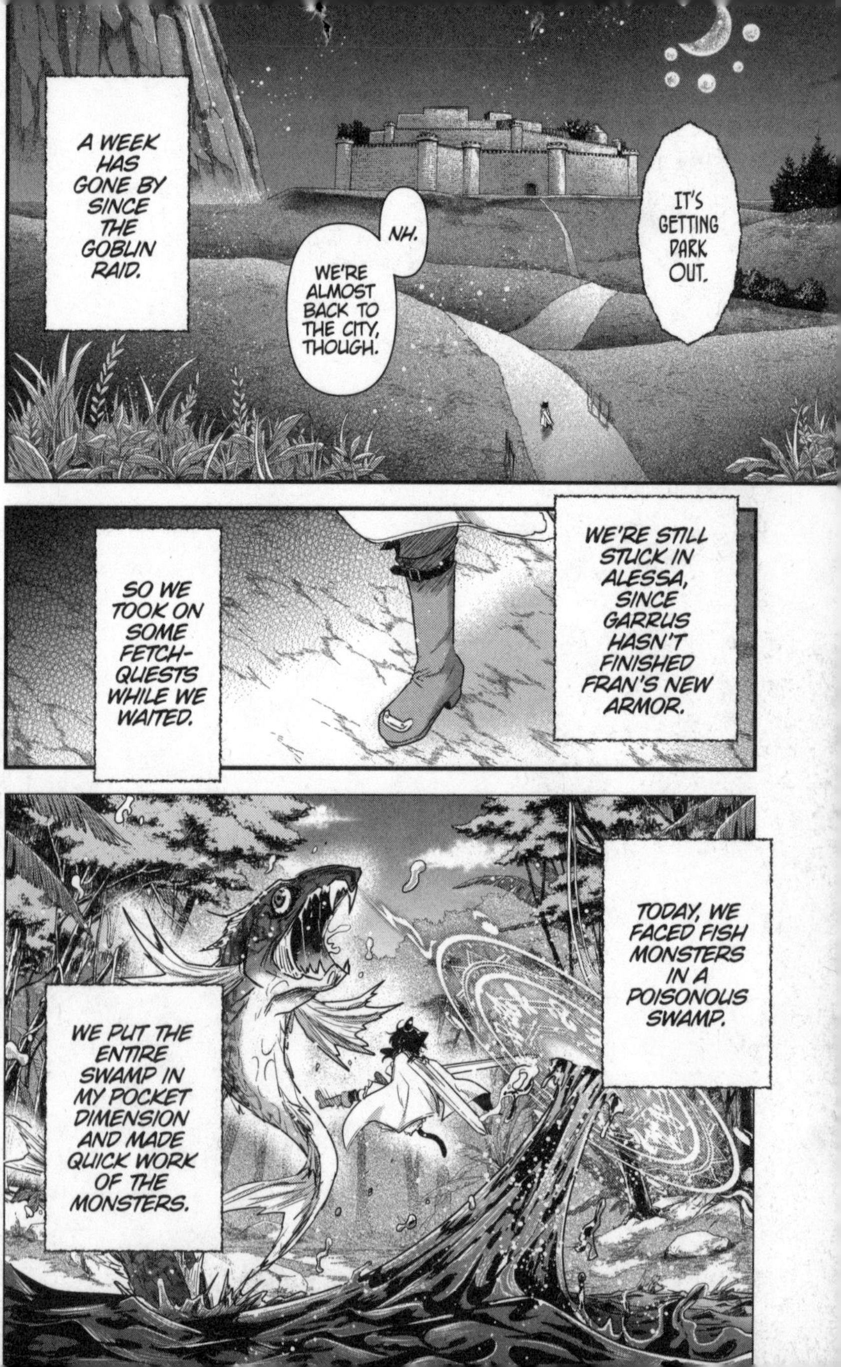
IT'S GETTING DARK OUT.
NH.
WE'RE ALMOST BACK TO THE CITY, THOUGH.
A WEEK HAS GONE BY SINCE THE GOBLIN RAID.
WE'RE STILL STUCK IN ALESSA, SINCE GARRUS HASN'T FINISHED FRAN'S NEW ARMOR.
SO WE TOOK ON SOME FETCH-QUESTS WHILE WE WAITED.
TODAY, WE FACED FISH MONSTERS IN A POISONOUS SWAMP.
WE PUT THE ENTIRE SWAMP IN MY POCKET DIMENSION AND MADE QUICK WORK OF THE MONSTERS.

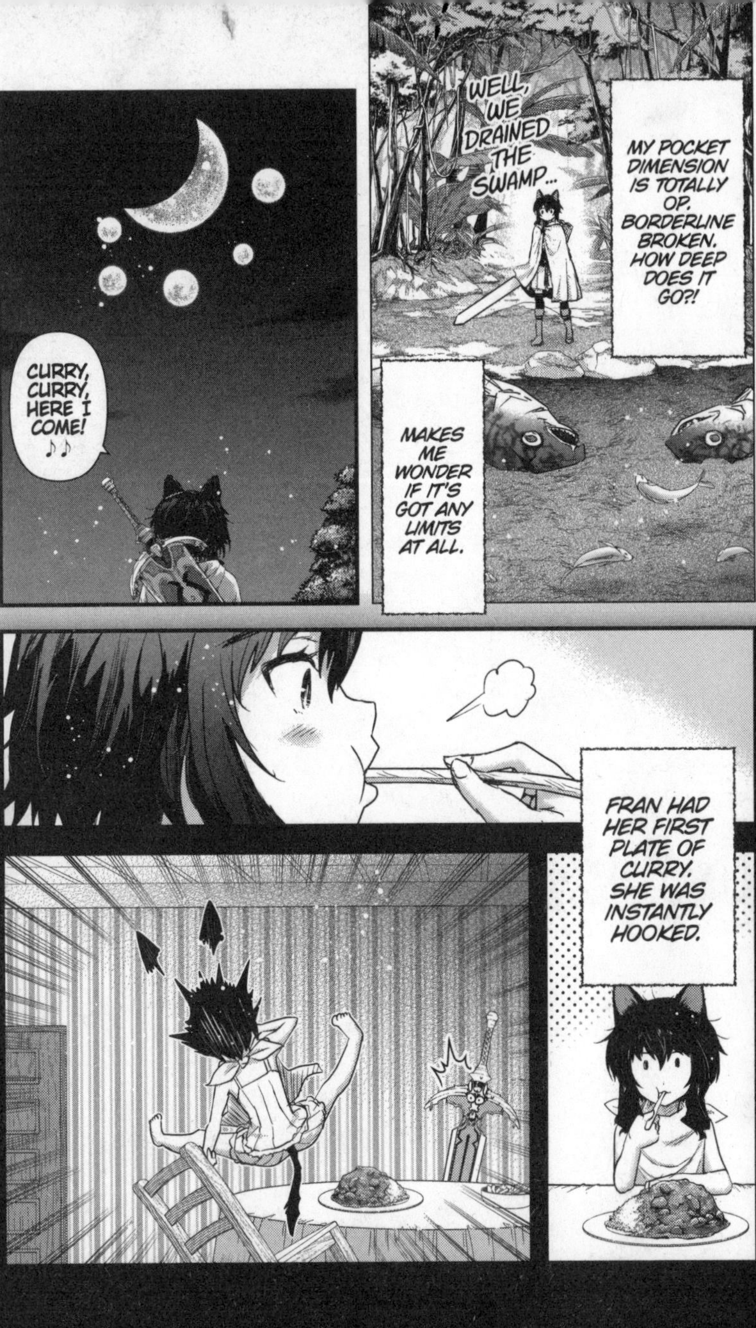
WELL, WE DRAINED THE SWAMP...
MY POCKET DIMENSION IS TOTALLY OP. BORDERLINE BROKEN. HOW DEEP DOES IT GO?!
MAKES ME WONDER IF IT'S GOT ANY LIMITS AT ALL.
CURRY, CURRY, HERE I COME! ♪♪
FRAN HAD HER FIRST PLATE OF CURRY. SHE WAS INSTANTLY HOOKED.

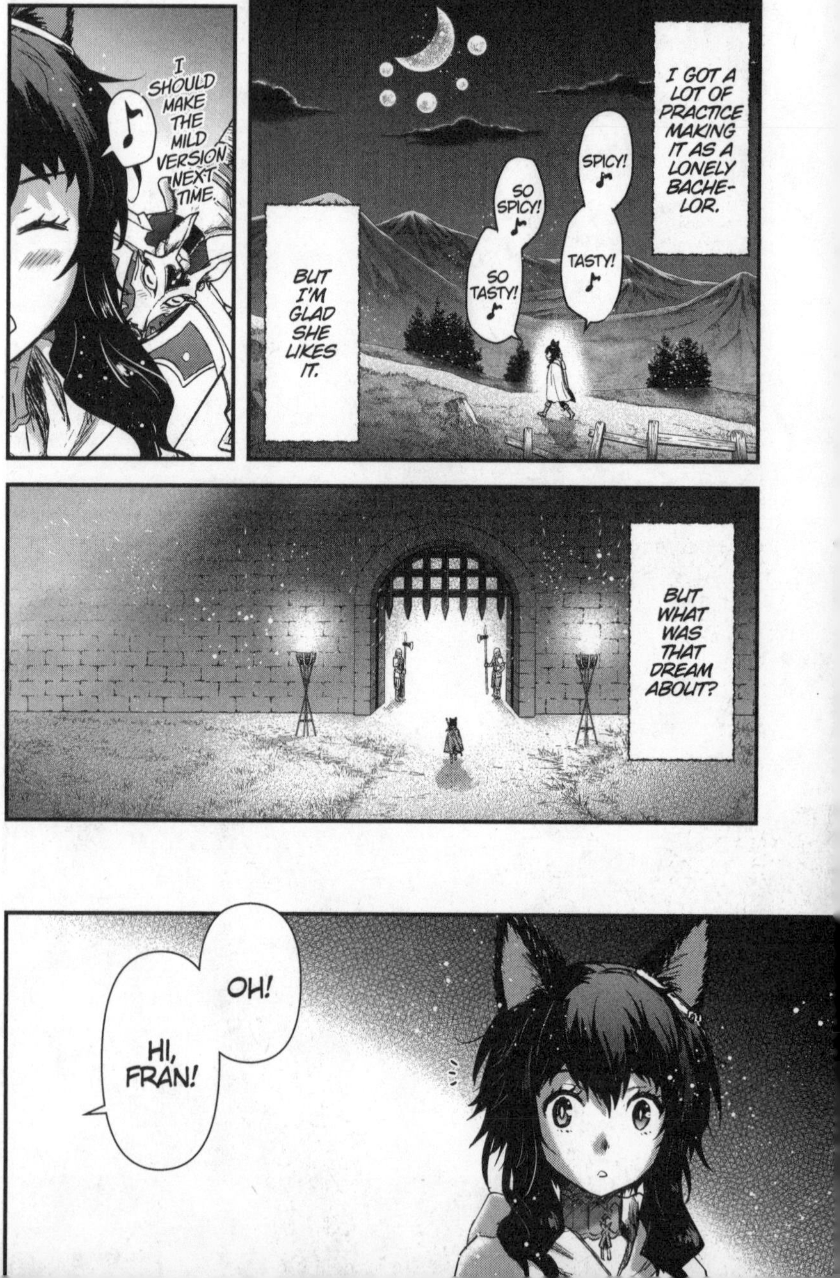
I GOT A LOT OF PRACTICE MAKING IT AS A LONELY BACHELOR.
SPICY! ♪
TASTY! ♪
SO SPICY! ♪
SO TASTY! ♪
BUT I'M GLAD SHE LIKES IT.
♪
I SHOULD MAKE THE MILD VERSION NEXT TIME.
BUT WHAT WAS THAT DREAM ABOUT?
OH!
HI, FRAN!

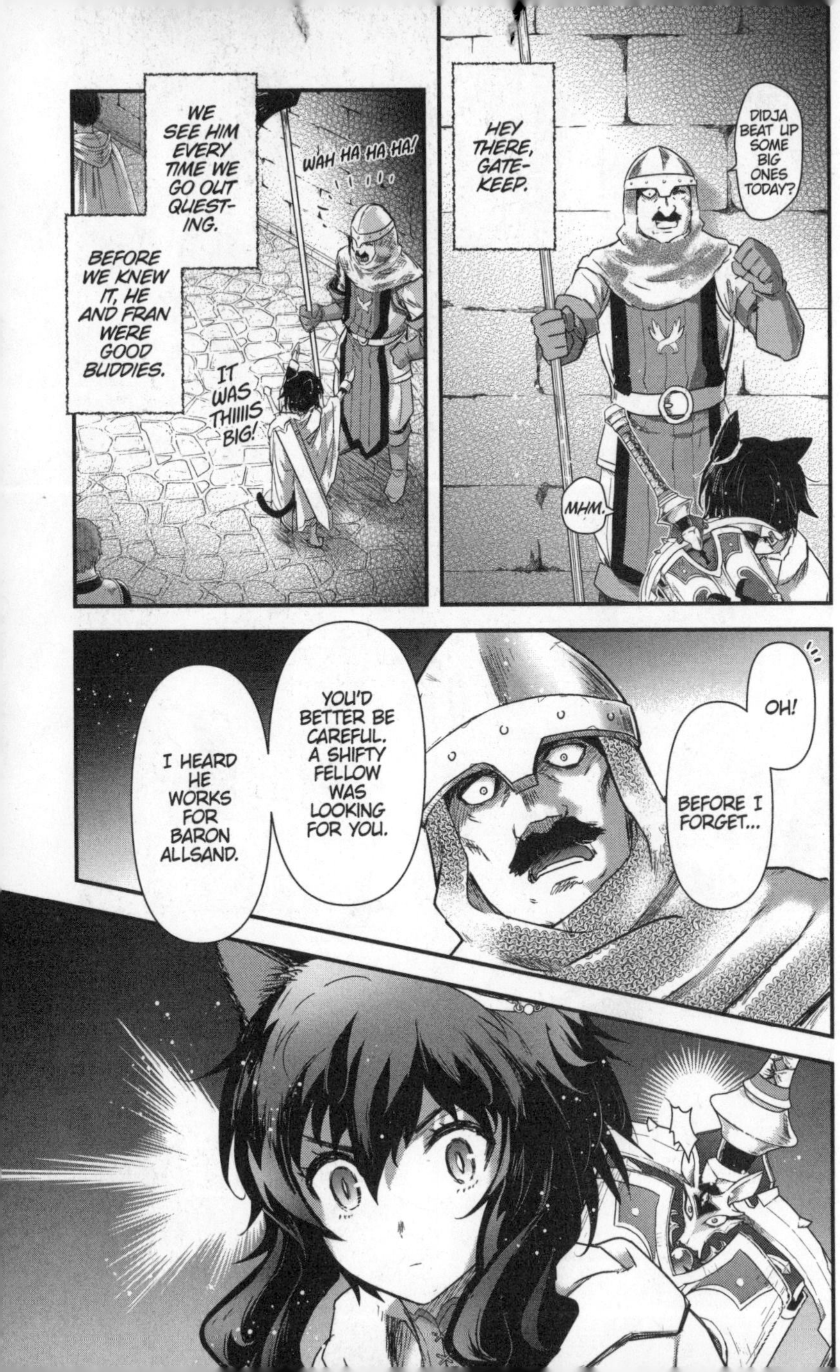
HEY THERE, GATE-KEEP.
DIDJA BEAT UP SOME BIG ONES TODAY?
MHM.
WE SEE HIM EVERY TIME WE GO OUT QUEST-ING.
WAH HA HA HA!
IT WAS THIIIIS BIG!
BEFORE WE KNEW IT, HE AND FRAN WERE GOOD BUDDIES.
OH!
BEFORE I FORGET...
YOU'D BETTER BE CAREFUL. A SHIFTY FELLOW WAS LOOKING FOR YOU.
I HEARD HE WORKS FOR BARON ALLSAND.

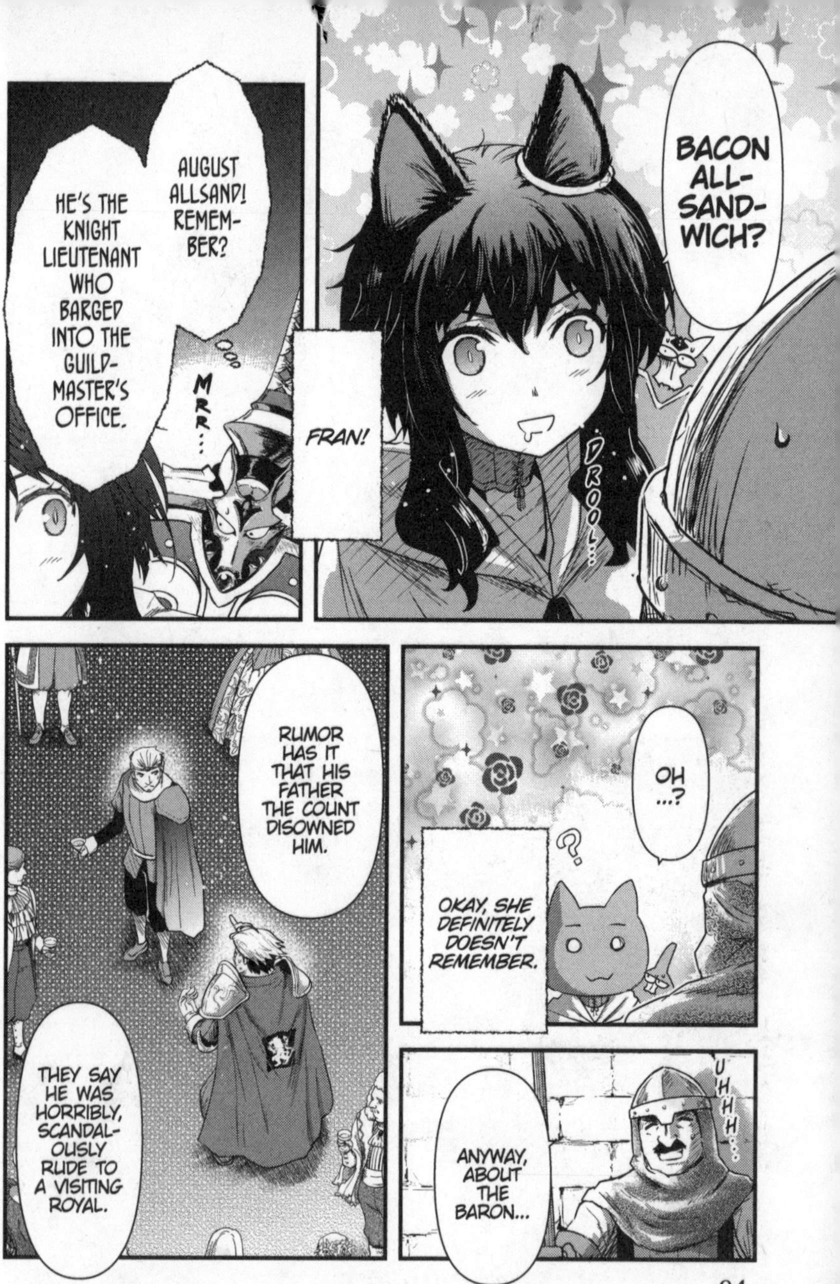
BACON ALL-SANDWICH?
FRAN!
DROOL...
AUGUST ALLSAND! REMEMBER?
HE'S THE KNIGHT LIEUTENANT WHO BARGED INTO THE GUILD-MASTER'S OFFICE.
MRR...
OH ...?
OKAY, SHE DEFINITELY DOESN'T REMEMBER.
UHHH...
ANYWAY, ABOUT THE BARON...
RUMOR HAS IT THAT HIS FATHER THE COUNT DISOWNED HIM.
THEY SAY HE WAS HORRIBLY, SCANDALOUSLY RUDE TO A VISITING ROYAL.

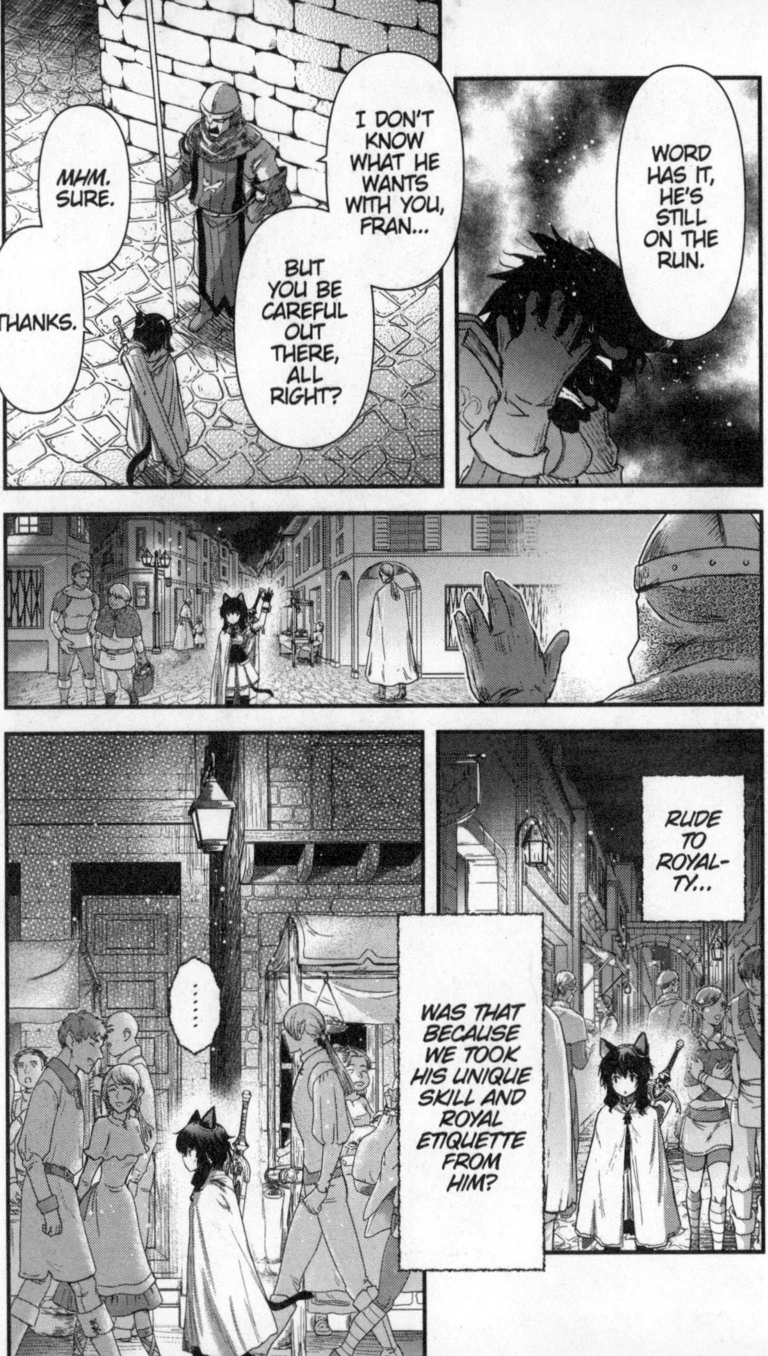
WORD HAS IT, HE'S STILL ON THE RUN.
I DON'T KNOW WHAT HE WANTS WITH YOU, FRAN...
BUT YOU BE CAREFUL OUT THERE, ALL RIGHT?
MHM. SURE.
THANKS.
RUDE TO ROYAL-TY...
WAS THAT BECAUSE WE TOOK HIS UNIQUE SKILL AND ROYAL ETIQUETTE FROM HIM?
......

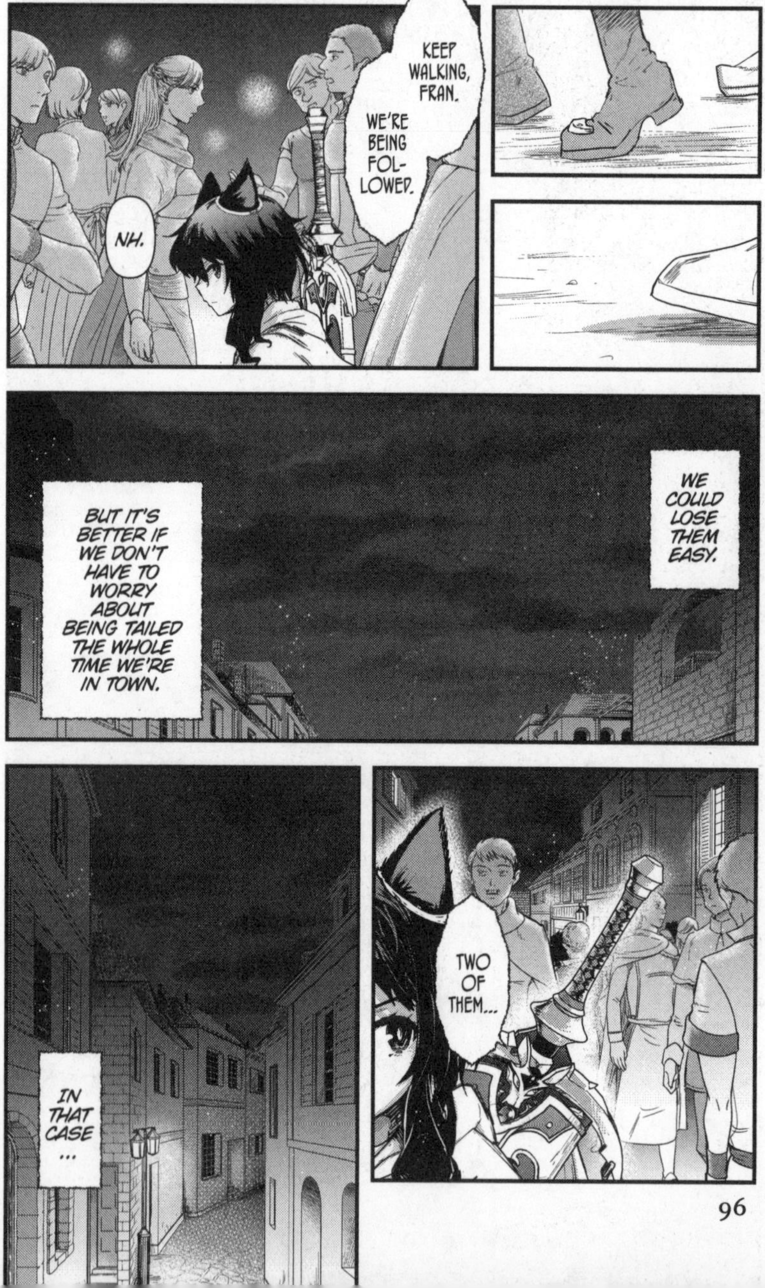
KEEP WALKING, FRAN.
WE'RE BEING FOL-LOWED.
NH.
WE COULD LOSE THEM EASY.
BUT IT'S BETTER IF WE DON'T HAVE TO WORRY ABOUT BEING TAILED THE WHOLE TIME WE'RE IN TOWN.
TWO OF THEM...
IN THAT CASE ...

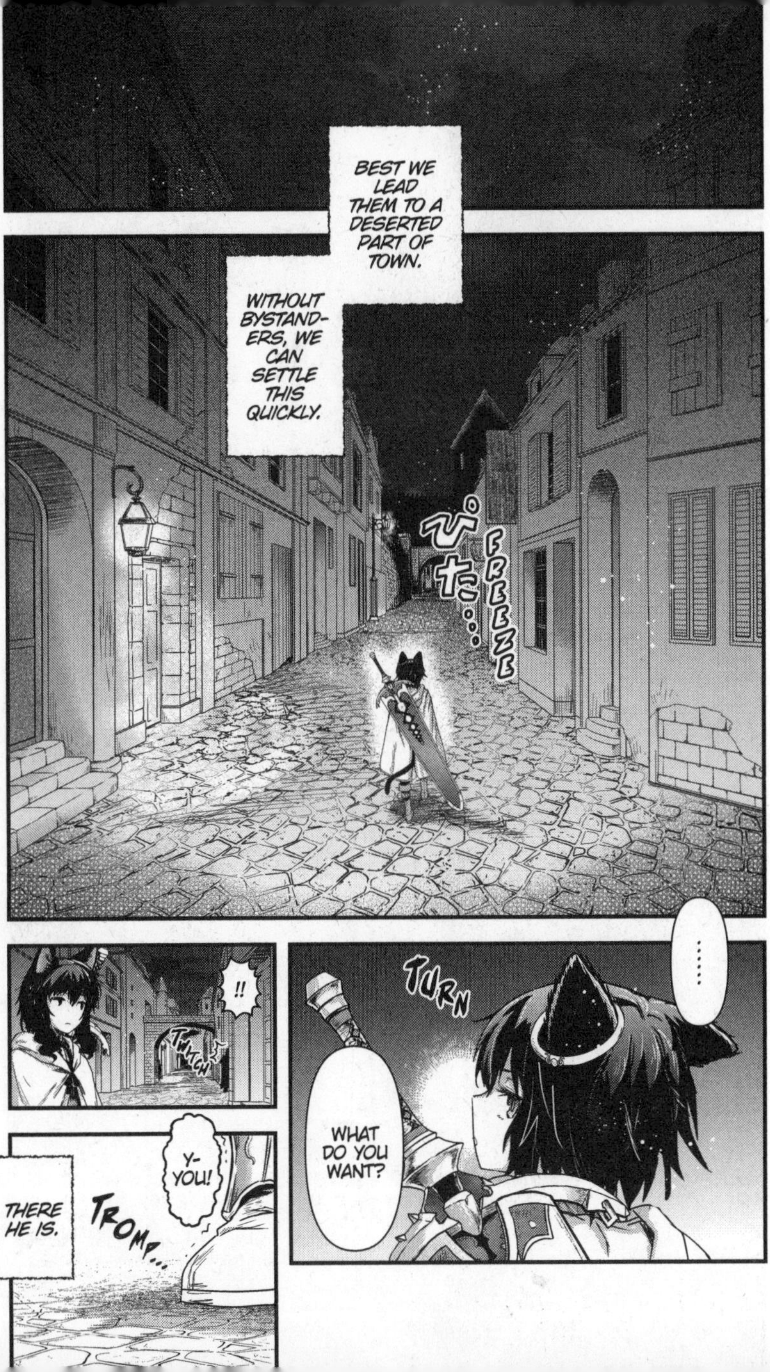
BEST WE LEAD THEM TO A DESERTED PART OF TOWN.
WITHOUT BYSTAND-ERS, WE CAN SETTLE THIS QUICKLY.
ぴた…
FREEZE
......
TURN
WHAT DO YOU WANT?
!!
TWITCH
THERE HE IS.
Y-YOU!
TROMP...

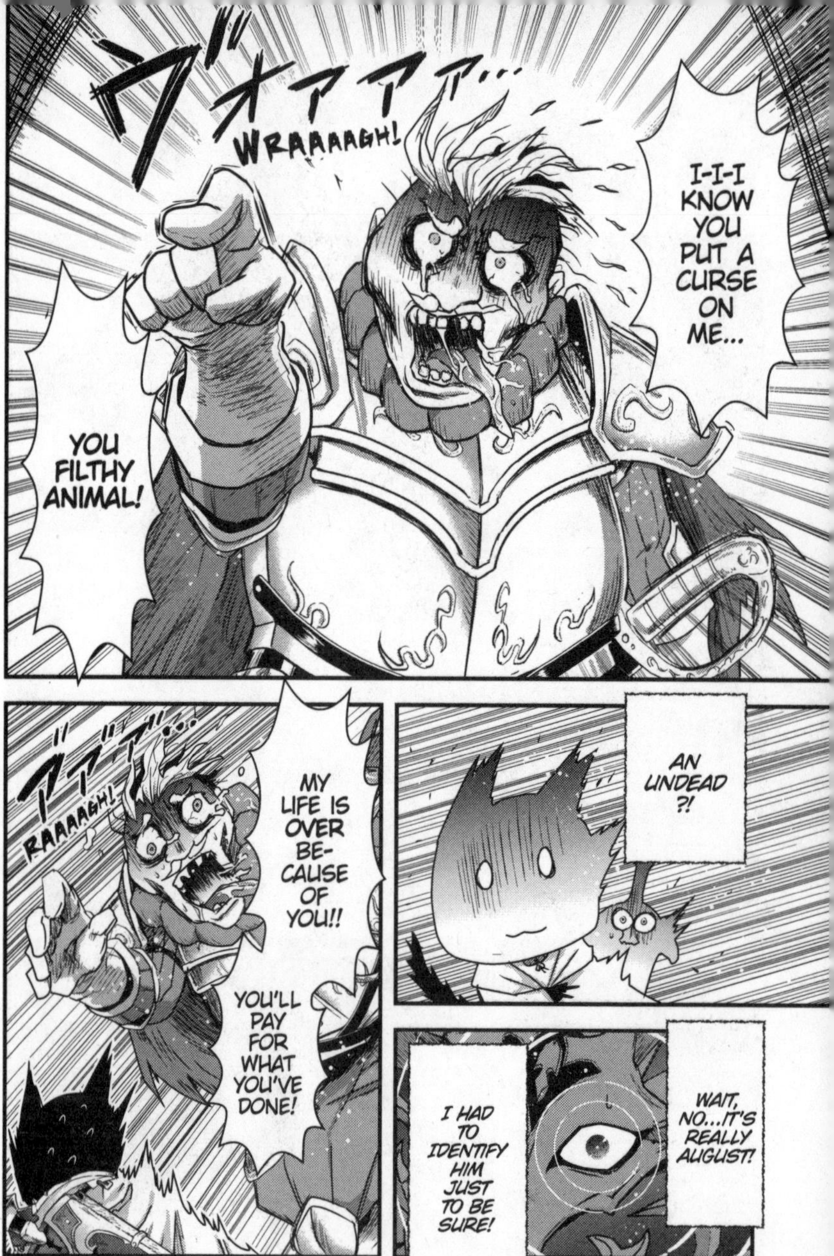
I-I-I KNOW YOU PUT A CURSE ON ME...
ヴォアアア…
WRAAAAGH!
YOU FILTHY ANIMAL!
AN UNDEAD ?!
WAIT, NO...IT'S REALLY AUGUST!
I HAD TO IDENTIFY HIM JUST TO BE SURE!
RAAAAGH!
MY LIFE IS OVER BE-CAUSE OF YOU!!
YOU'LL PAY FOR WHAT YOU'VE DONE!

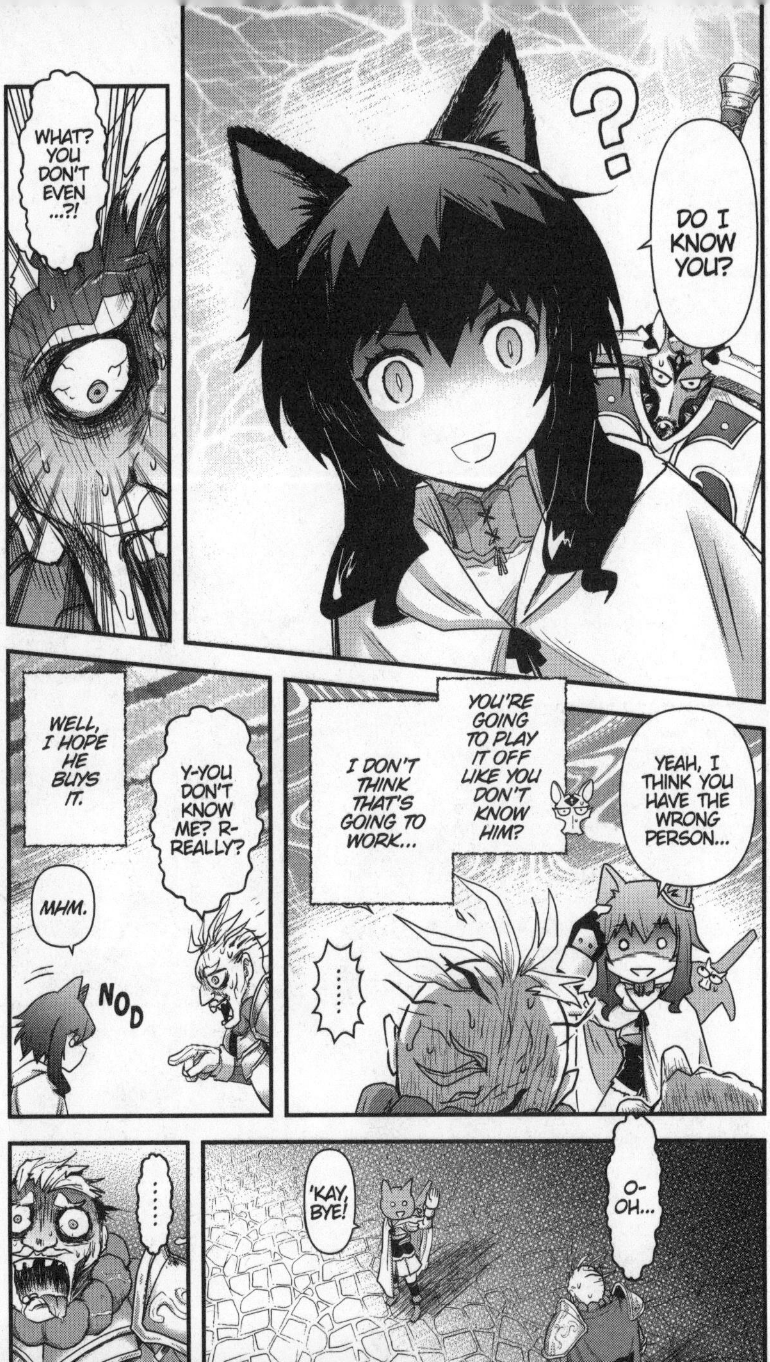
?
DO I KNOW YOU?
WHAT? YOU DON'T EVEN ...?!
YEAH, I THINK YOU HAVE THE WRONG PERSON...
YOU'RE GOING TO PLAY IT OFF LIKE YOU DON'T KNOW HIM?
I DON'T THINK THAT'S GOING TO WORK...
......
WELL, I HOPE HE BUYS IT.
Y-YOU DON'T KNOW ME? R-REALLY?
MHM.
NOD
O-OH...
'KAY, BYE!
......

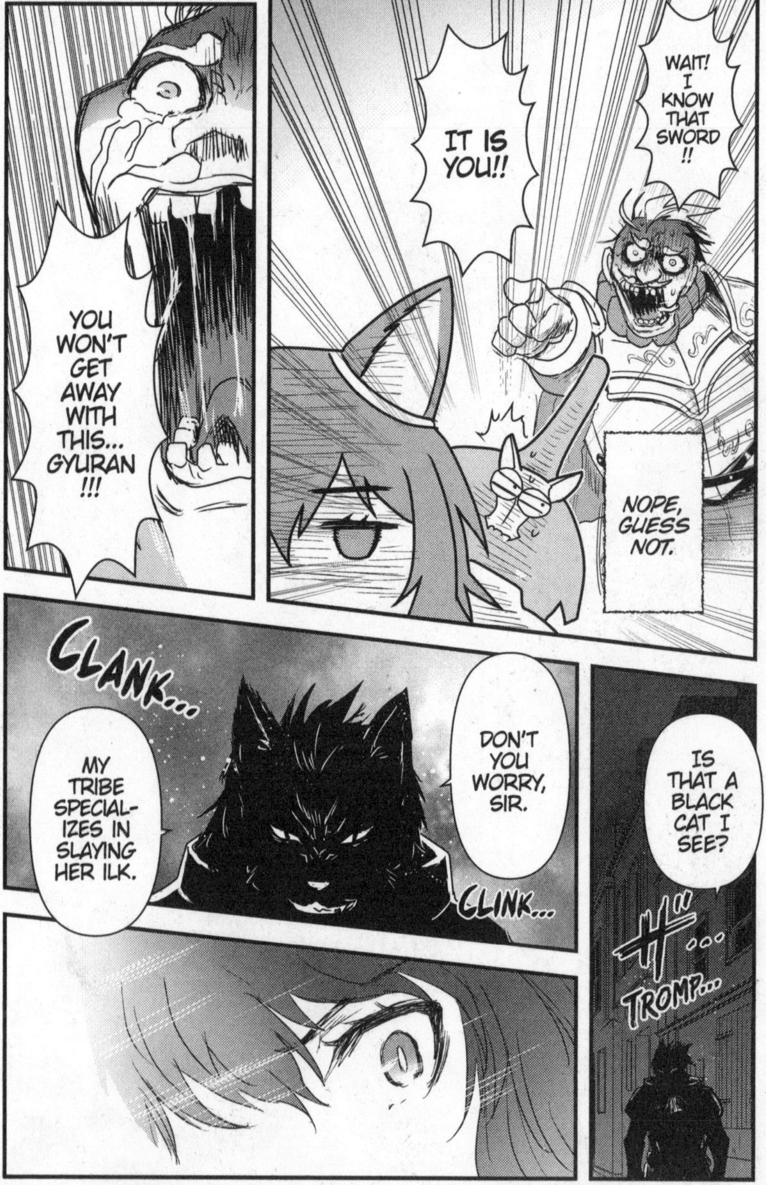
WAIT! I KNOW THAT SWORD!!
IT IS YOU!!
NOPE, GUESS NOT.
YOU WON'T GET AWAY WITH THIS... GYURAN!!!
IS THAT A BLACK CAT I SEE?
TROMP...
CLANK...
DON'T YOU WORRY, SIR.
MY TRIBE SPECIAL-IZES IN SLAYING HER ILK.
CLINK...

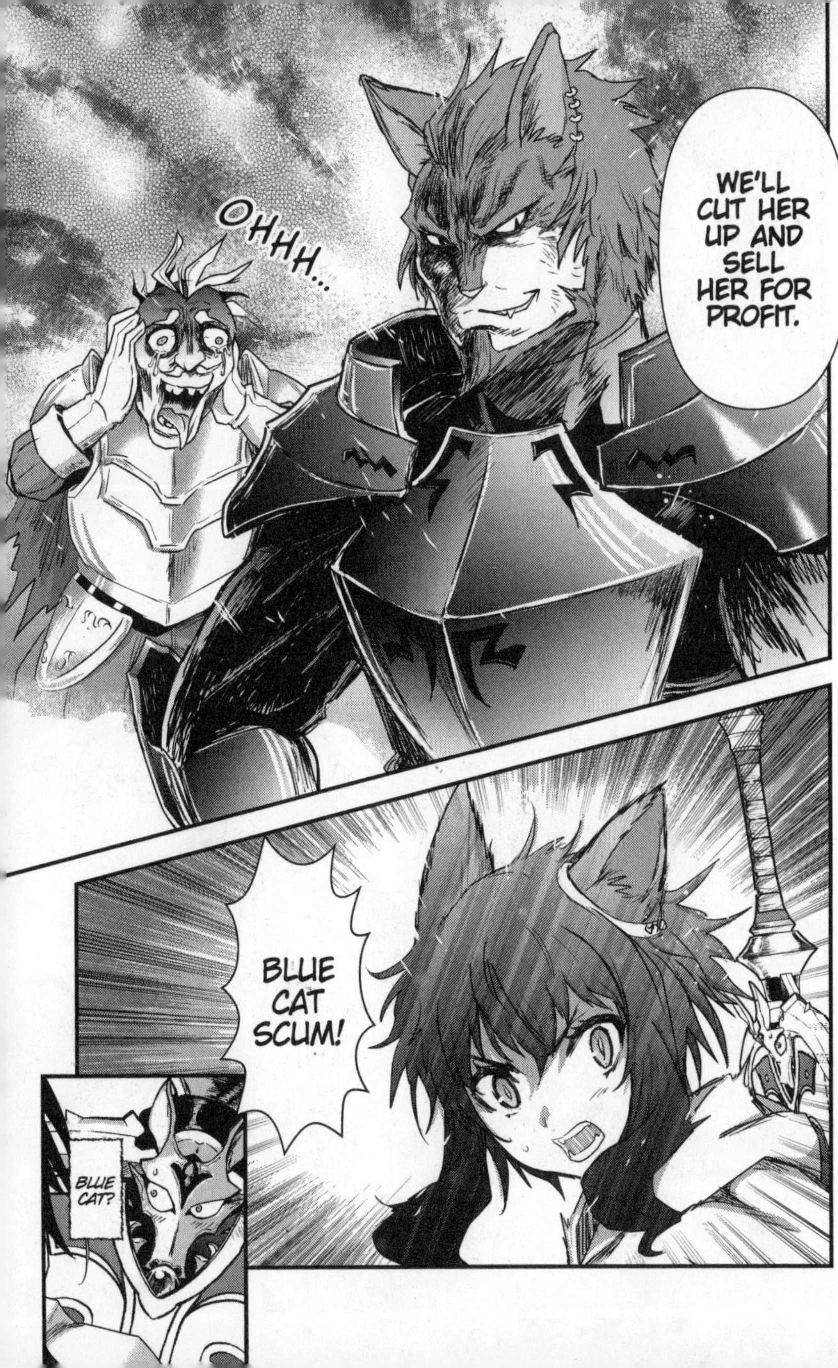
WE'LL CUT HER UP AND SELL HER FOR PROFIT.
OHHH...
BLUE CAT SCUM!
BLUE CAT?

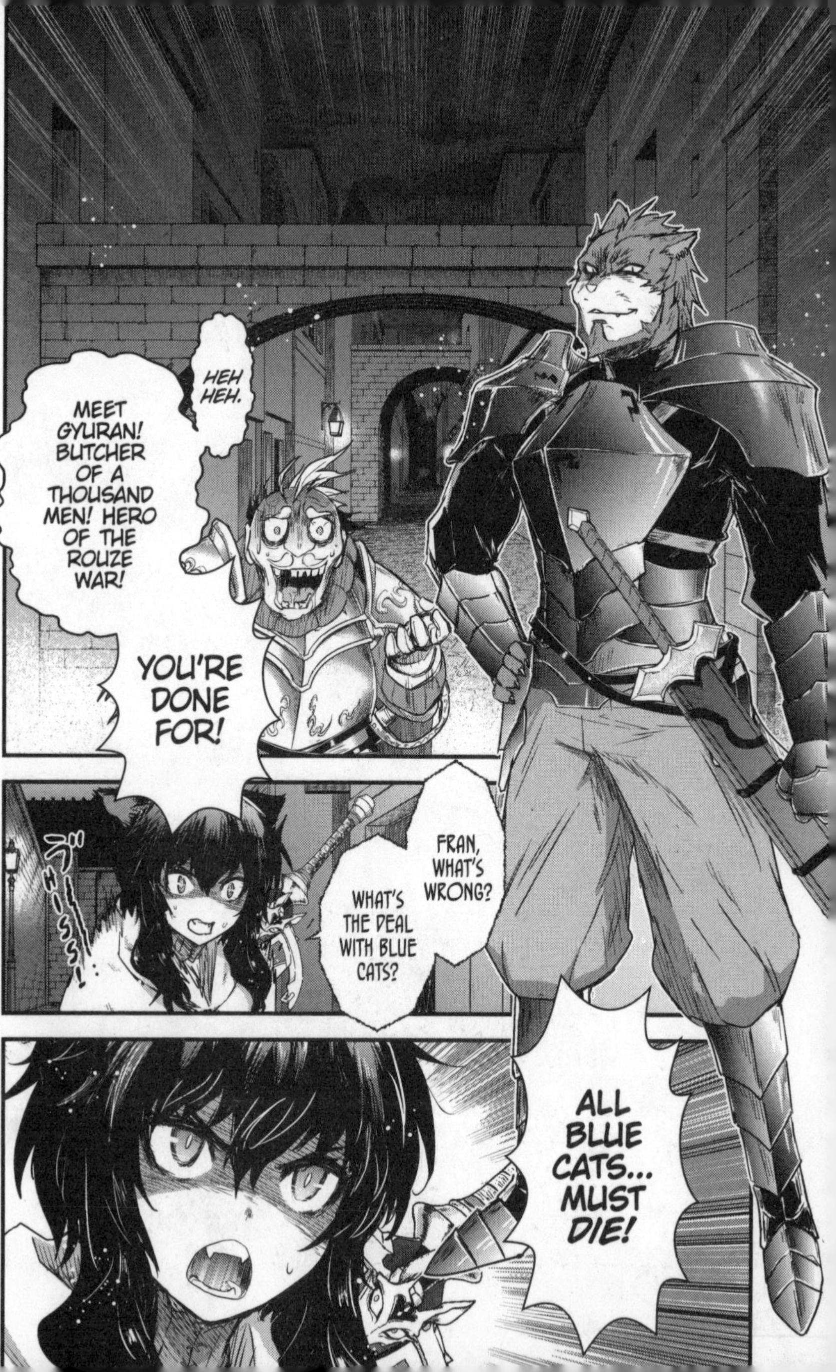
HEH HEH.
MEET GYURAN! BUTCHER OF A THOUSAND MEN! HERO OF THE ROUZE WAR!
YOU'RE DONE FOR!
FRAN, WHAT'S WRONG?
WHAT'S THE DEAL WITH BLUE CATS?
HISSS!
ALL BLUE CATS... MUST DIE!

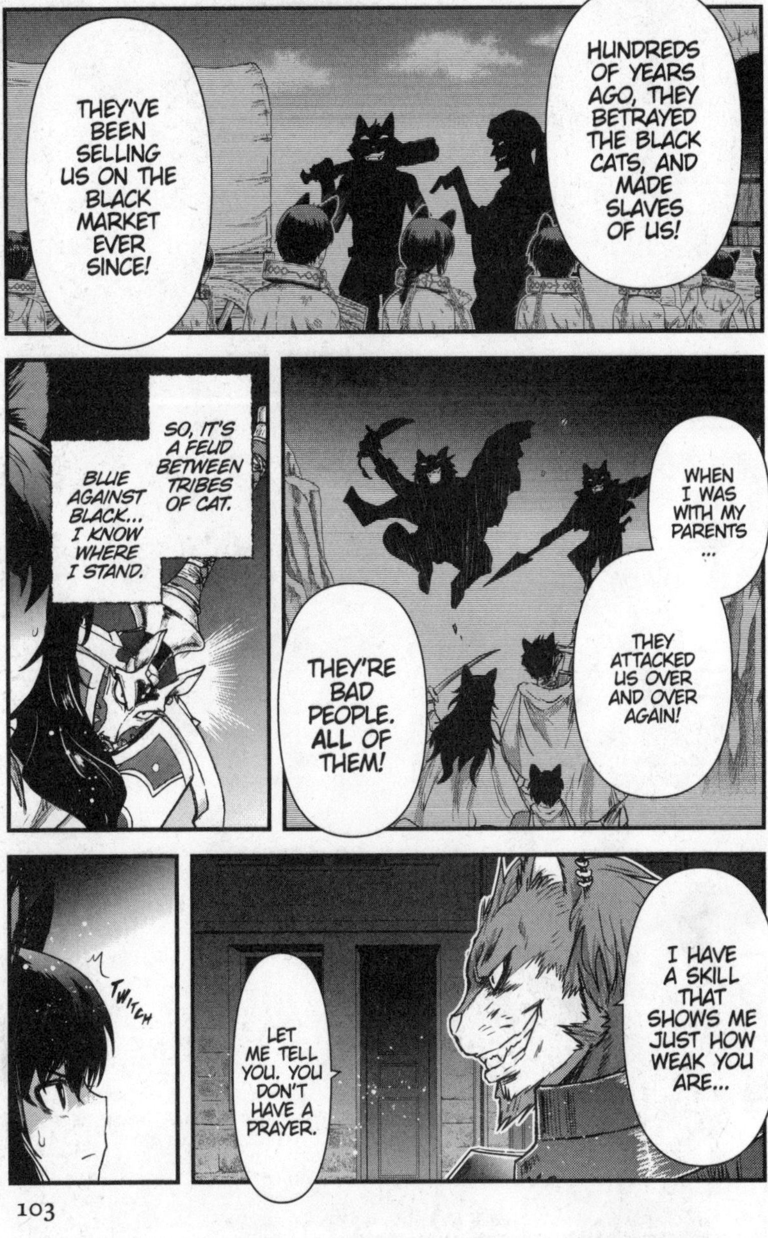
HUNDREDS OF YEARS AGO, THEY BETRAYED THE BLACK CATS, AND MADE SLAVES OF US!
THEY'VE BEEN SELLING US ON THE BLACK MARKET EVER SINCE!
WHEN I WAS WITH MY PARENTS...
THEY ATTACKED US OVER AND OVER AGAIN!
THEY'RE BAD PEOPLE. ALL OF THEM!
SO, IT'S A FEUD BETWEEN TRIBES OF CAT.
BLUE AGAINST BLACK... I KNOW WHERE I STAND.
I HAVE A SKILL THAT SHOWS ME JUST HOW WEAK YOU ARE...
LET ME TELL YOU. YOU DON'T HAVE A PRAYER.
TWITCH

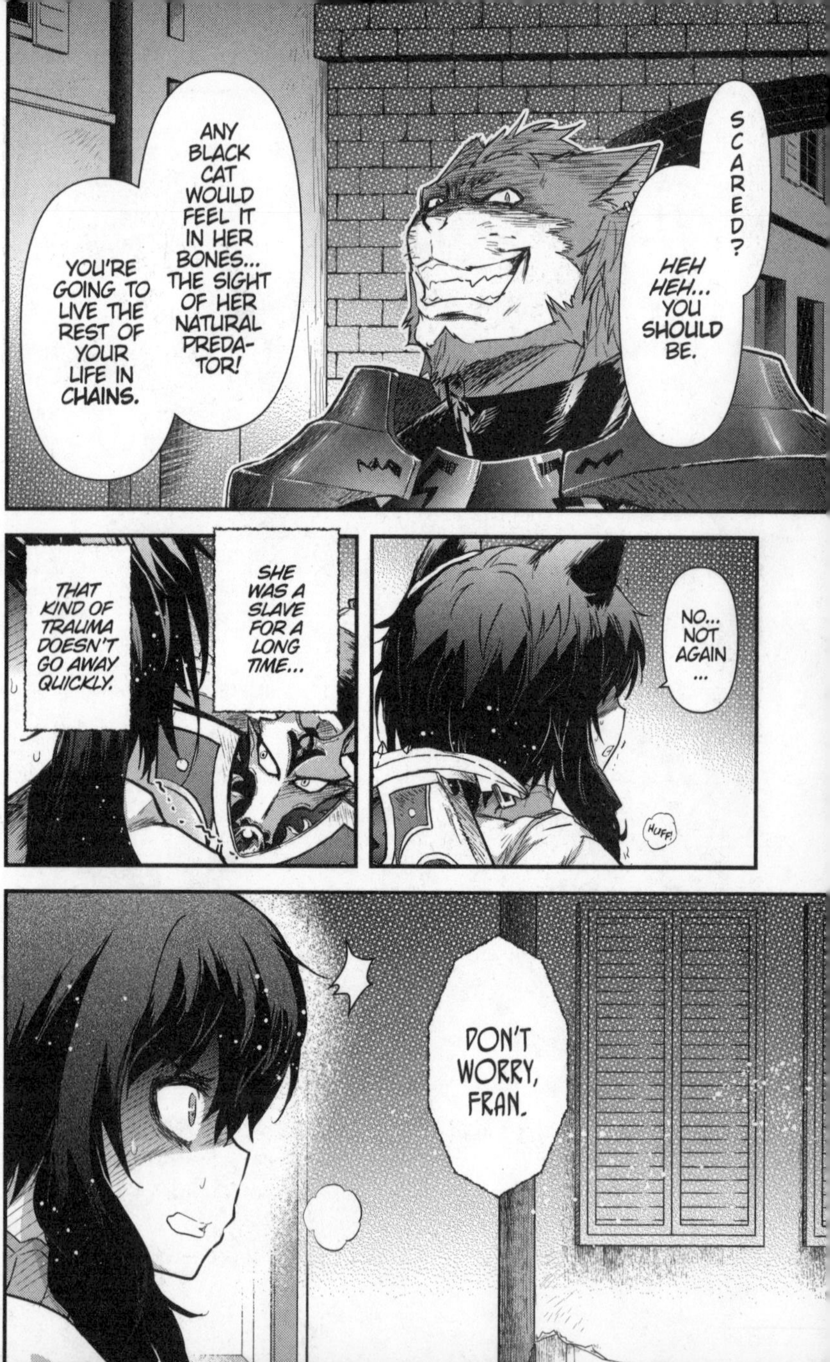
SCARED?
HEH HEH... YOU SHOULD BE.
ANY BLACK CAT WOULD FEEL IT IN HER BONES... THE SIGHT OF HER NATURAL PREDA-TOR!
YOU'RE GOING TO LIVE THE REST OF YOUR LIFE IN CHAINS.
NO... NOT AGAIN...
HUFF!
SHE WAS A SLAVE FOR A LONG TIME...
THAT KIND OF TRAUMA DOESN'T GO AWAY QUICKLY.
DON'T WORRY, FRAN.

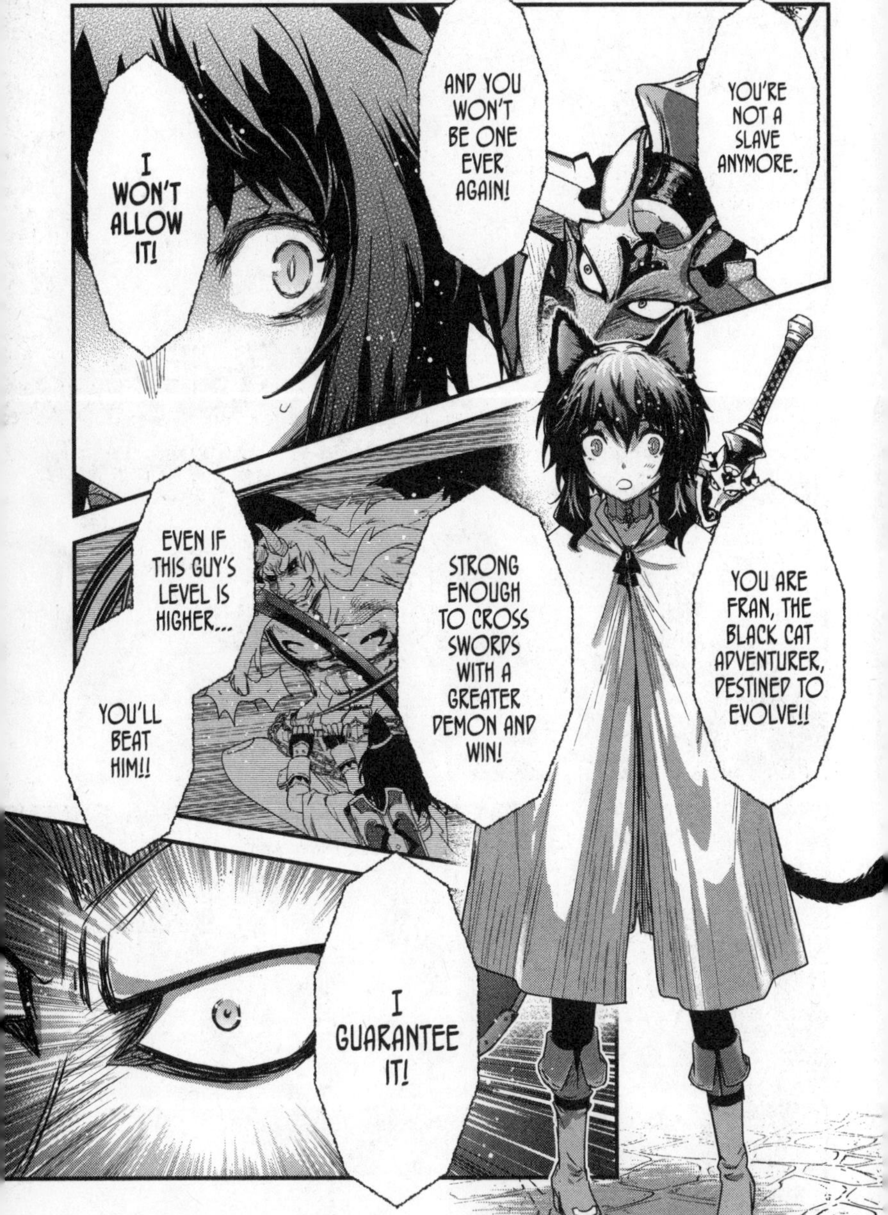
YOU'RE NOT A SLAVE ANYMORE.
AND YOU WON'T BE ONE EVER AGAIN!
I WON'T ALLOW IT!
YOU ARE FRAN, THE BLACK CAT ADVENTURER, DESTINED TO EVOLVE!!
STRONG ENOUGH TO CROSS SWORDS WITH A GREATER DEMON AND WIN!
EVEN IF THIS GUY'S LEVEL IS HIGHER...
YOU'LL BEAT HIM!!
I GUARANTEE IT!

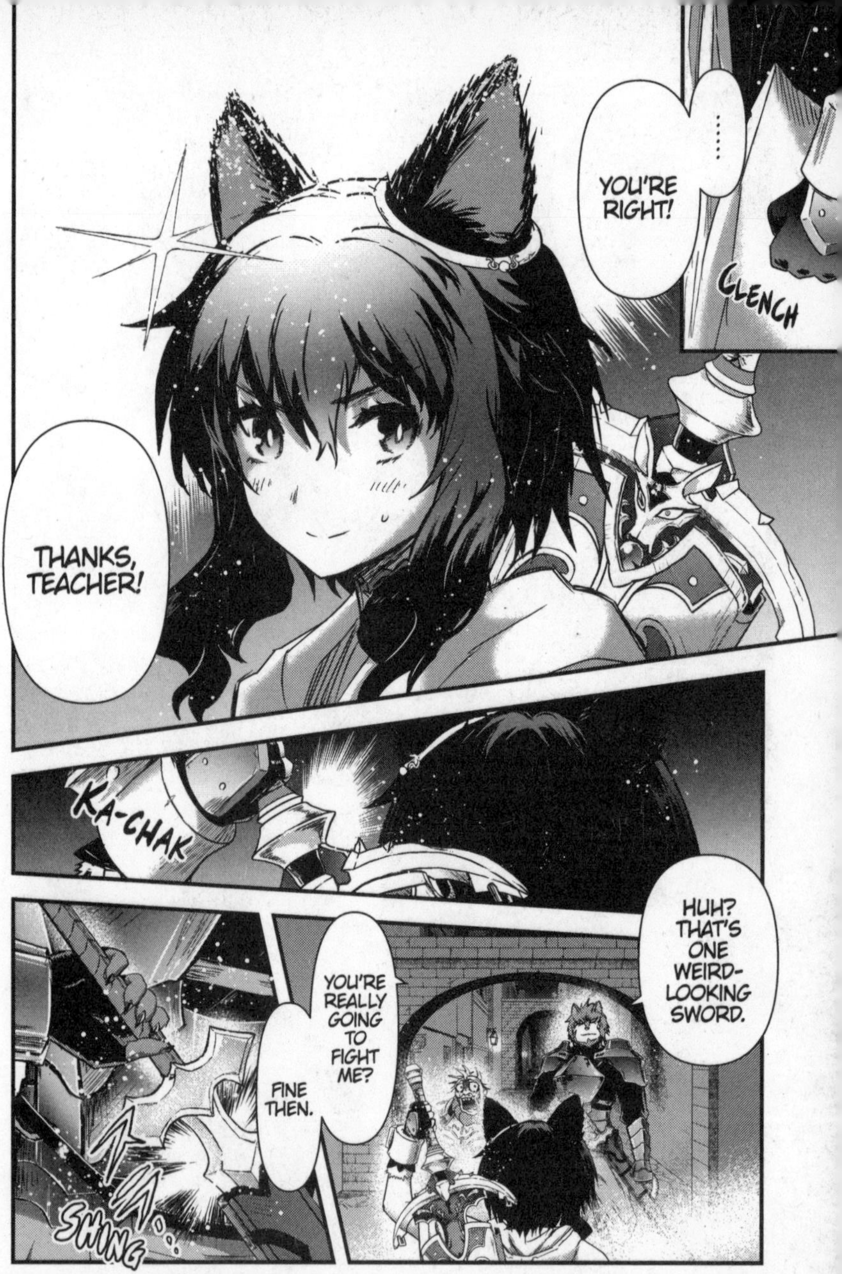
......
YOU'RE RIGHT!
CLENCH
THANKS, TEACHER!
KA-CHAK
HUH? THAT'S ONE WEIRD-LOOKING SWORD.
YOU'RE REALLY GOING TO FIGHT ME?
FINE THEN.
SHING

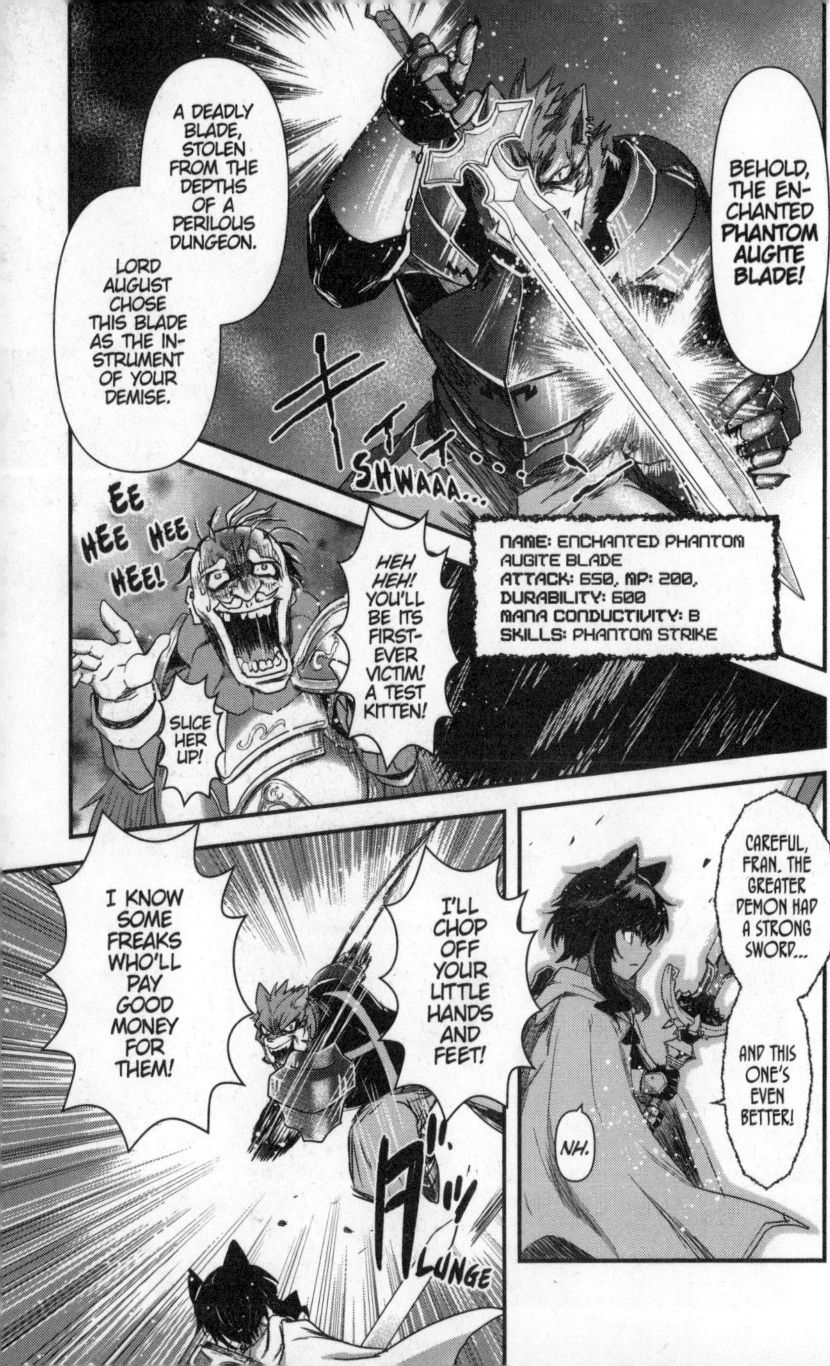

BEHOLD, THE ENCHANTED PHANTOM AUGITE BLADE!
A DEADLY BLADE, STOLEN FROM THE DEPTHS OF A PERILOUS DUNGEON.
LORD AUGUST CHOSE THIS BLADE AS THE INSTRUMENT OF YOUR DEMISE.
SHWAAA...
NAME: ENCHANTED PHANTOM AUGITE BLADE
ATTACK: 650, MP: 200, DURABILITY: 600
MANA CONDUCTIVITY: B
SKILLS: PHANTOM STRIKE
HEH HEH! YOU'LL BE ITS FIRST-EVER VICTIM! A TEST KITTEN!
EE HEE HEE HEE!
SLICE HER UP!
CAREFUL, FRAN. THE GREATER DEMON HAD A STRONG SWORD...
AND THIS ONE'S EVEN BETTER!
NH.
I'LL CHOP OFF YOUR LITTLE HANDS AND FEET!
I KNOW SOME FREAKS WHO'LL PAY GOOD MONEY FOR THEM!
LUNGE

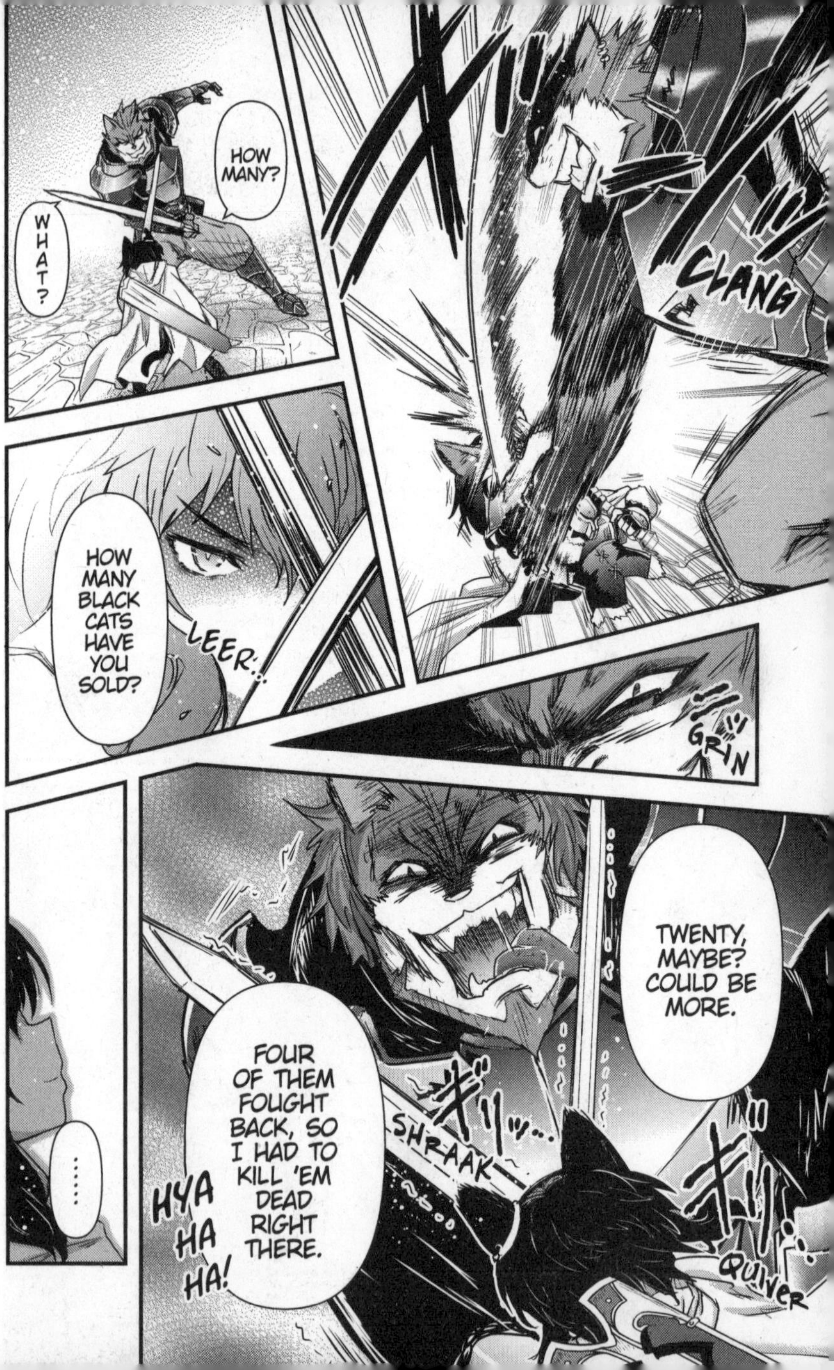
CLANG
HOW MANY?
WHAT?
HOW MANY BLACK CATS HAVE YOU SOLD?
LEER...
GRIN
TWENTY, MAYBE? COULD BE MORE.
FOUR OF THEM FOUGHT BACK, SO I HAD TO KILL 'EM DEAD RIGHT THERE.
HYA HA HA!
SHRAAK
QUIVER
......

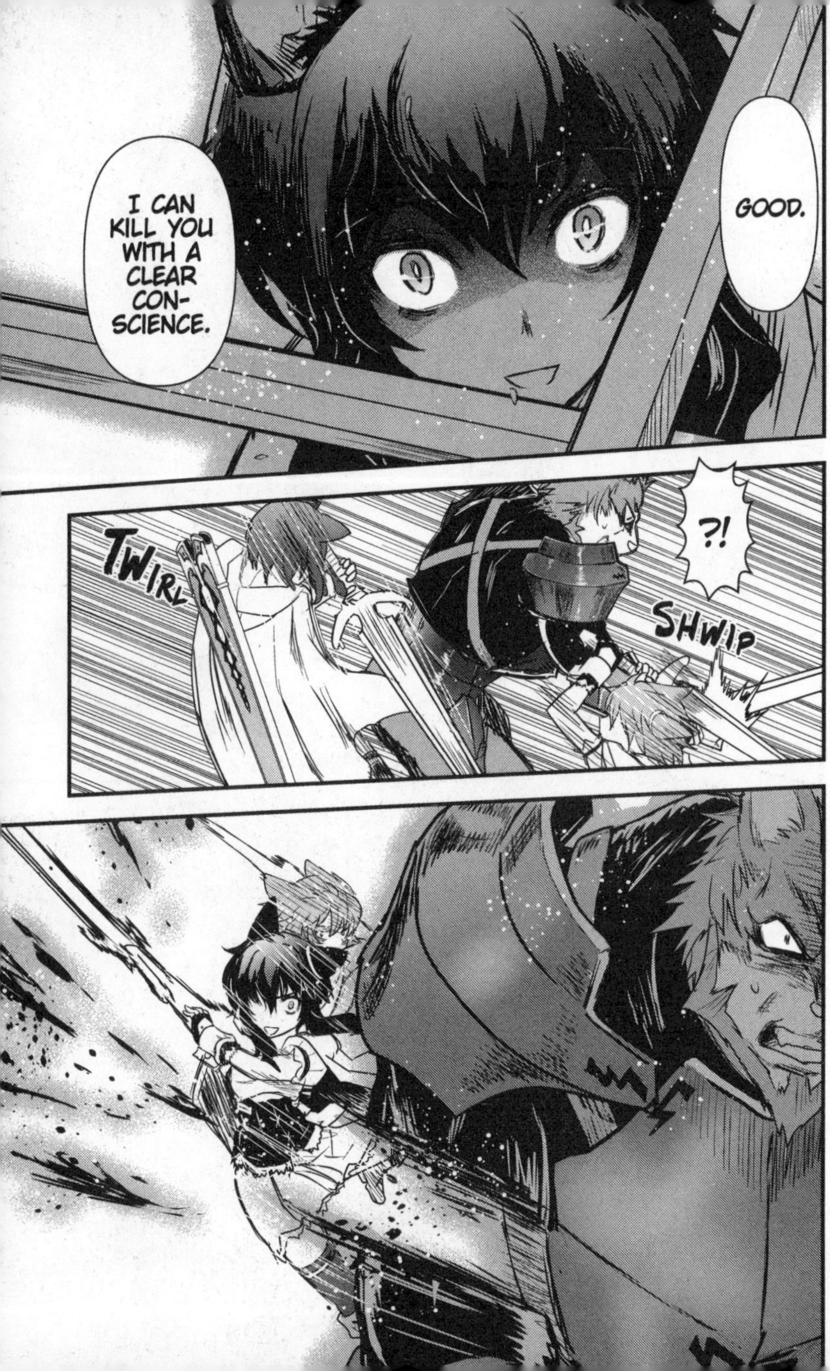
GOOD.
I CAN KILL YOU WITH A CLEAR CON-SCIENCE.
?!
SHWIP
TWIRL

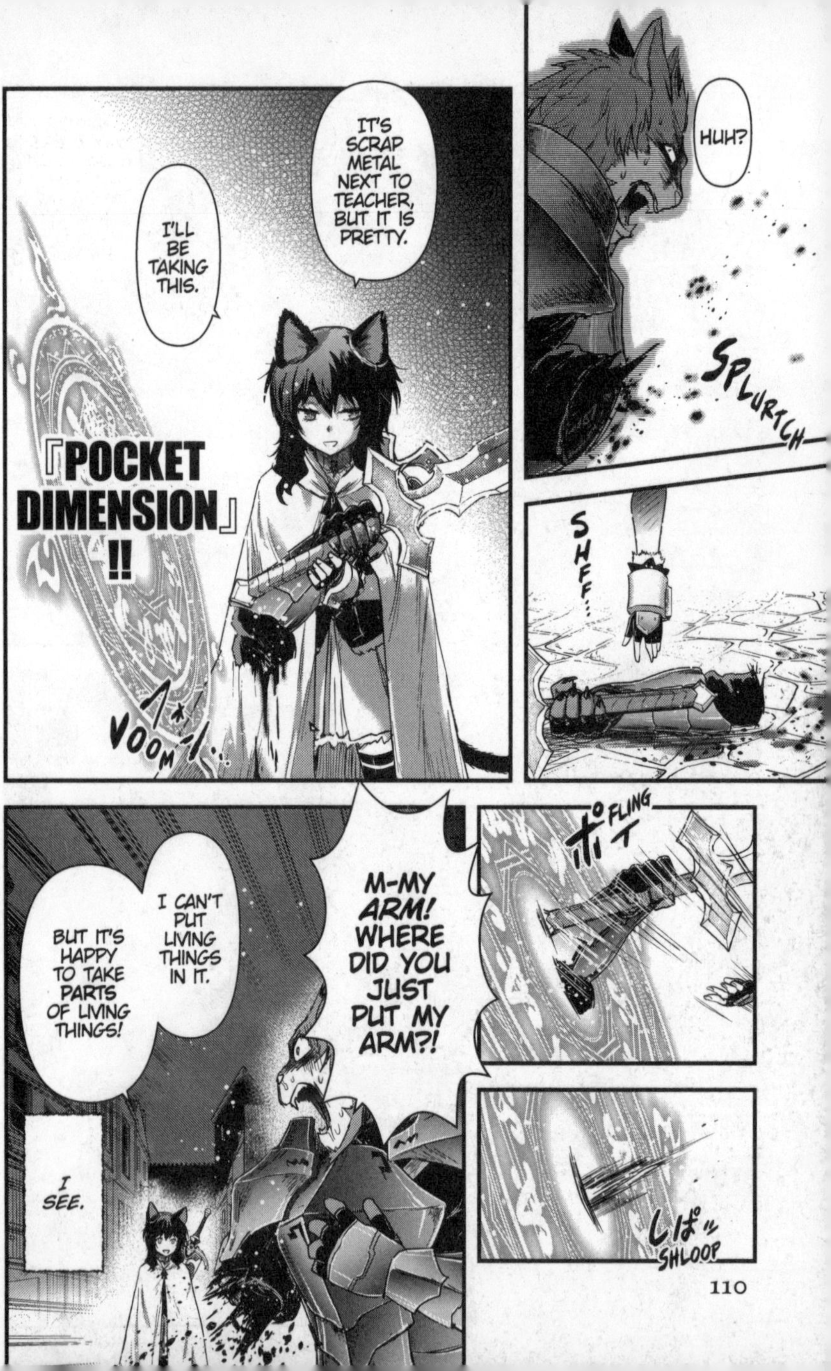
HUH?
SPLURTCH
SHFF...
IT'S SCRAP METAL NEXT TO TEACHER, BUT IT IS PRETTY.
I'LL BE TAKING THIS.
『POCKET DIMENSION』!!
VOOM
ポイ
FLING
しぱッ
SHLOOP
M-MY ARM! WHERE DID YOU JUST PUT MY ARM?!
I CAN'T PUT LIVING THINGS IN IT.
BUT IT'S HAPPY TO TAKE PARTS OF LIVING THINGS!
I SEE.

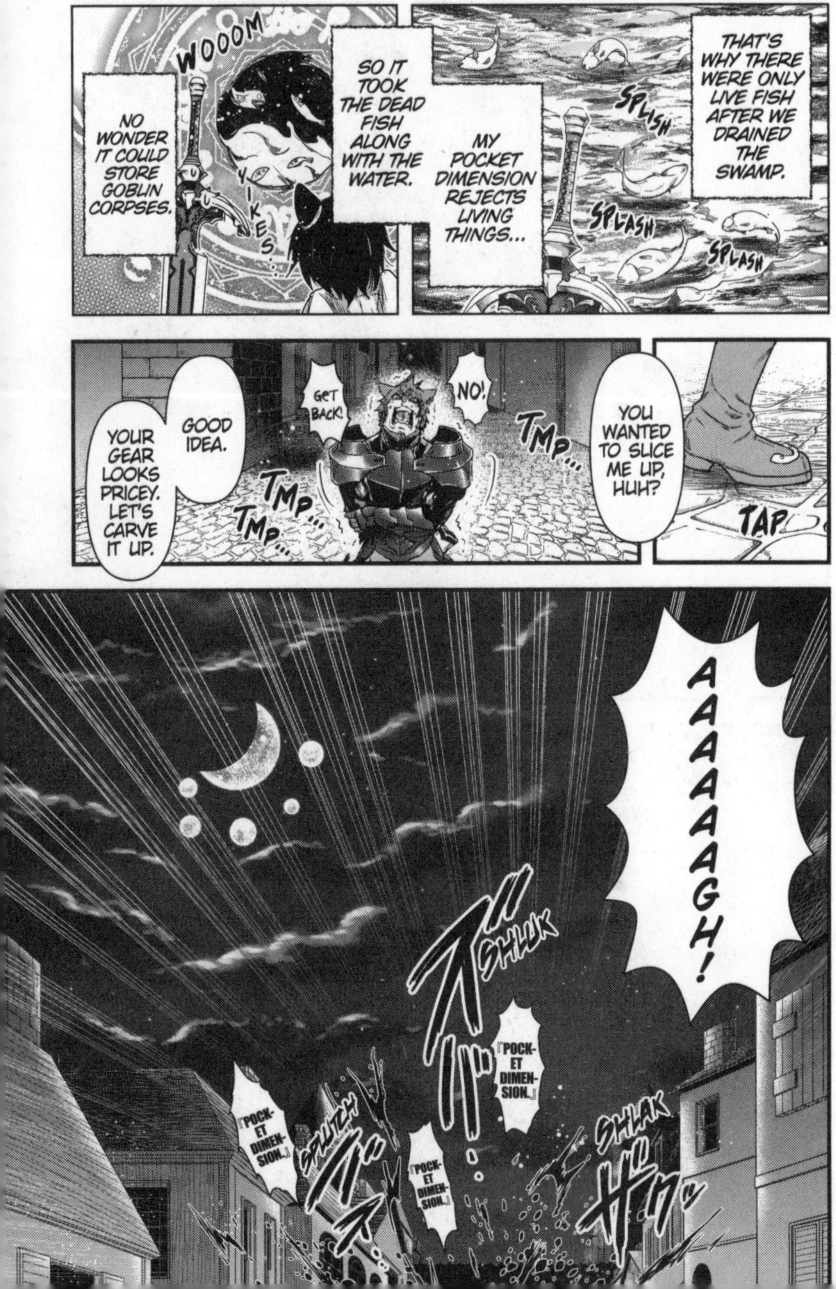
THAT'S WHY THERE WERE ONLY LIVE FISH AFTER WE DRAINED THE SWAMP.
MY POCKET DIMENSION REJECTS LIVING THINGS...
SPLISH
SPLASH
SPLASH
SO IT TOOK THE DEAD FISH ALONG WITH THE WATER.
WOOOM
NO WONDER IT COULD STORE GOBLIN CORPSES.
YIKES...
YOU WANTED TO SLICE ME UP, HUH?
TAP
NO!
GET BACK!
TMP...
GOOD IDEA.
YOUR GEAR LOOKS PRICEY. LET'S CARVE IT UP.
TMP...
TMP...
AAAAAAAAGH!
SHLUK
『POCK-ET DIMEN-SION.』
SHLAK
『POCK-ET DIMEN-SION.』
SPLUTCH
『POCK-ET DIMEN-SION.』

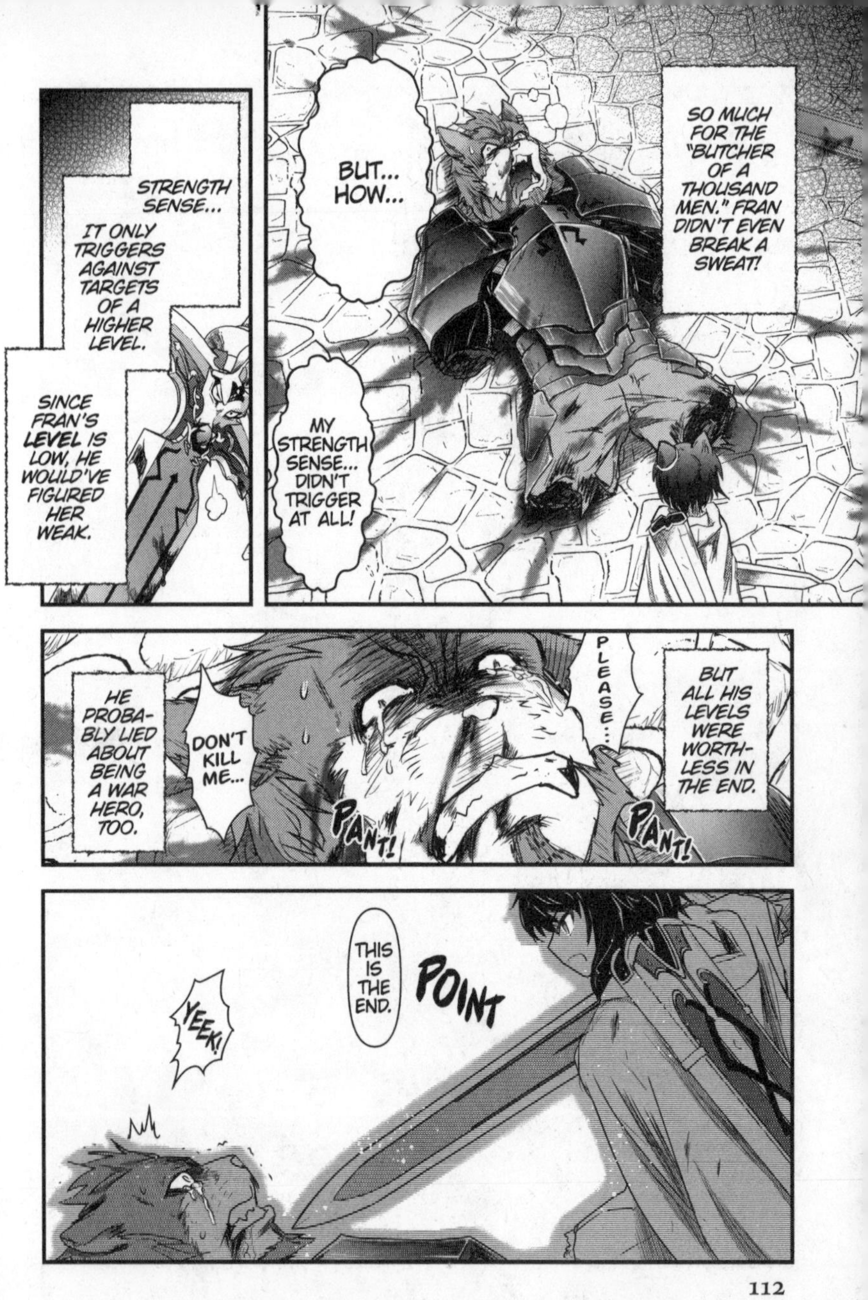
SO MUCH FOR THE "BUTCHER OF A THOUSAND MEN." FRAN DIDN'T EVEN BREAK A SWEAT!
BUT... HOW...
MY STRENGTH SENSE... DIDN'T TRIGGER AT ALL!
STRENGTH SENSE...
IT ONLY TRIGGERS AGAINST TARGETS OF A HIGHER LEVEL.
SINCE FRAN'S **LEVEL** IS LOW, HE WOULD'VE FIGURED HER WEAK.
BUT ALL HIS LEVELS WERE WORTHLESS IN THE END.
PLEASE...
PANT!
PANT!
DON'T KILL ME...
HE PROBABLY LIED ABOUT BEING A WAR HERO, TOO.
POINT
THIS IS THE END.
YEEK!

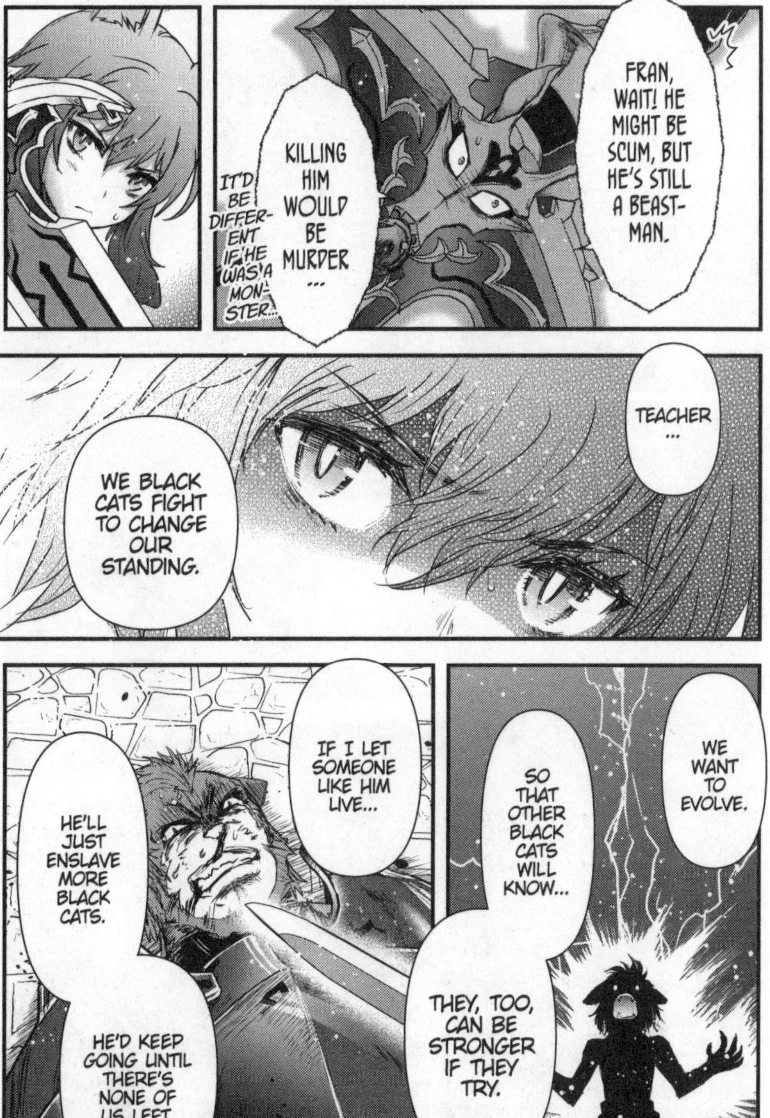
FRAN, WAIT! HE MIGHT BE SCUM, BUT HE'S STILL A BEAST-MAN.
KILLING HIM WOULD BE MURDER...
IT'D BE DIFFERENT IF HE WAS A MONSTER...
TEACHER...
WE BLACK CATS FIGHT TO CHANGE OUR STANDING.
WE WANT TO EVOLVE.
SO THAT OTHER BLACK CATS WILL KNOW...
THEY, TOO, CAN BE STRONGER IF THEY TRY.
IF I LET SOMEONE LIKE HIM LIVE...
HE'LL JUST ENSLAVE MORE BLACK CATS.
HE'D KEEP GOING UNTIL THERE'S NONE OF US LEFT.

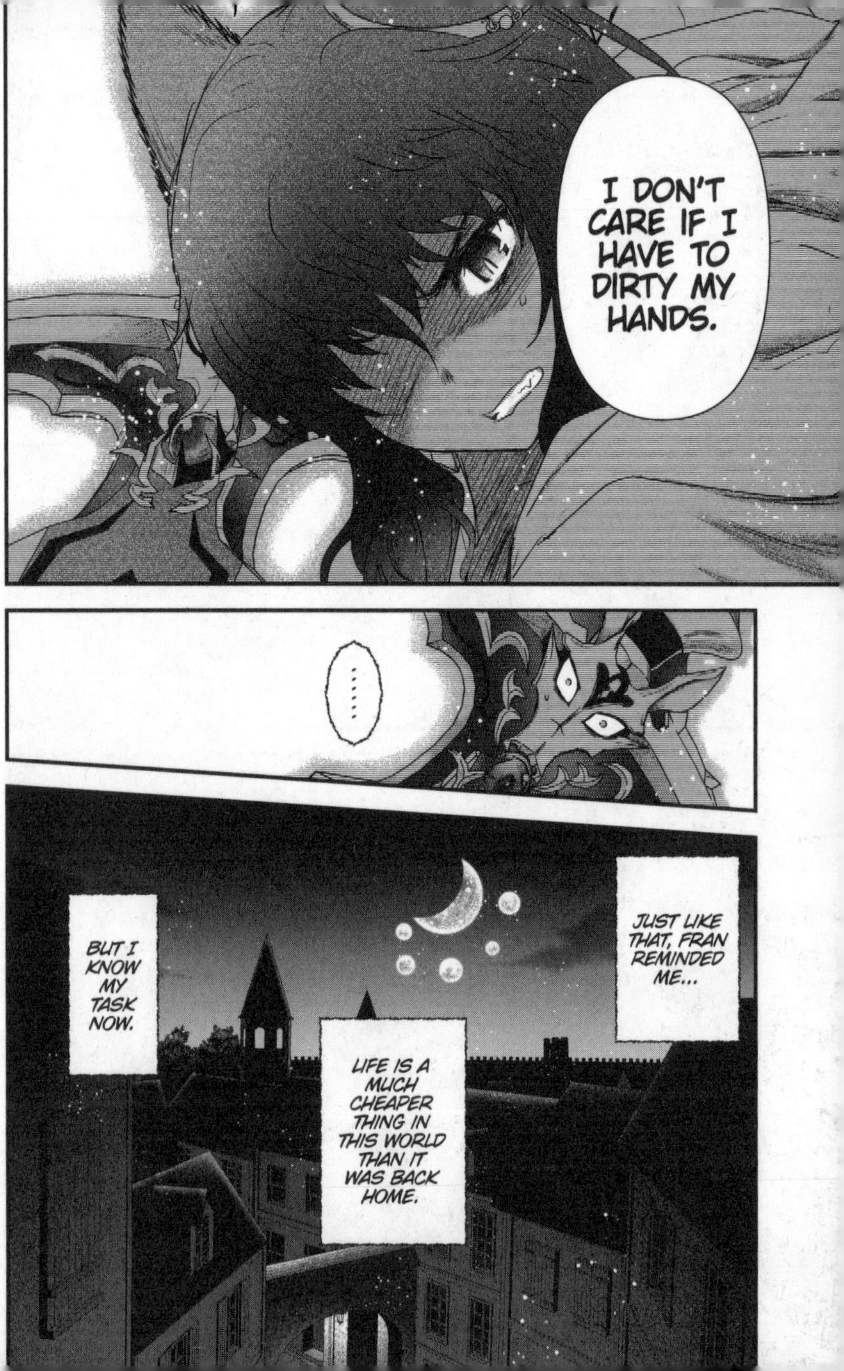
I DON'T CARE IF I HAVE TO DIRTY MY HANDS.
......
JUST LIKE THAT, FRAN REMINDED ME...
LIFE IS A MUCH CHEAPER THING IN THIS WORLD THAN IT WAS BACK HOME.
BUT I KNOW MY TASK NOW.

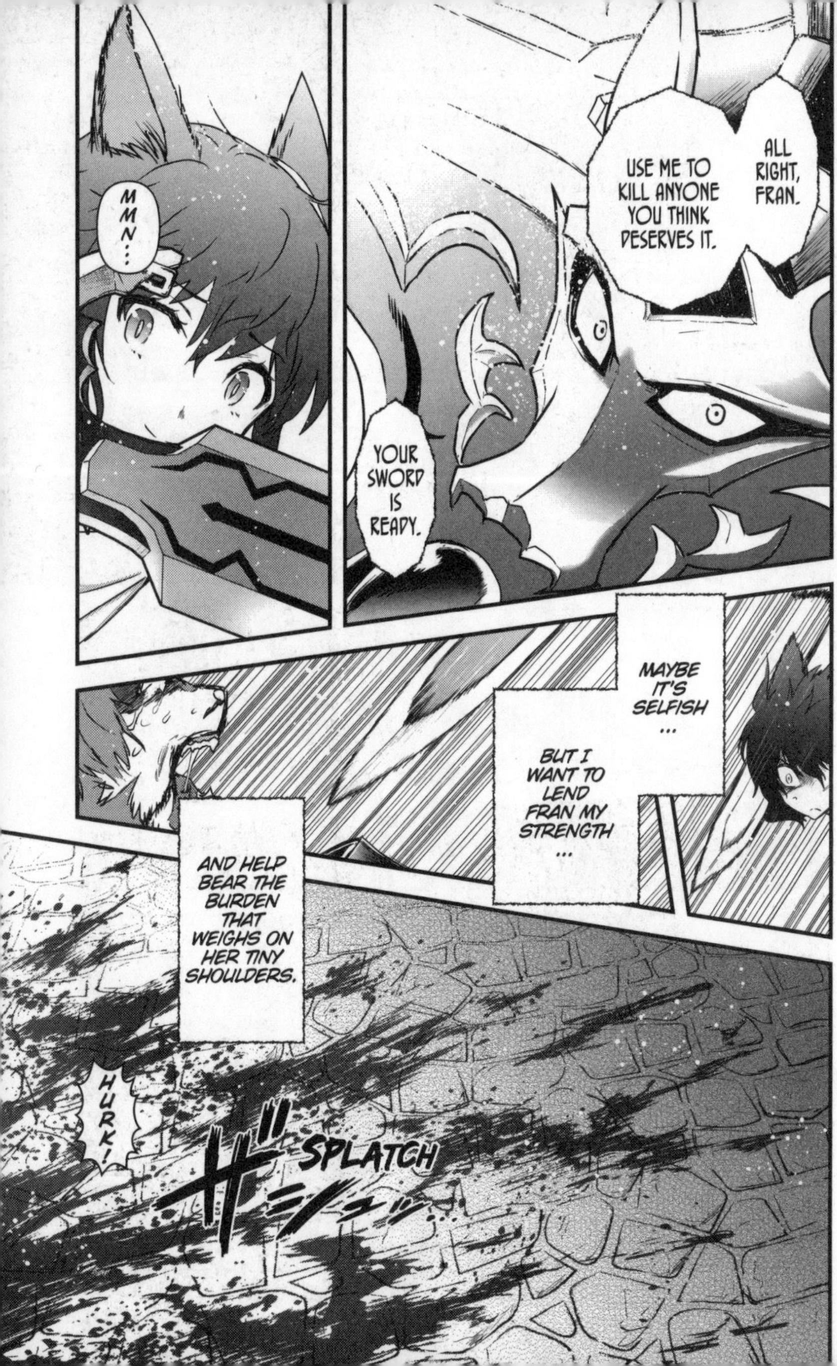
ALL RIGHT, FRAN.
USE ME TO KILL ANYONE YOU THINK DESERVES IT.
YOUR SWORD IS READY.
MMN...
MAYBE IT'S SELFISH...
BUT I WANT TO LEND FRAN MY STRENGTH...
AND HELP BEAR THE BURDEN THAT WEIGHS ON HER TINY SHOULDERS.
HURK!
SPLATCH

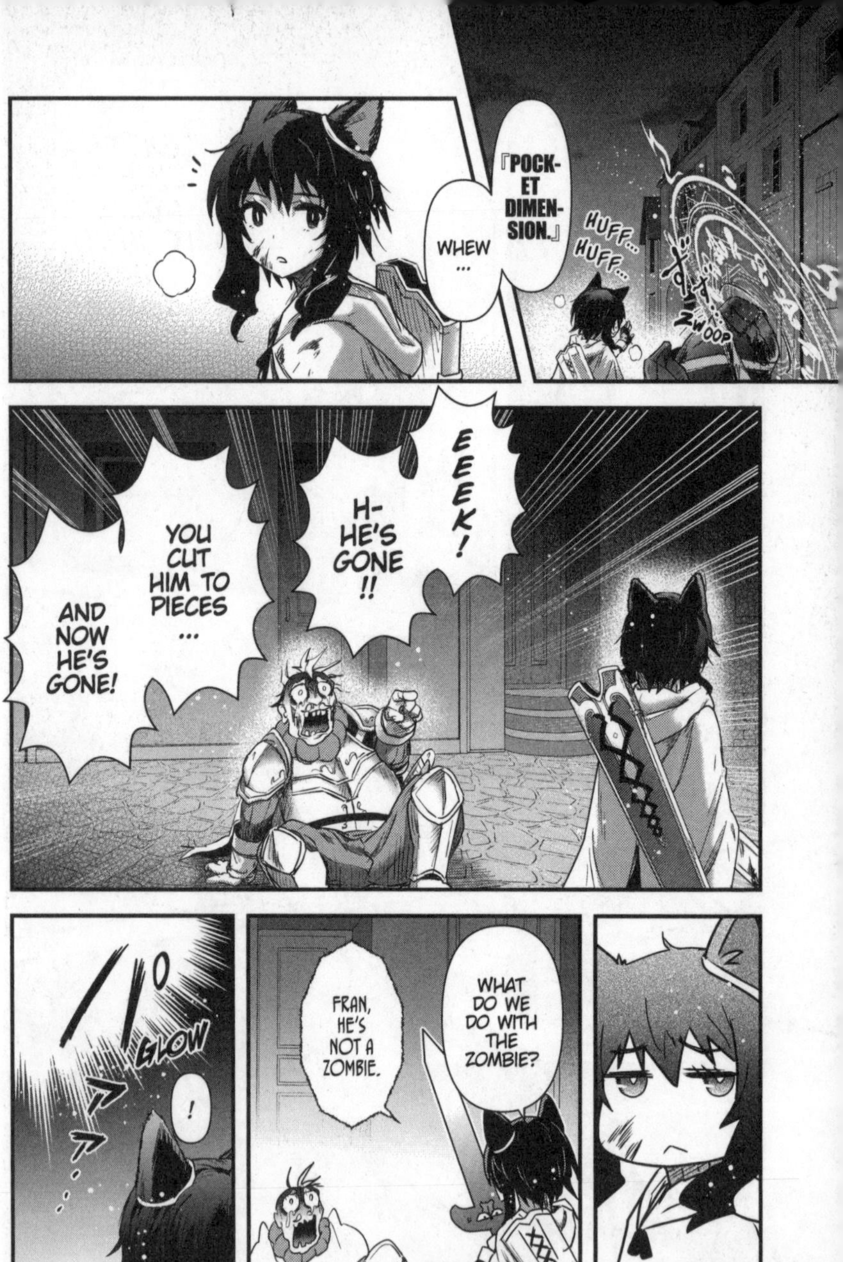
『POCK-ET DIMEN-SION.』
HUFF... HUFF...
ZWOOP
WHEW ...
EEEEK!
H-HE'S GONE !!
YOU CUT HIM TO PIECES ...
AND NOW HE'S GONE!
WHAT DO WE DO WITH THE ZOMBIE?
FRAN, HE'S NOT A ZOMBIE.
GLOW
!

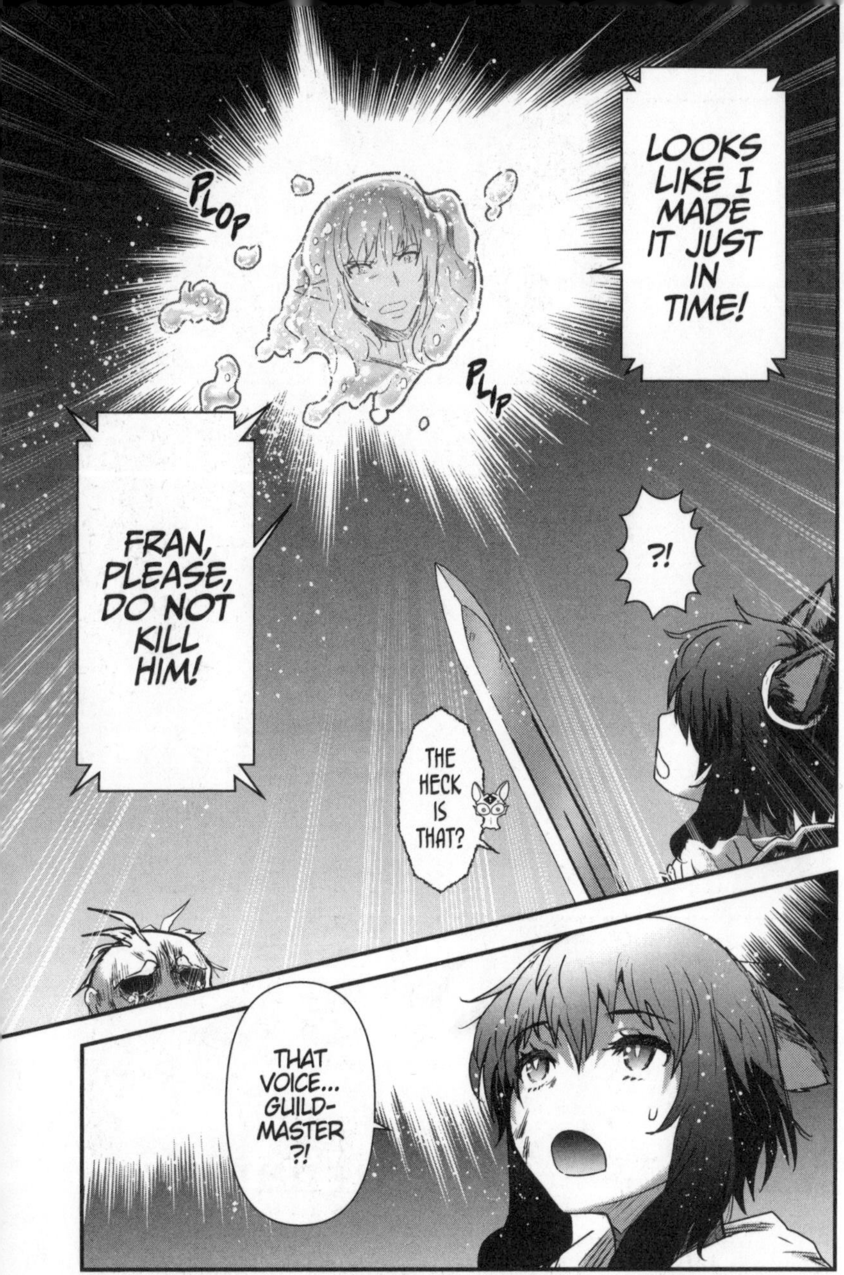
LOOKS LIKE I MADE IT JUST IN TIME!
PLOP
PLIP
FRAN, PLEASE, DO NOT KILL HIM!
?!
THE HECK IS THAT?
THAT VOICE... GUILD-MASTER?!

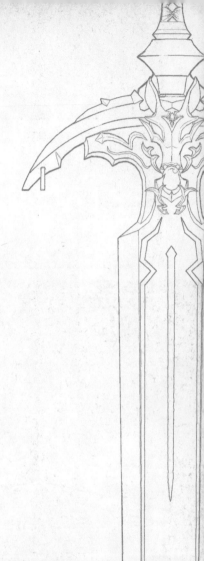

Reincarnated
as a Sword

Chapter 16: Return of the A-Rank

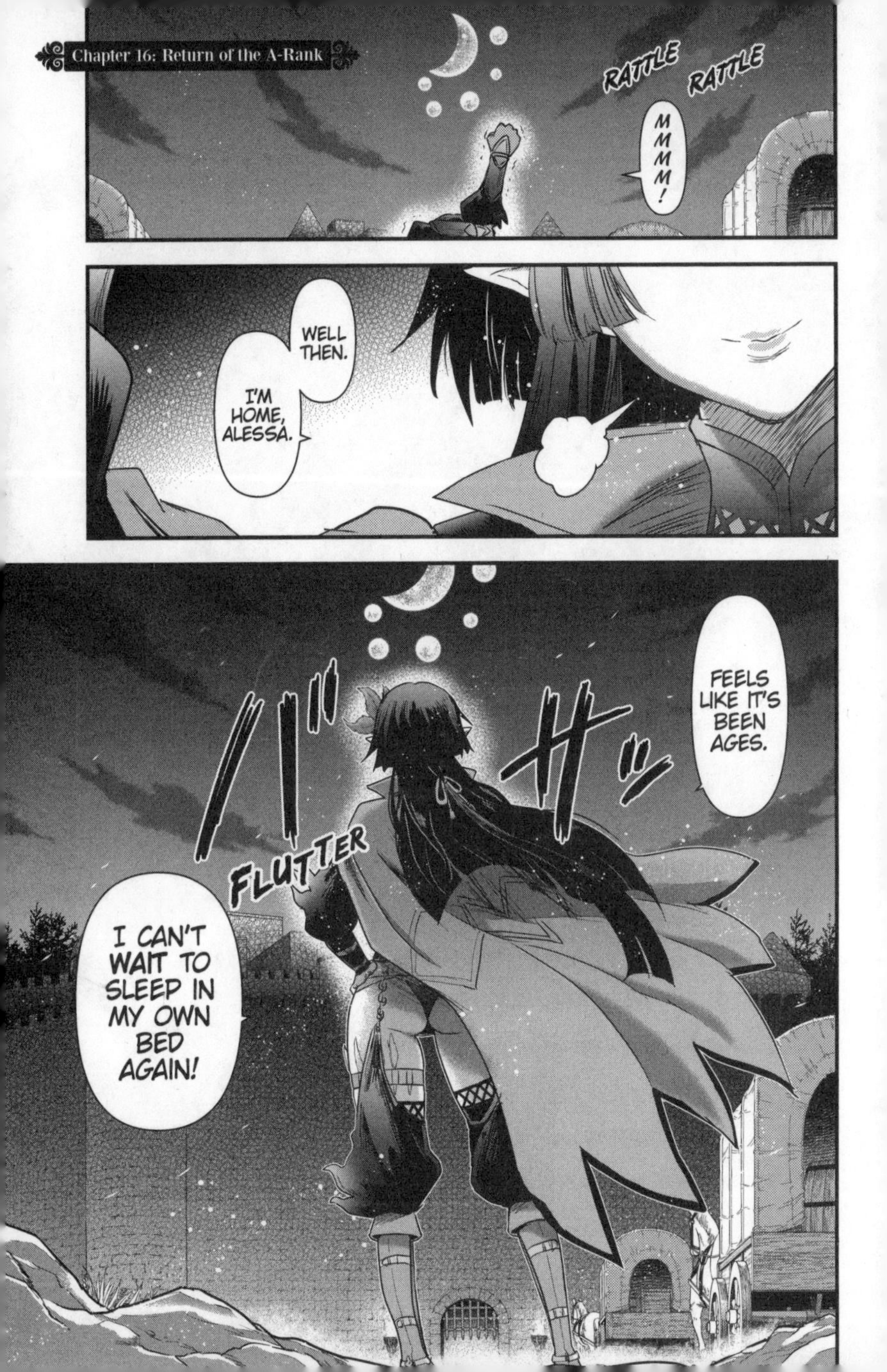
RATTLE RATTLE
MMMM!
WELL THEN.
I'M HOME, ALESSA.
FEELS LIKE IT'S BEEN AGES.
バサッ
FLUTTER
I CAN'T WAIT TO SLEEP IN MY OWN BED AGAIN!

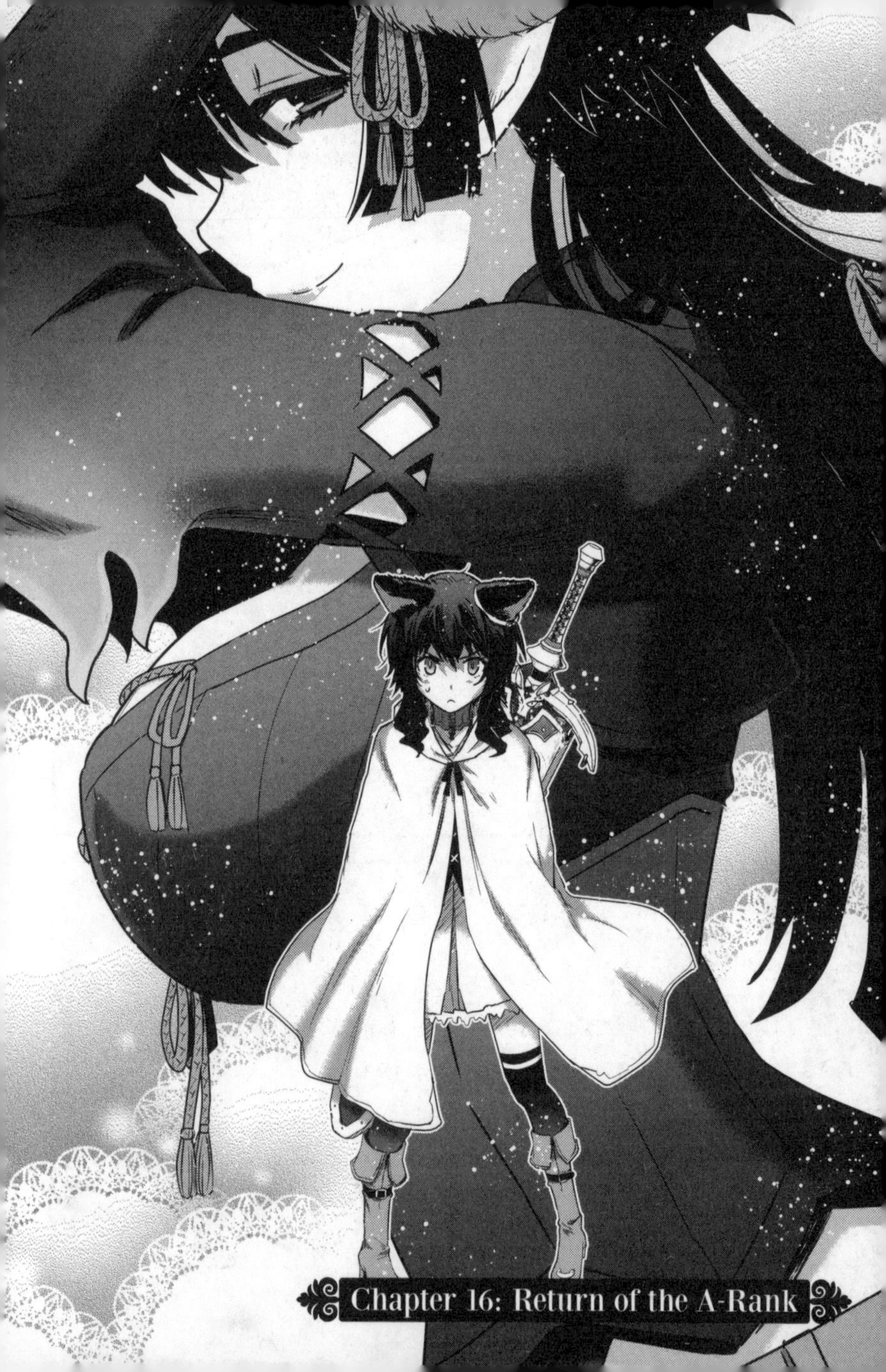
Chapter 16: Return of the A-Rank

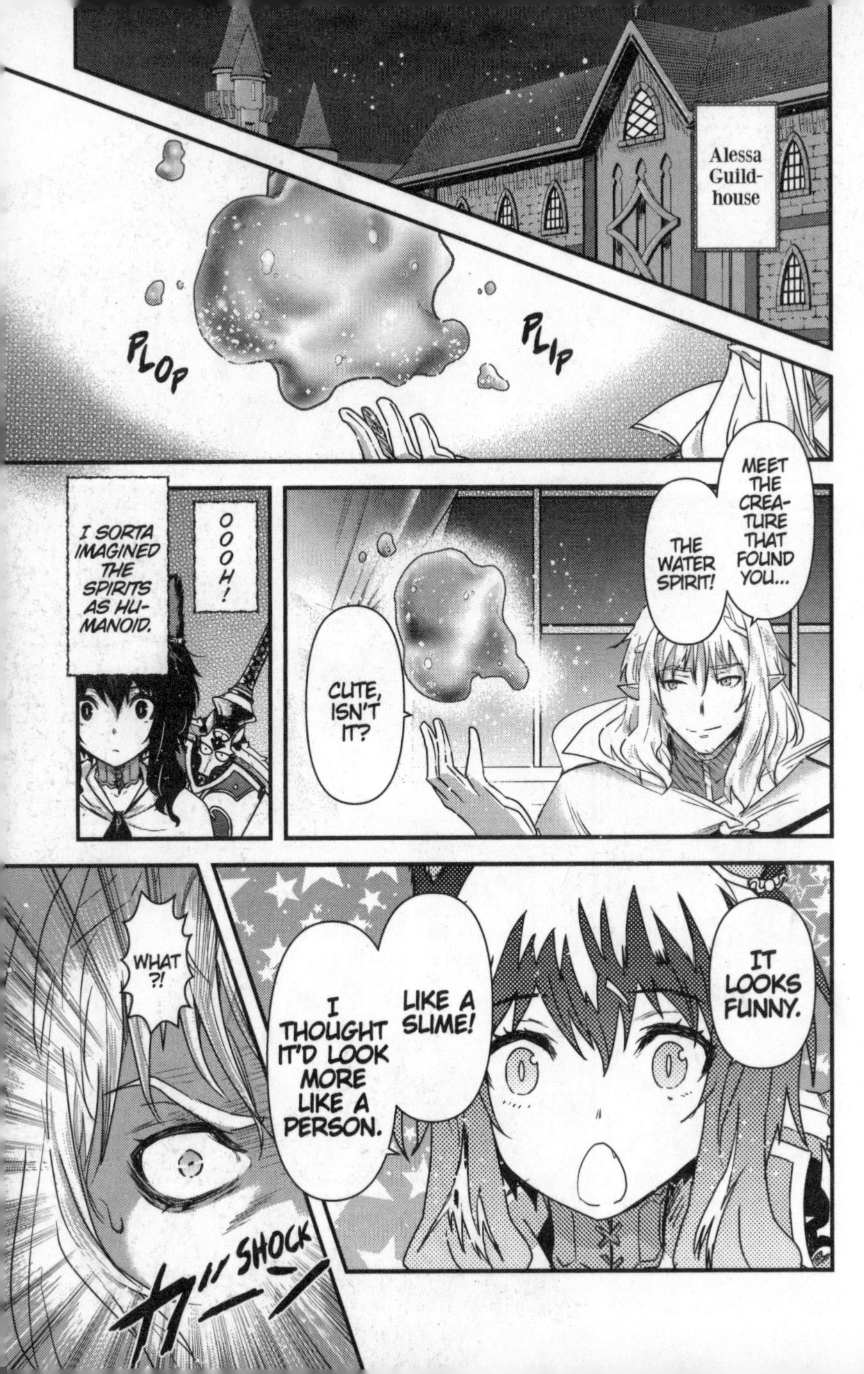
Alessa Guild-house
PLIP
PLOP
MEET THE CREA-TURE THAT FOUND YOU...
THE WATER SPIRIT!
CUTE, ISN'T IT?
OOOH!
I SORTA IMAGINED THE SPIRITS AS HU-MANOID.
IT LOOKS FUNNY.
LIKE A SLIME!
I THOUGHT IT'D LOOK MORE LIKE A PERSON.
WHAT?!
SHOCK

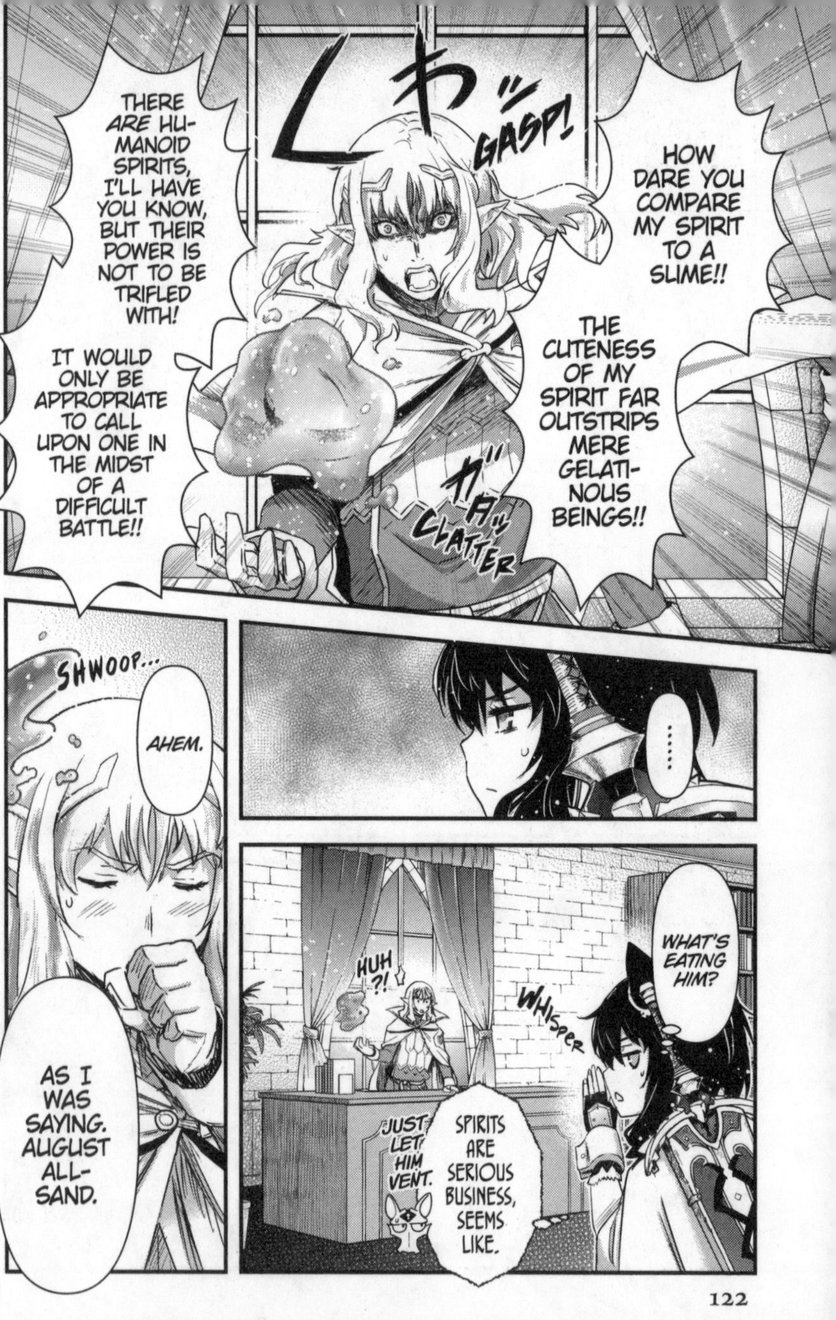
HOW DARE YOU COMPARE MY SPIRIT TO A SLIME!!
GASP!
THE CUTENESS OF MY SPIRIT FAR OUTSTRIPS MERE GELATINOUS BEINGS!!
THERE ARE HUMANOID SPIRITS, I'LL HAVE YOU KNOW, BUT THEIR POWER IS NOT TO BE TRIFLED WITH!
IT WOULD ONLY BE APPROPRIATE TO CALL UPON ONE IN THE MIDST OF A DIFFICULT BATTLE!!
CLATTER
......
WHAT'S EATING HIM?
WHISPER
HUH ?!
SPIRITS ARE SERIOUS BUSINESS, SEEMS LIKE.
JUST LET HIM VENT.
SHWOOP...
AHEM.
AS I WAS SAYING. AUGUST ALL-SAND.

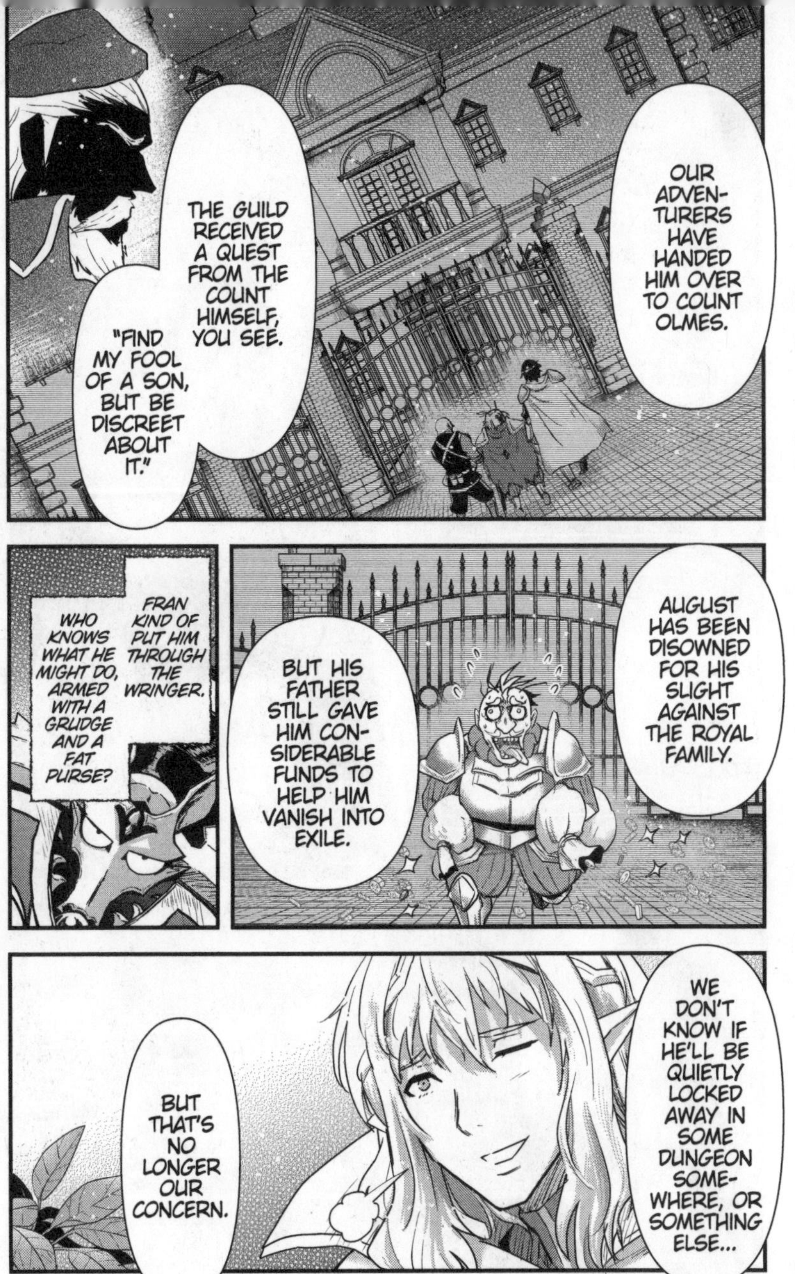
OUR ADVENTURERS HAVE HANDED HIM OVER TO COUNT OLMES.
THE GUILD RECEIVED A QUEST FROM THE COUNT HIMSELF, YOU SEE.
"FIND MY FOOL OF A SON, BUT BE DISCREET ABOUT IT."
AUGUST HAS BEEN DISOWNED FOR HIS SLIGHT AGAINST THE ROYAL FAMILY.
BUT HIS FATHER STILL GAVE HIM CONSIDERABLE FUNDS TO HELP HIM VANISH INTO EXILE.
FRAN KIND OF PUT HIM THROUGH THE WRINGER.
WHO KNOWS WHAT HE MIGHT DO, ARMED WITH A GRUDGE AND A FAT PURSE?
WE DON'T KNOW IF HE'LL BE QUIETLY LOCKED AWAY IN SOME DUNGEON SOMEWHERE, OR SOMETHING ELSE...
BUT THAT'S NO LONGER OUR CONCERN.

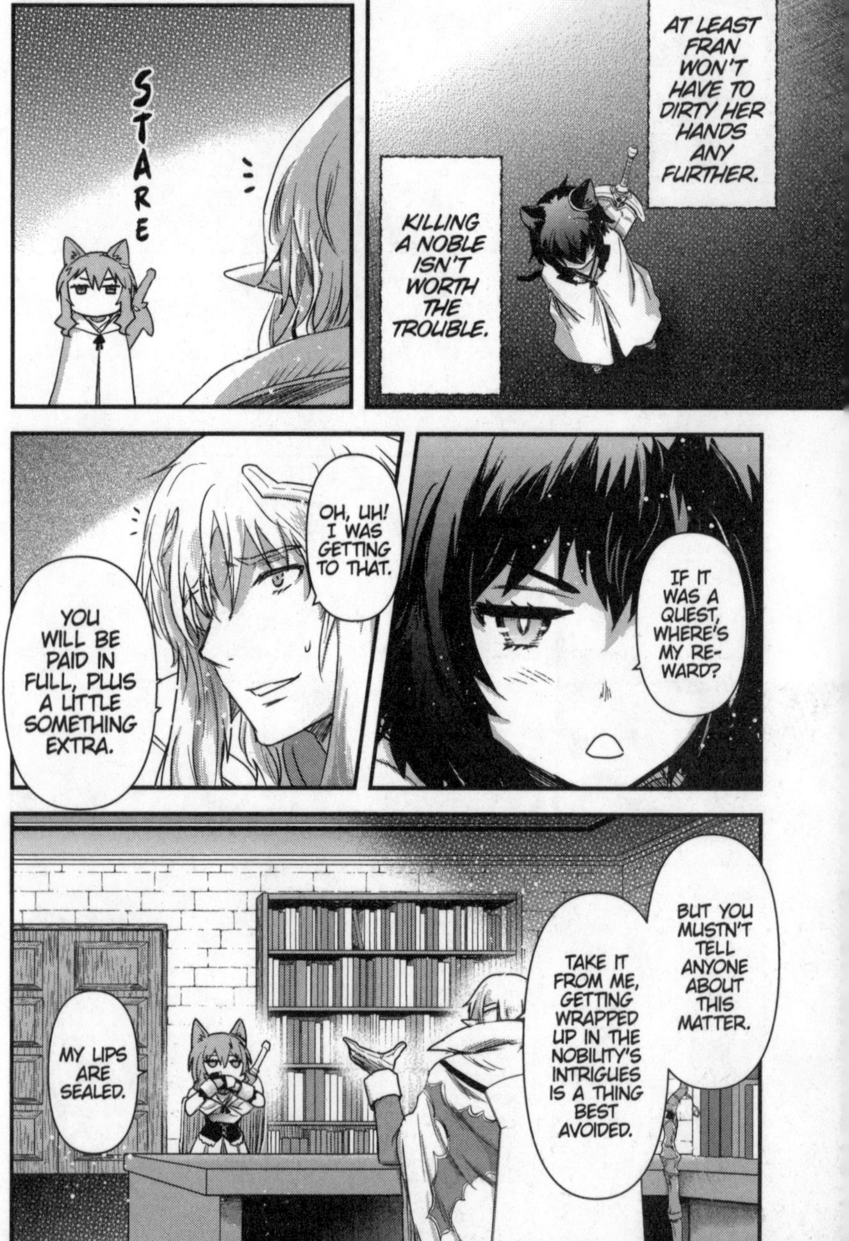
AT LEAST FRAN WON'T HAVE TO DIRTY HER HANDS ANY FURTHER.
KILLING A NOBLE ISN'T WORTH THE TROUBLE.
STARE
IF IT WAS A QUEST, WHERE'S MY RE-WARD?
OH, UH! I WAS GETTING TO THAT.
YOU WILL BE PAID IN FULL, PLUS A LITTLE SOMETHING EXTRA.
BUT YOU MUSTN'T TELL ANYONE ABOUT THIS MATTER.
TAKE IT FROM ME, GETTING WRAPPED UP IN THE NOBILITY'S INTRIGUES IS A THING BEST AVOIDED.
MY LIPS ARE SEALED.

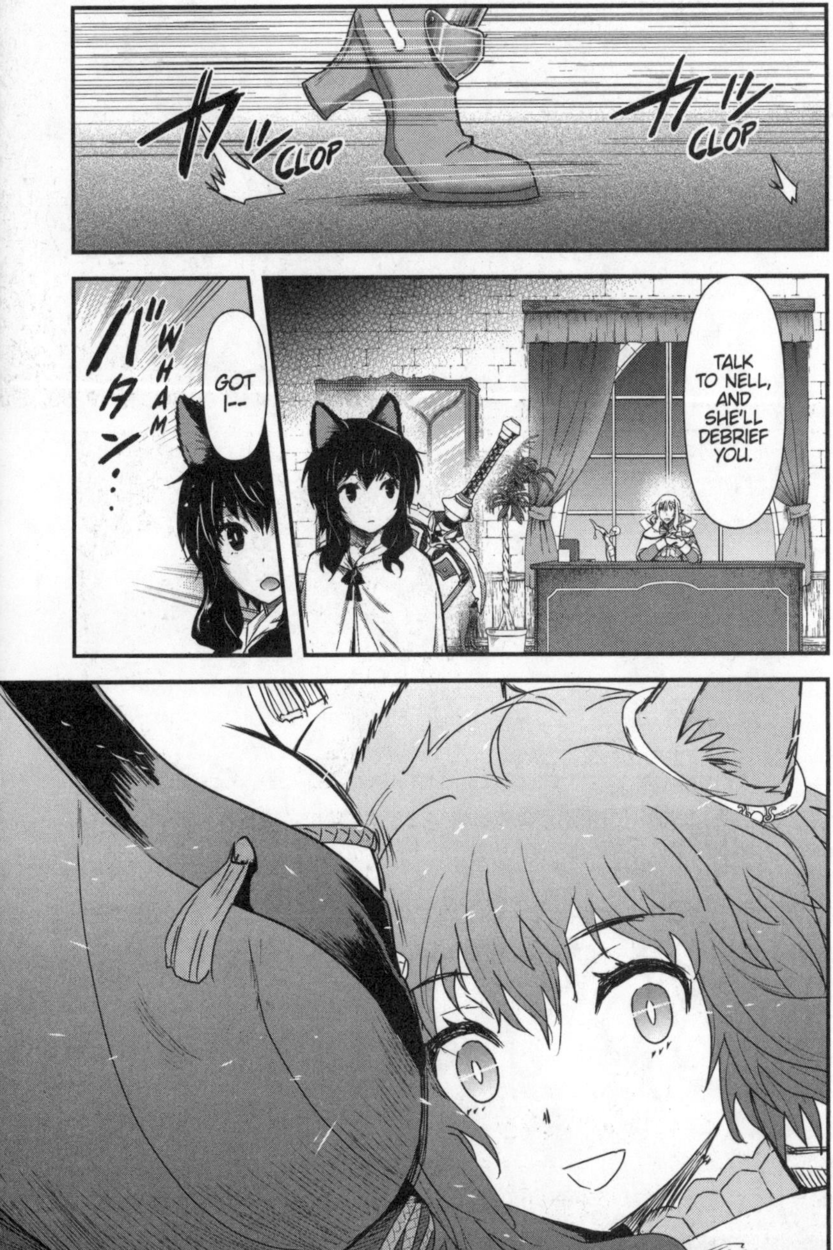
ガッ
CLOP
ガッ
CLOP
TALK TO NELL, AND SHE'LL DEBRIEF YOU.
GOT I--
バタン…
WHAM

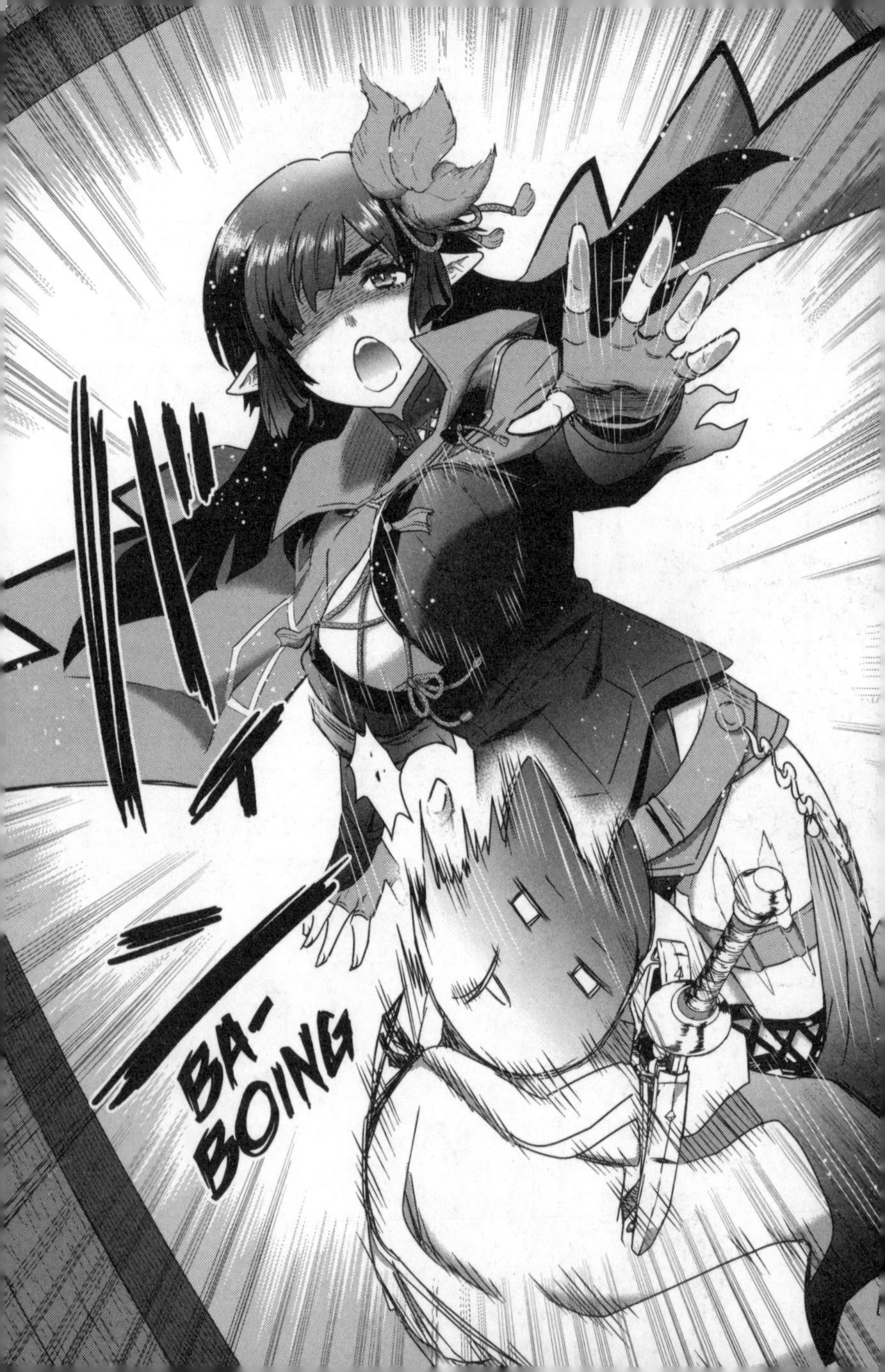
BA-
BOING

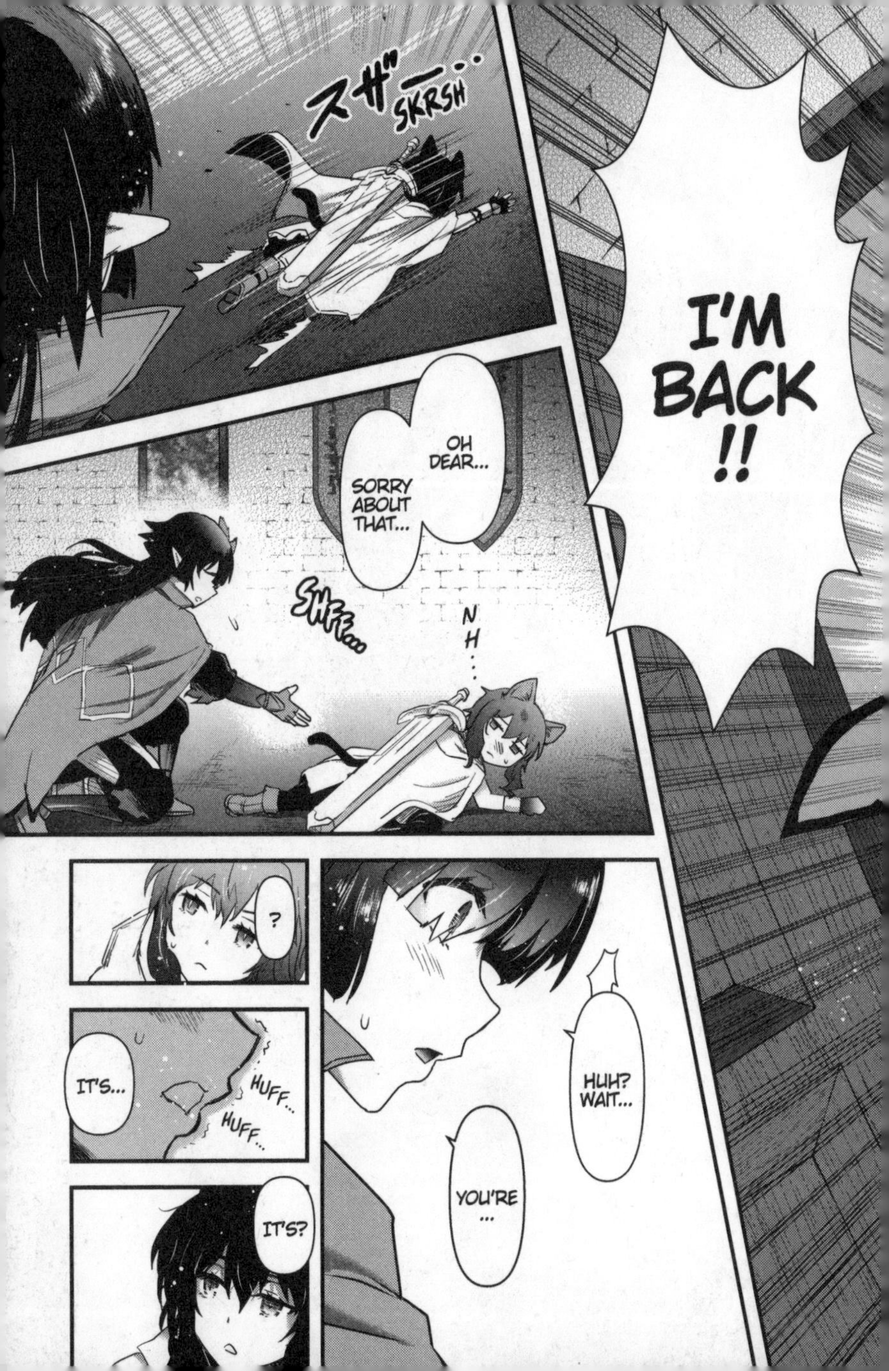
I'M BACK!!
スザー
SKRSH
OH DEAR... SORRY ABOUT THAT...
NH...
SHFF...
HUH? WAIT...
YOU'RE...
?
IT'S...
HUFF... HUFF...
IT'S?

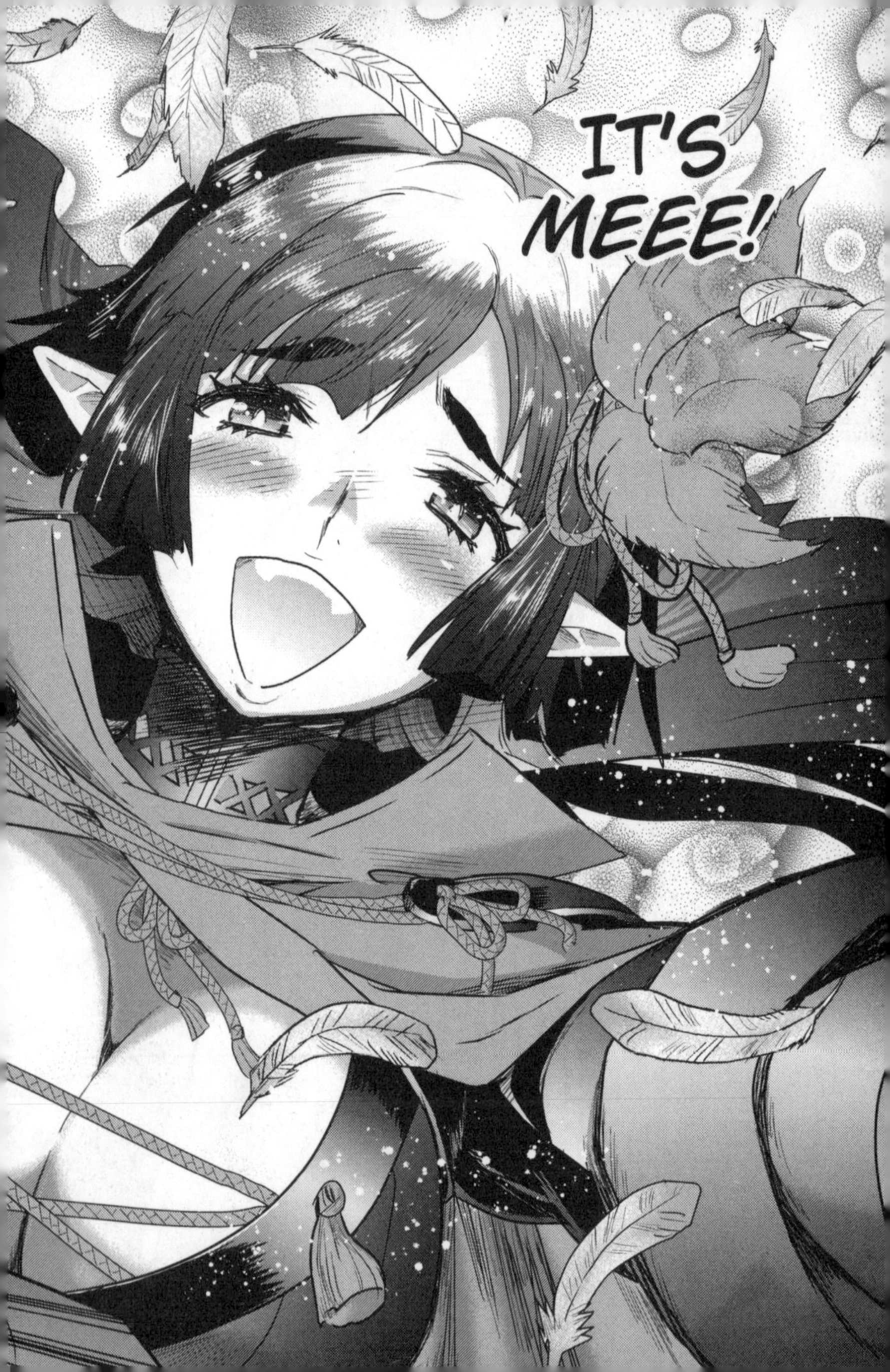
IT'S MEEE!

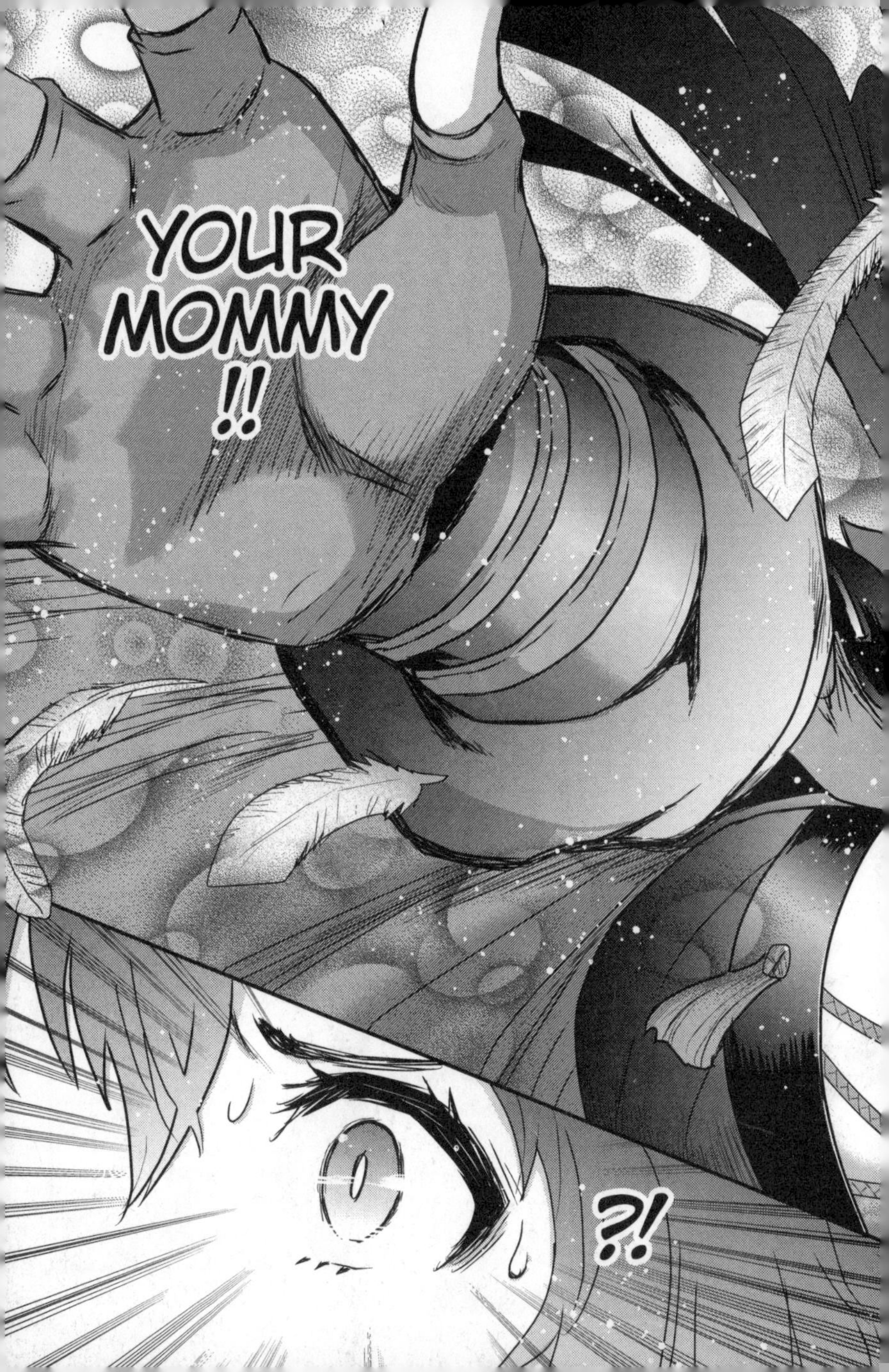
YOUR MOMMY !!
?!

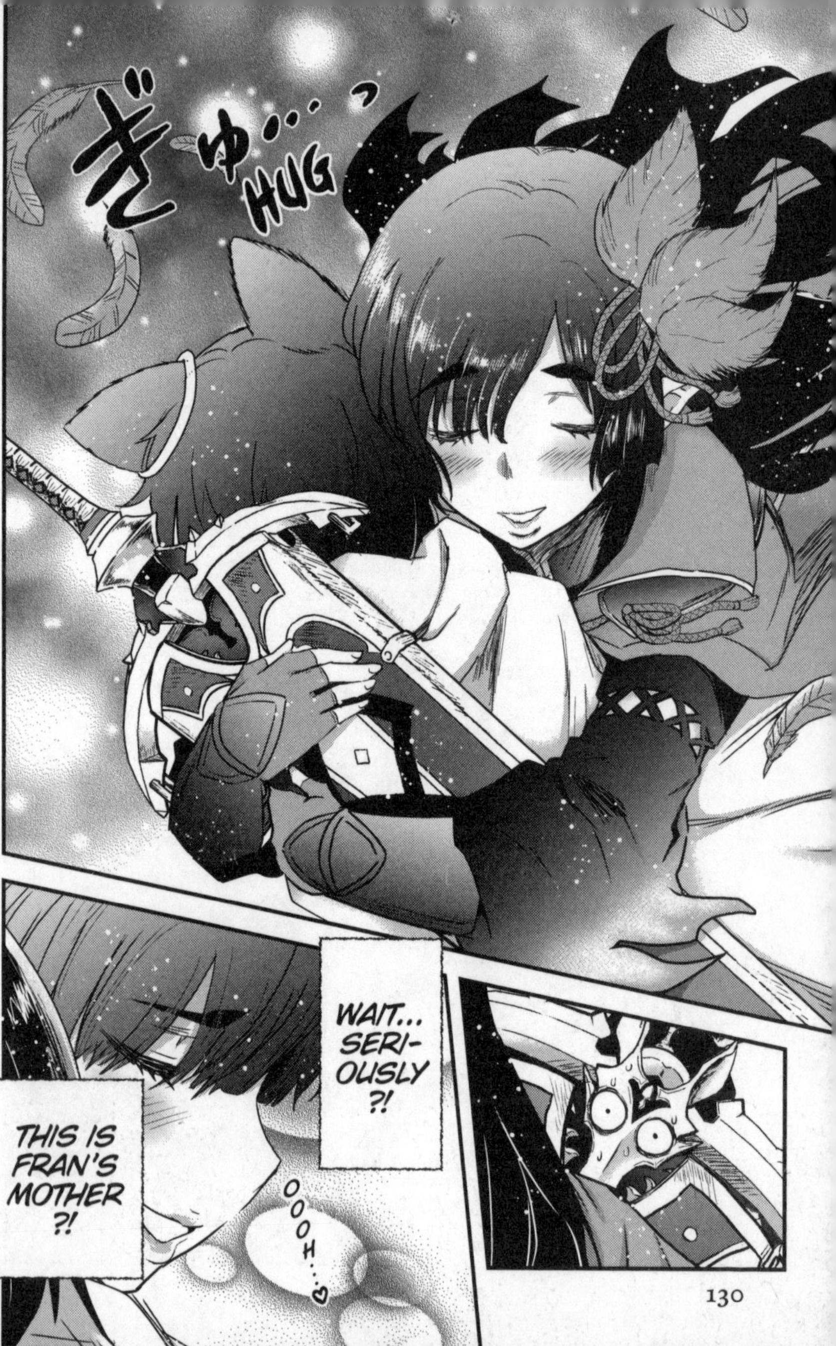
ぎゅ…っ
HUG
WAIT... SERI-OUSLY ?!
THIS IS FRAN'S MOTHER ?!
OOOH...♥

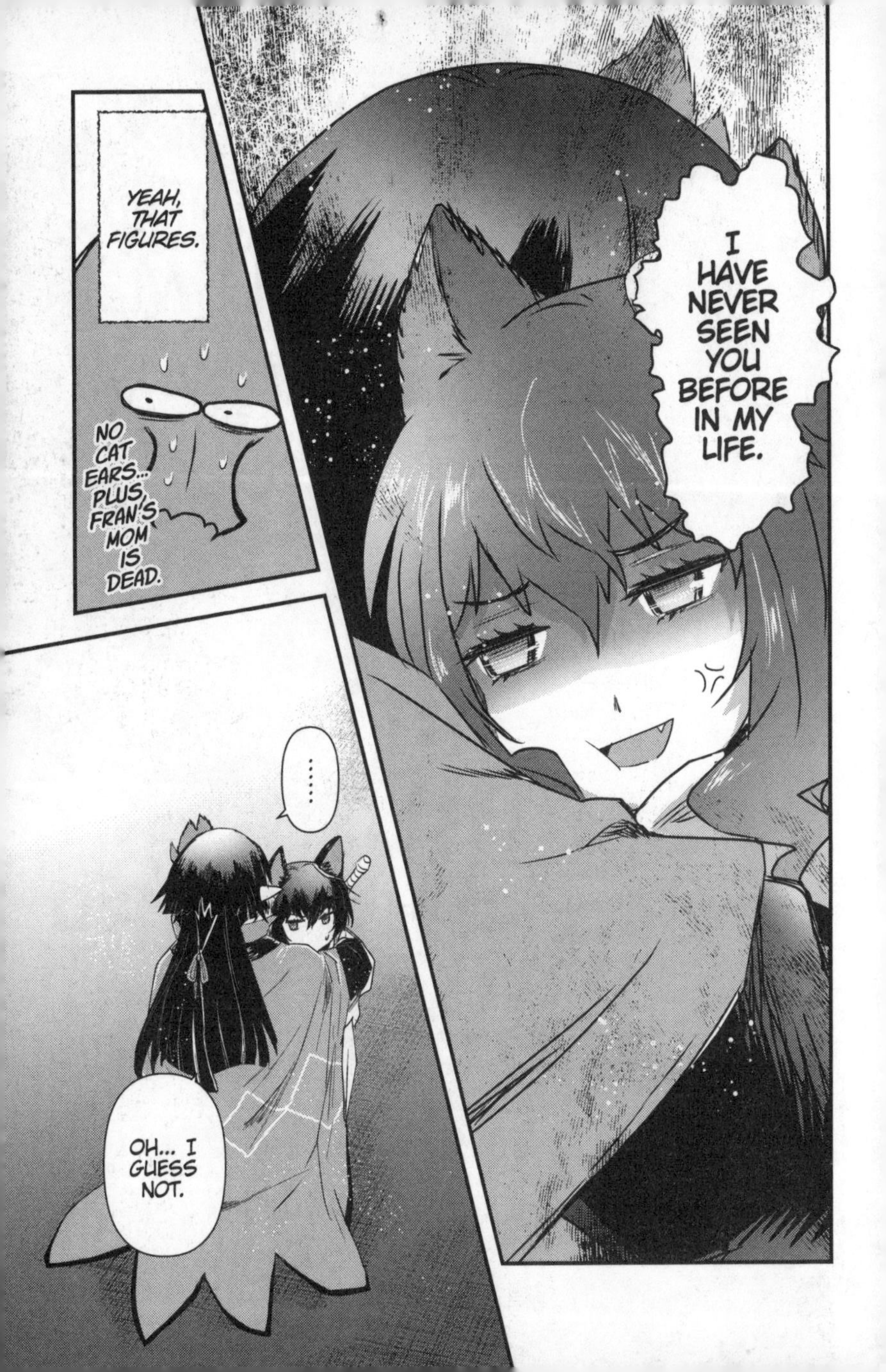
I HAVE NEVER SEEN YOU BEFORE IN MY LIFE.
YEAH, THAT FIGURES.
NO CAT EARS... PLUS, FRAN'S MOM IS DEAD.
......
OH... I GUESS NOT.

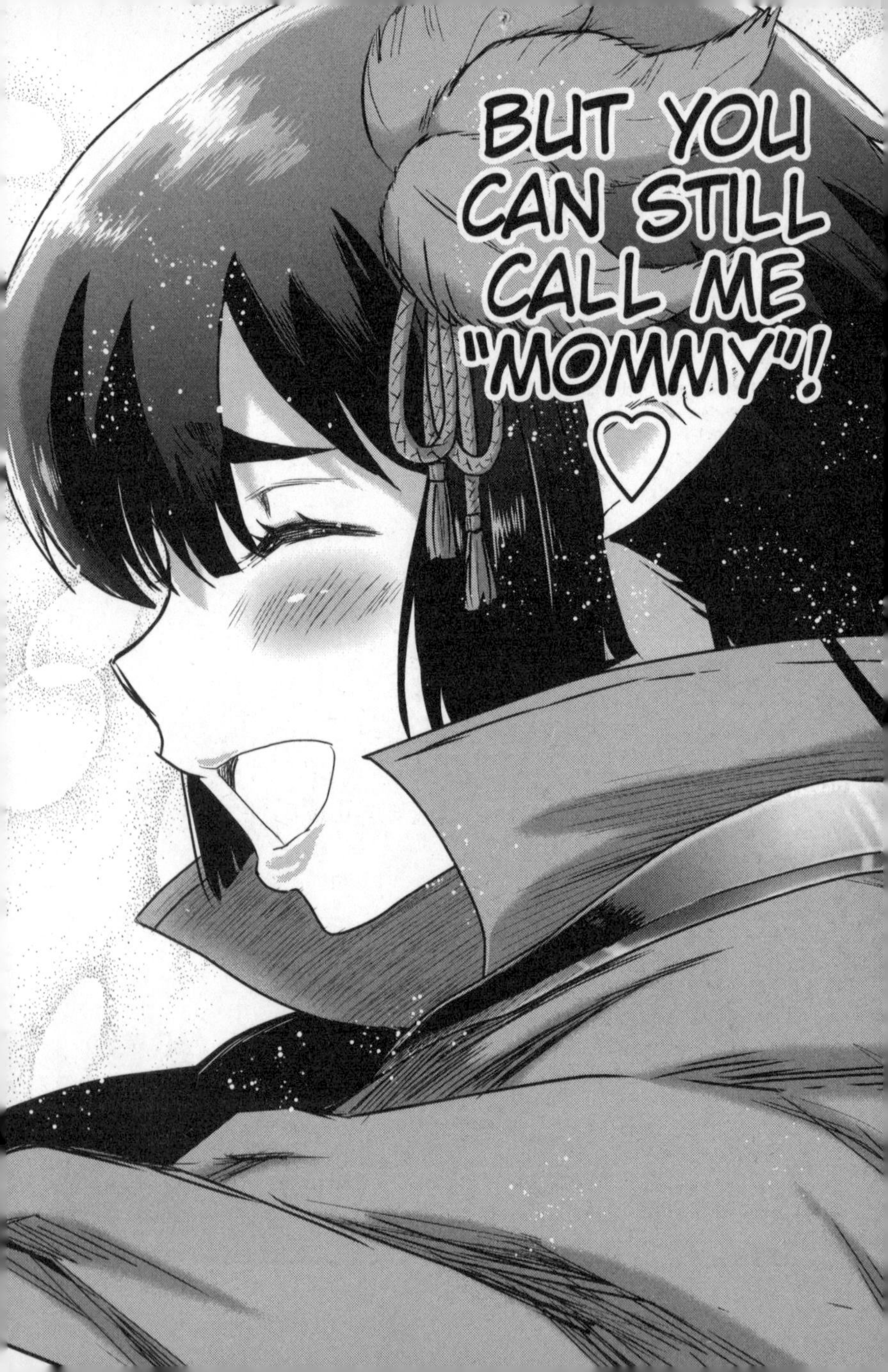
BUT YOU CAN STILL CALL ME "MOMMY"! ♡

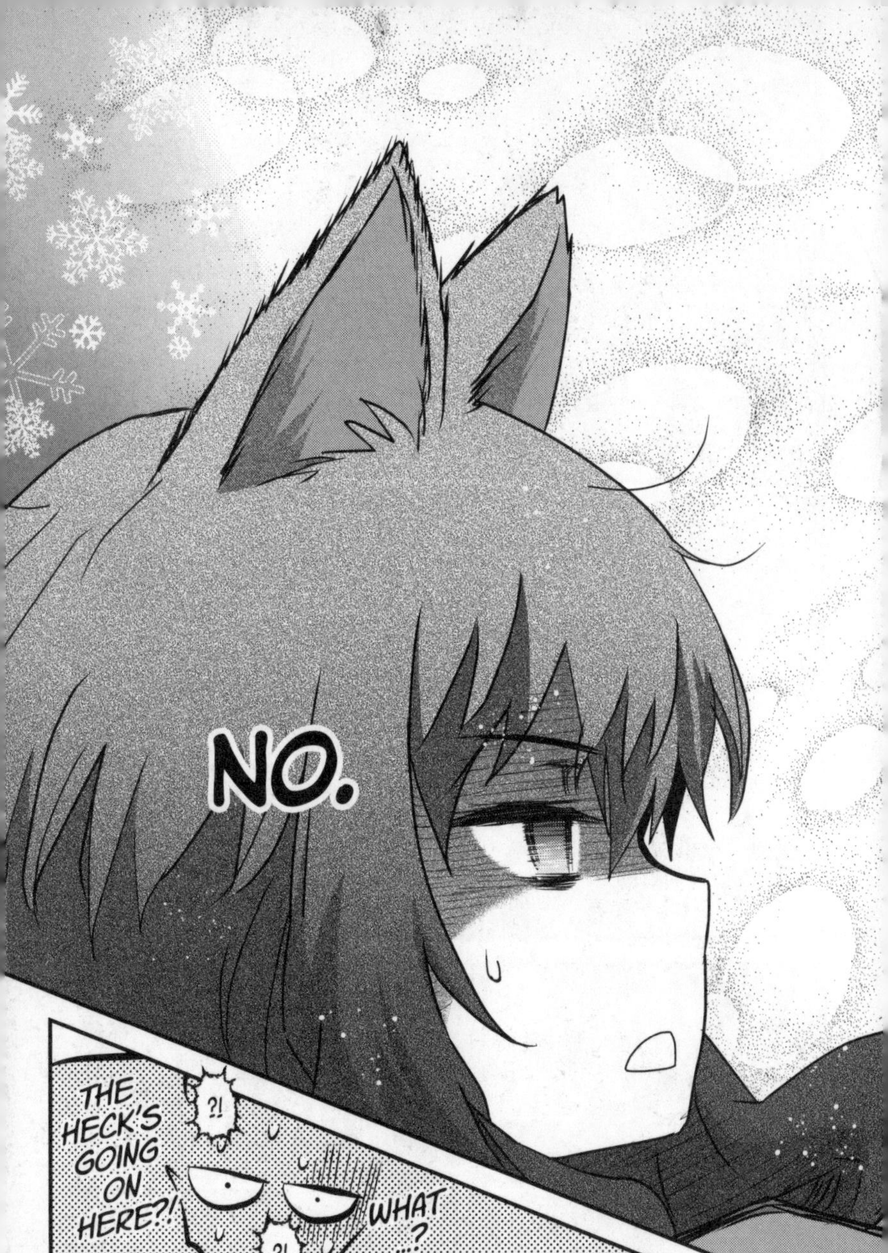
NO.
WHAT ...?
?!
THE HECK'S GOING ON HERE?!
?!

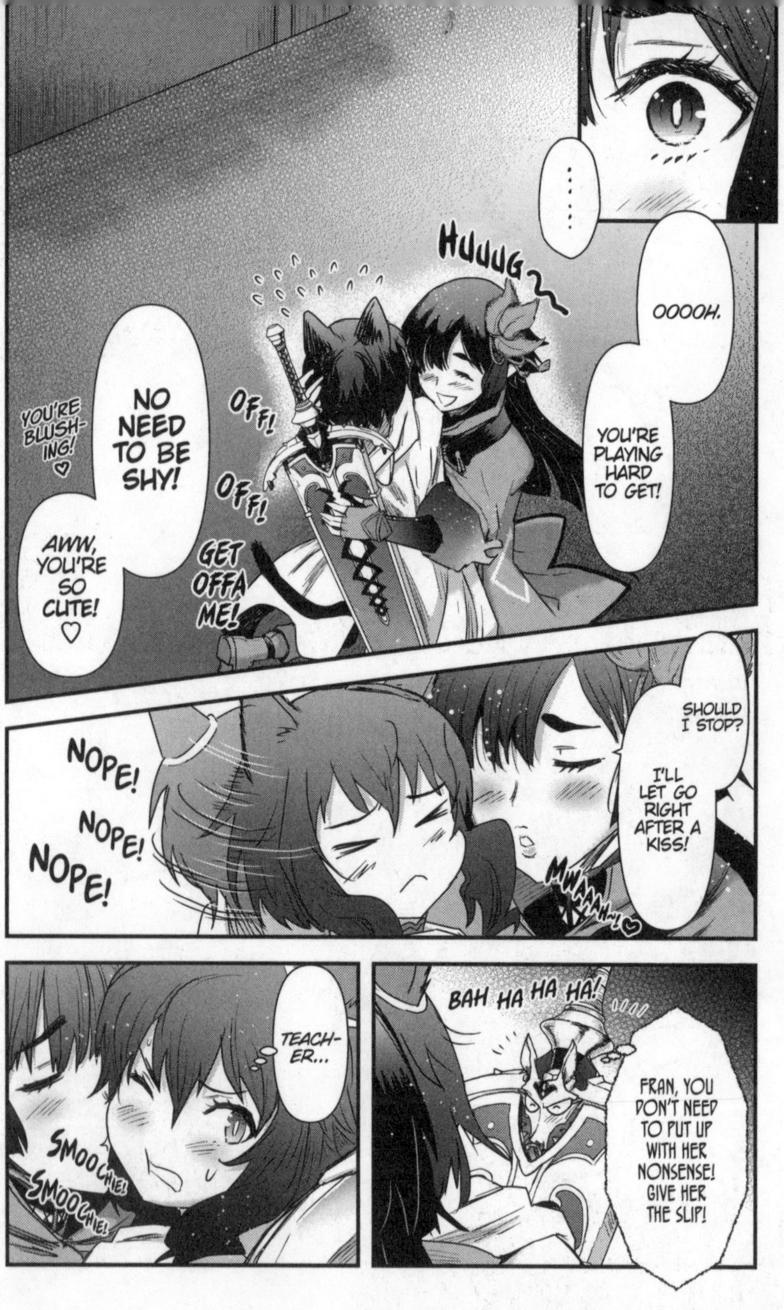
......
HUUUG~
OOOOH.
YOU'RE PLAYING HARD TO GET!
OFF!
OFF!
GET OFFA ME!
NO NEED TO BE SHY!
YOU'RE BLUSHING! ♡
AWW, YOU'RE SO CUTE! ♡
SHOULD I STOP?
I'LL LET GO RIGHT AFTER A KISS!
MWAAAH~! ♡
NOPE!
NOPE!
NOPE!
BAH HA HA HA!
FRAN, YOU DON'T NEED TO PUT UP WITH HER NONSENSE! GIVE HER THE SLIP!
TEACHER...
SMOOCHIE!
SMOOCHIE!

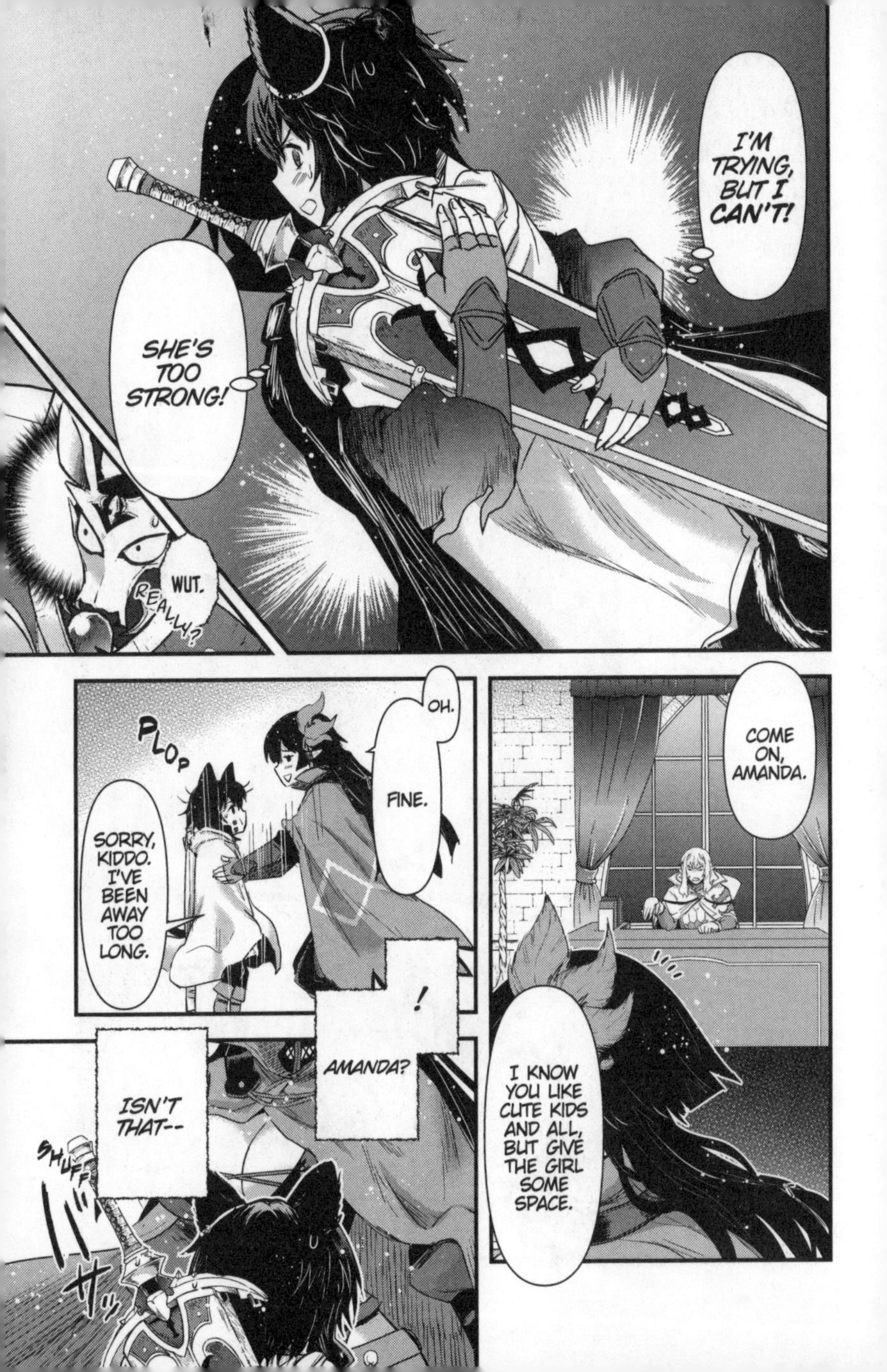
I'M TRYING, BUT I CAN'T!
SHE'S TOO STRONG!
WUT.
REALLY?
COME ON, AMANDA.
I KNOW YOU LIKE CUTE KIDS AND ALL, BUT GIVE THE GIRL SOME SPACE.
OH.
FINE.
PLOP
SORRY, KIDDO. I'VE BEEN AWAY TOO LONG.
!
AMANDA?
ISN'T THAT--
SHUFF

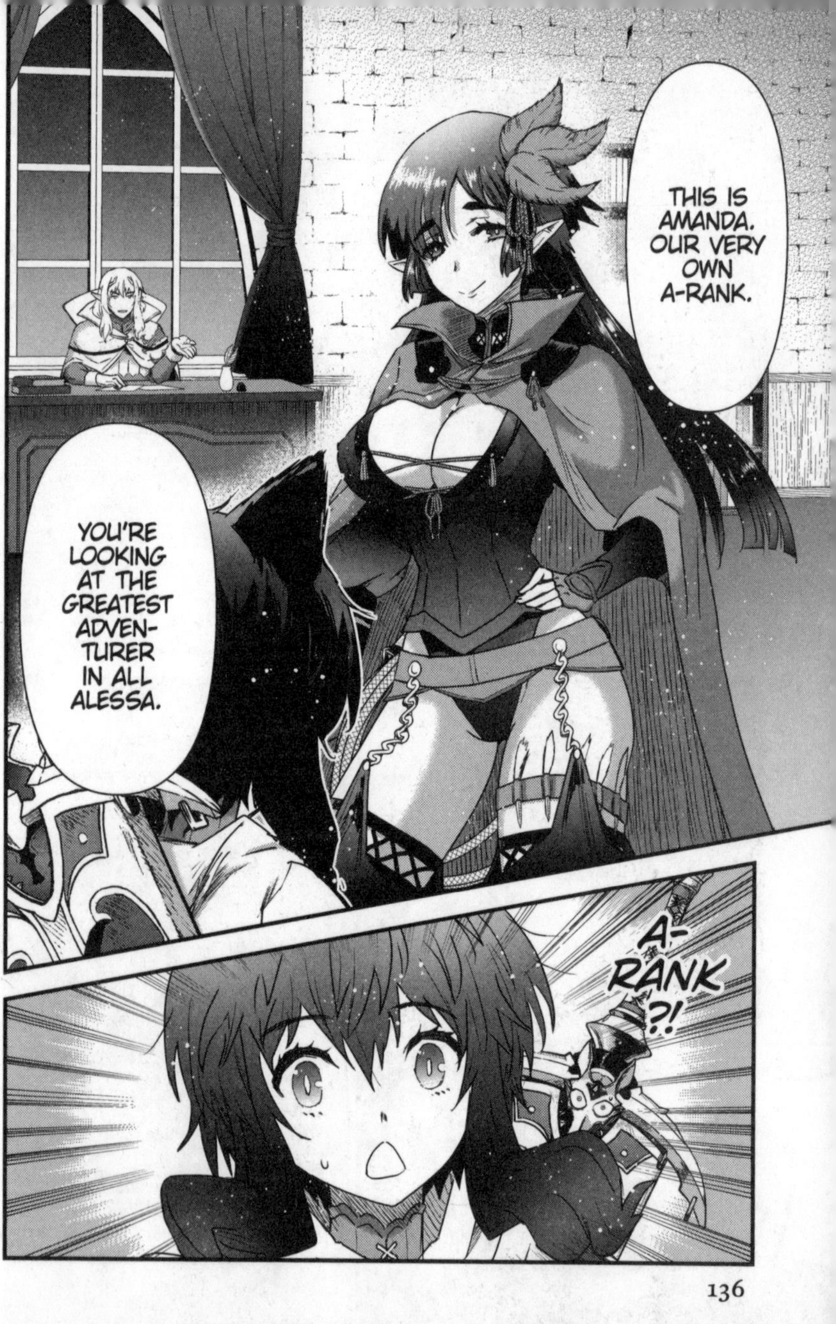
THIS IS AMANDA. OUR VERY OWN A-RANK.
YOU'RE LOOKING AT THE GREATEST ADVEN-TURER IN ALL ALESSA.
A-RANK?!

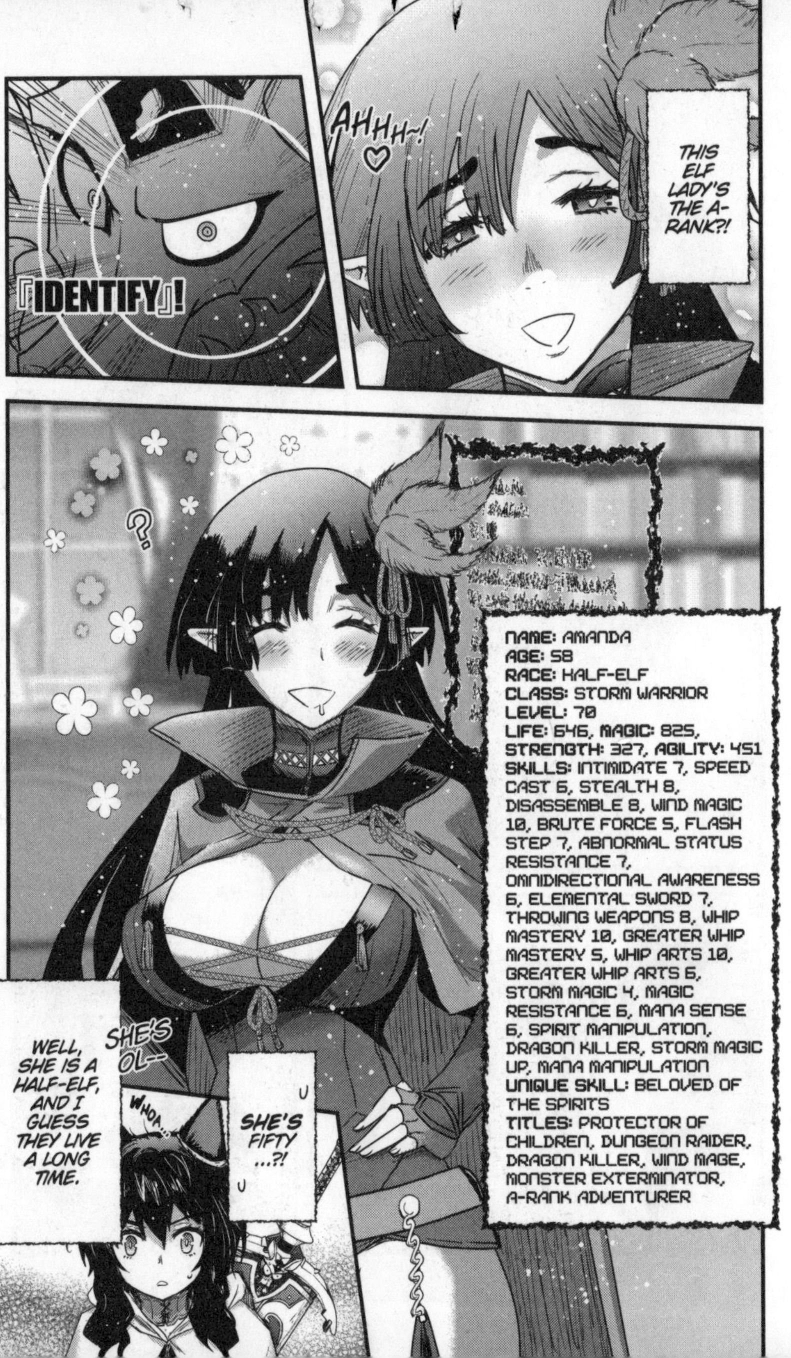
THIS ELF LADY'S THE A-RANK?!
AHHH~! ♥
『IDENTIFY』!
NAME: AMANDA
AGE: 58
RACE: HALF-ELF
CLASS: STORM WARRIOR
LEVEL: 70
LIFE: 646, MAGIC: 825,
STRENGTH: 327, AGILITY: 451
SKILLS: INTIMIDATE 7, SPEED CAST 6, STEALTH 8, DISASSEMBLE 8, WIND MAGIC 10, BRUTE FORCE 5, FLASH STEP 7, ABNORMAL STATUS RESISTANCE 7, OMNIDIRECTIONAL AWARENESS 6, ELEMENTAL SWORD 7, THROWING WEAPONS 8, WHIP MASTERY 10, GREATER WHIP MASTERY 5, WHIP ARTS 10, GREATER WHIP ARTS 6, STORM MAGIC 4, MAGIC RESISTANCE 6, MANA SENSE 6, SPIRIT MANIPULATION, DRAGON KILLER, STORM MAGIC UP, MANA MANIPULATION
UNIQUE SKILL: BELOVED OF THE SPIRITS
TITLES: PROTECTOR OF CHILDREN, DUNGEON RAIDER, DRAGON KILLER, WIND MAGE, MONSTER EXTERMINATOR, A-RANK ADVENTURER
SHE'S OL--
SHE'S FIFTY ...?!
WELL, SHE IS A HALF-ELF, AND I GUESS THEY LIVE A LONG TIME.
WHOA...

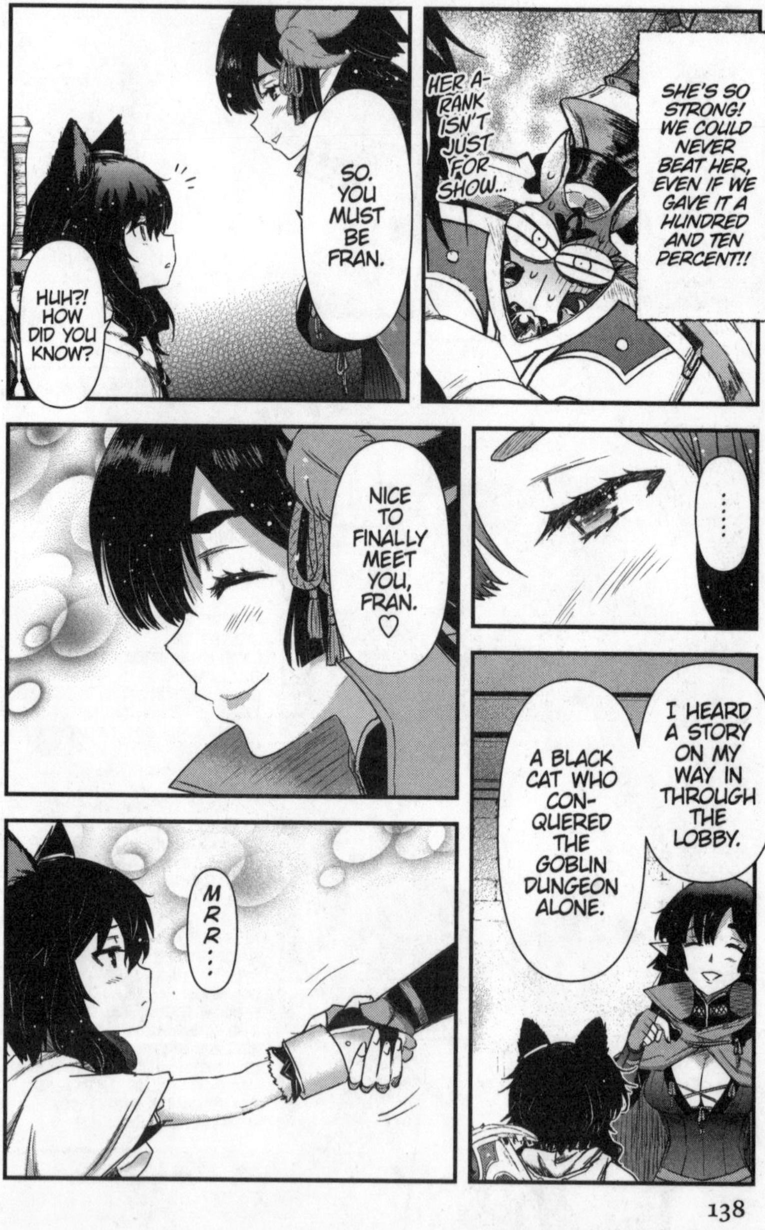
SHE'S SO STRONG! WE COULD NEVER BEAT HER, EVEN IF WE GAVE IT A HUNDRED AND TEN PERCENT!!
HER A-RANK ISN'T JUST FOR SHOW...
SO. YOU MUST BE FRAN.
HUH?! HOW DID YOU KNOW?
......
I HEARD A STORY ON MY WAY IN THROUGH THE LOBBY.
A BLACK CAT WHO CON-QUERED THE GOBLIN DUNGEON ALONE.
NICE TO FINALLY MEET YOU, FRAN. ♡
MRR...

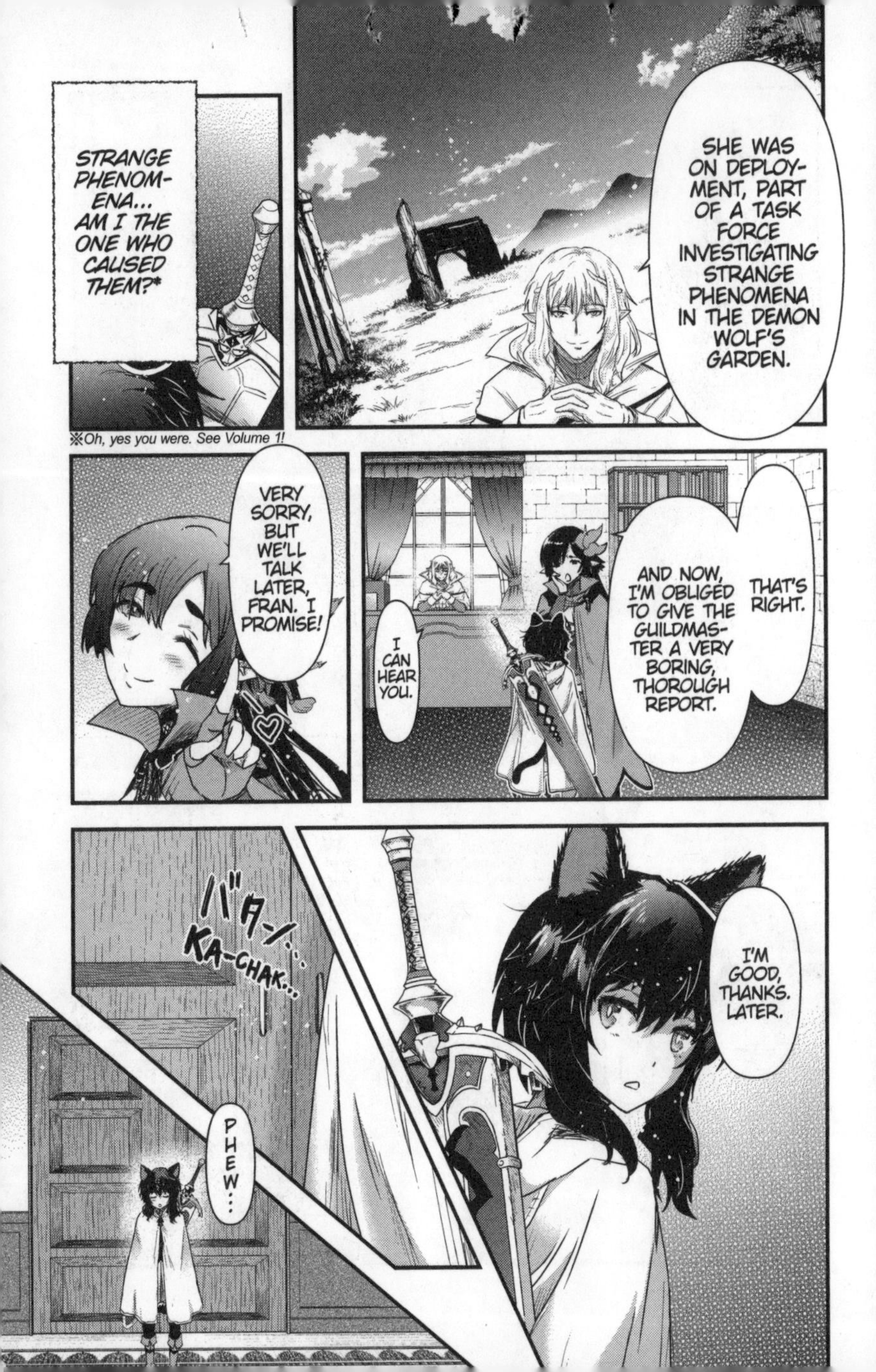
SHE WAS ON DEPLOYMENT, PART OF A TASK FORCE INVESTIGATING STRANGE PHENOMENA IN THE DEMON WOLF'S GARDEN.
STRANGE PHENOMENA... AM I THE ONE WHO CAUSED THEM?*
※Oh, yes you were. See Volume 1!
THAT'S RIGHT.
AND NOW, I'M OBLIGED TO GIVE THE GUILDMASTER A VERY BORING, THOROUGH REPORT.
I CAN HEAR YOU.
VERY SORRY, BUT WE'LL TALK LATER, FRAN. I PROMISE!
I'M GOOD, THANKS. LATER.
バタン
KA-CHAK...
PHEW...

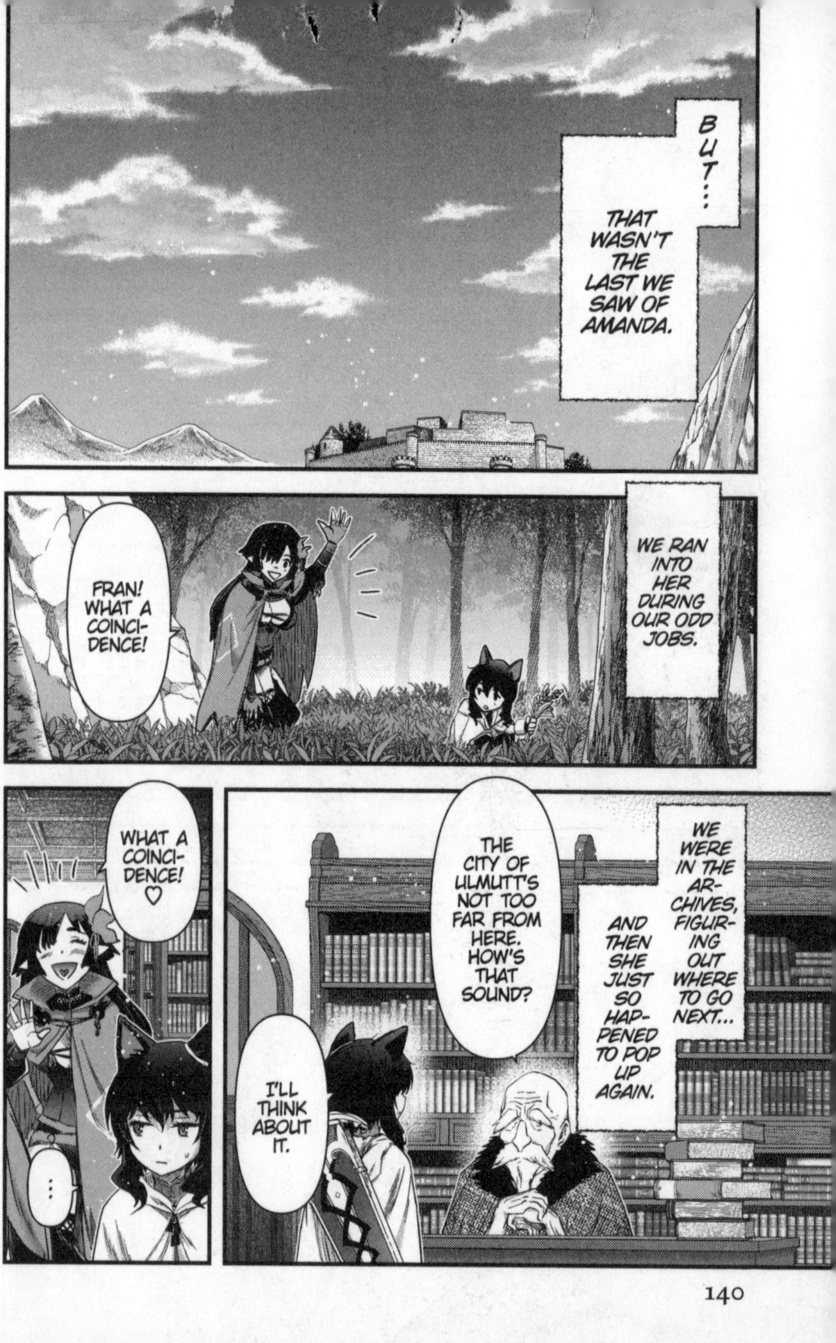
BUT...
THAT WASN'T THE LAST WE SAW OF AMANDA.
WE RAN INTO HER DURING OUR ODD JOBS.
FRAN! WHAT A COINCI-DENCE!
WE WERE IN THE AR-CHIVES, FIGUR-ING OUT WHERE TO GO NEXT...
AND THEN SHE JUST SO HAP-PENED TO POP UP AGAIN.
THE CITY OF ULMUTT'S NOT TOO FAR FROM HERE. HOW'S THAT SOUND?
I'LL THINK ABOUT IT.
WHAT A COINCI-DENCE! ♡
...

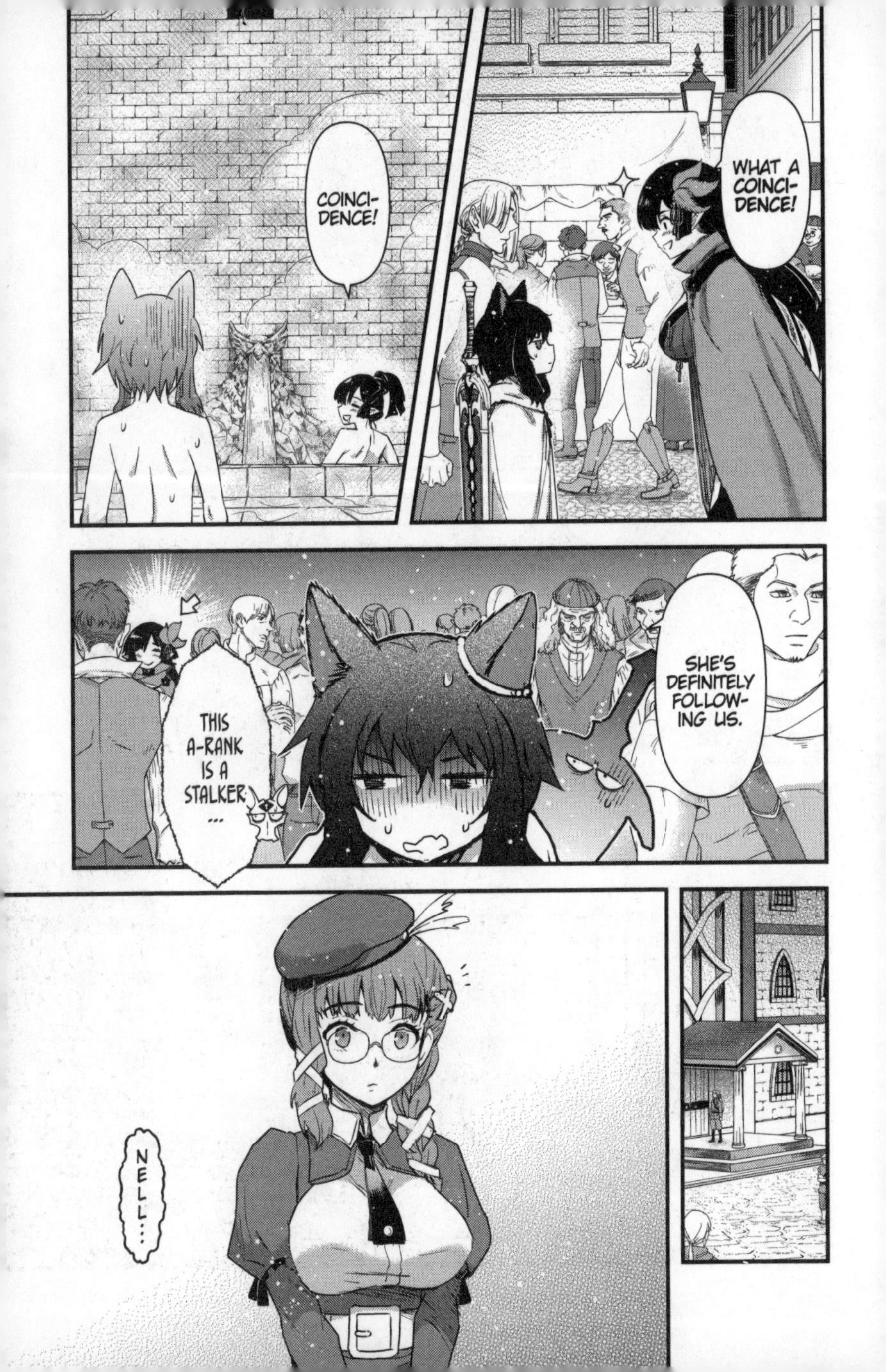
WHAT A COINCI-DENCE!
COINCI-DENCE!
SHE'S DEFINITELY FOLLOW-ING US.
THIS A-RANK IS A STALKER...
NELL...

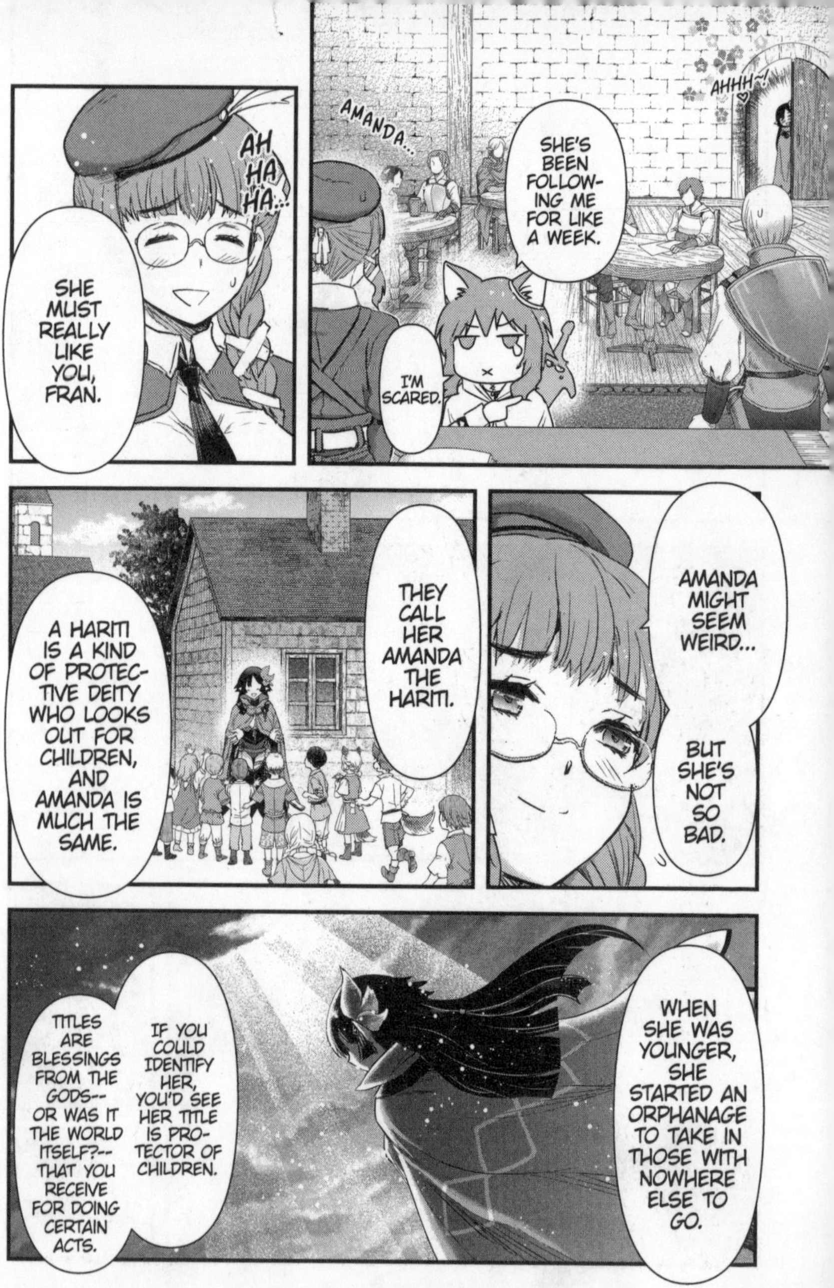
AHHH~!♥
AMANDA...
SHE'S BEEN FOLLOWING ME FOR LIKE A WEEK.
I'M SCARED.
AH HA HA...
SHE MUST REALLY LIKE YOU, FRAN.
AMANDA MIGHT SEEM WEIRD...
BUT SHE'S NOT SO BAD.
THEY CALL HER AMANDA THE HARITI.
A HARITI IS A KIND OF PROTECTIVE DEITY WHO LOOKS OUT FOR CHILDREN, AND AMANDA IS MUCH THE SAME.
WHEN SHE WAS YOUNGER, SHE STARTED AN ORPHANAGE TO TAKE IN THOSE WITH NOWHERE ELSE TO GO.
IF YOU COULD IDENTIFY HER, YOU'D SEE HER TITLE IS PROTECTOR OF CHILDREN.
TITLES ARE BLESSINGS FROM THE GODS--OR WAS IT THE WORLD ITSELF?--THAT YOU RECEIVE FOR DOING CERTAIN ACTS.

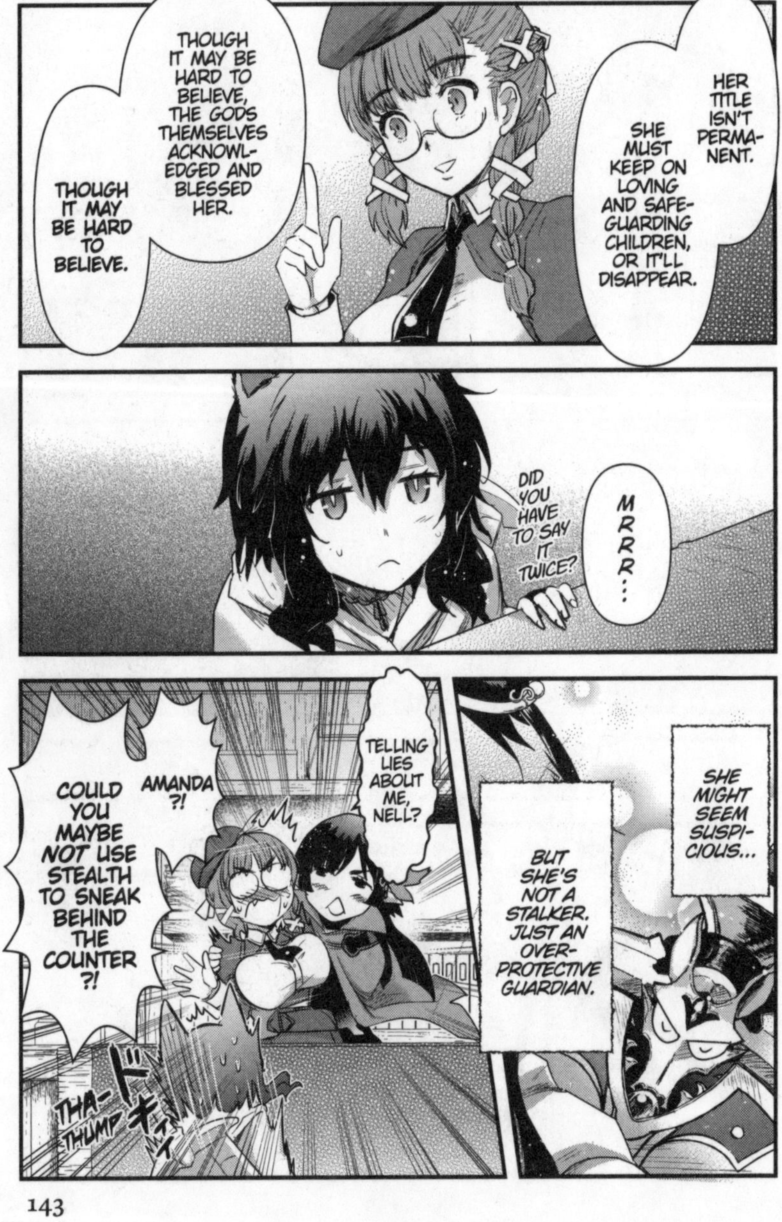
HER TITLE ISN'T PERMANENT.
SHE MUST KEEP ON LOVING AND SAFEGUARDING CHILDREN, OR IT'LL DISAPPEAR.
THOUGH IT MAY BE HARD TO BELIEVE, THE GODS THEMSELVES ACKNOWLEDGED AND BLESSED HER.
THOUGH IT MAY BE HARD TO BELIEVE.
MRRR...
DID YOU HAVE TO SAY IT TWICE?
SHE MIGHT SEEM SUSPICIOUS...
BUT SHE'S NOT A STALKER. JUST AN OVERPROTECTIVE GUARDIAN.
TELLING LIES ABOUT ME, NELL?
AMANDA?!
COULD YOU MAYBE NOT USE STEALTH TO SNEAK BEHIND THE COUNTER?!
THA-THUMP

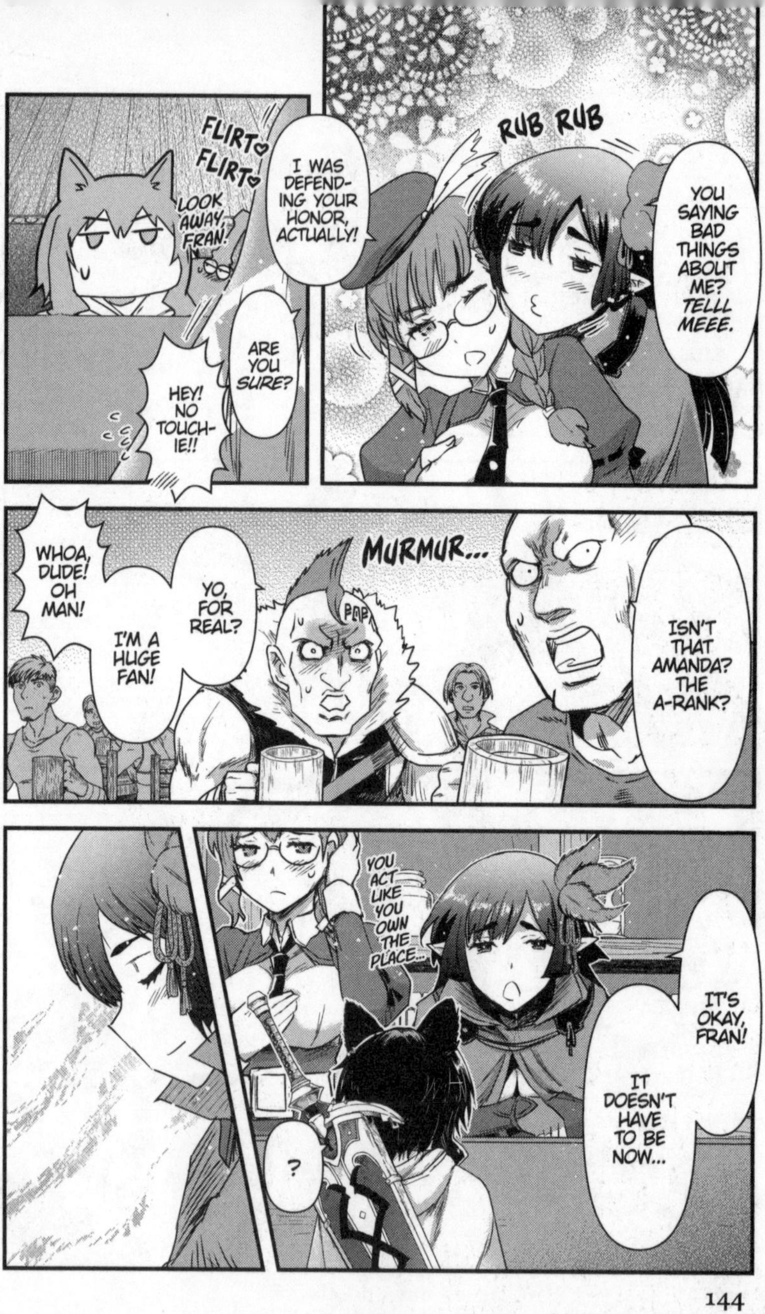
RUB RUB
YOU SAYING BAD THINGS ABOUT ME? TELLL MEEE.
I WAS DEFEND-ING YOUR HONOR, ACTUALLY!
ARE YOU SURE?
FLIRT♡ FLIRT♡
LOOK AWAY, FRAN.
HEY! NO TOUCH-IE!!
MURMUR...
ISN'T THAT AMANDA? THE A-RANK?
YO, FOR REAL?
I'M A HUGE FAN!
WHOA, DUDE! OH MAN!
IT'S OKAY, FRAN!
IT DOESN'T HAVE TO BE NOW...
YOU ACT LIKE YOU OWN THE PLACE...
?

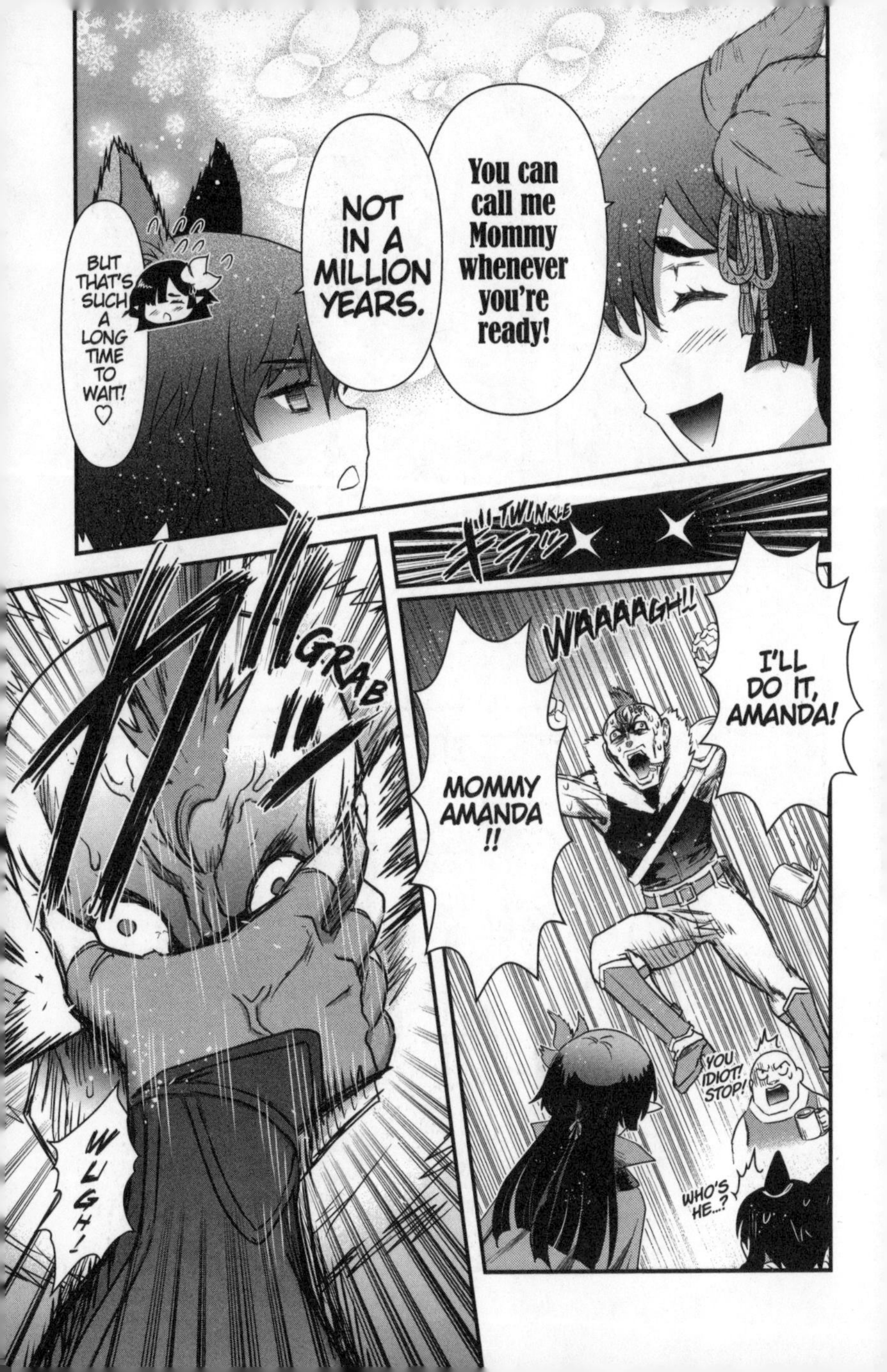
You can call me Mommy whenever you're ready!
NOT IN A MILLION YEARS.
BUT THAT'S SUCH A LONG TIME TO WAIT! ♡
TWINKLE
キラッ
I'LL DO IT, AMANDA!
WAAAAGH!!
MOMMY AMANDA!!
YOU IDIOT! STOP!
WHO'S HE...?
GRAB
WUGH!

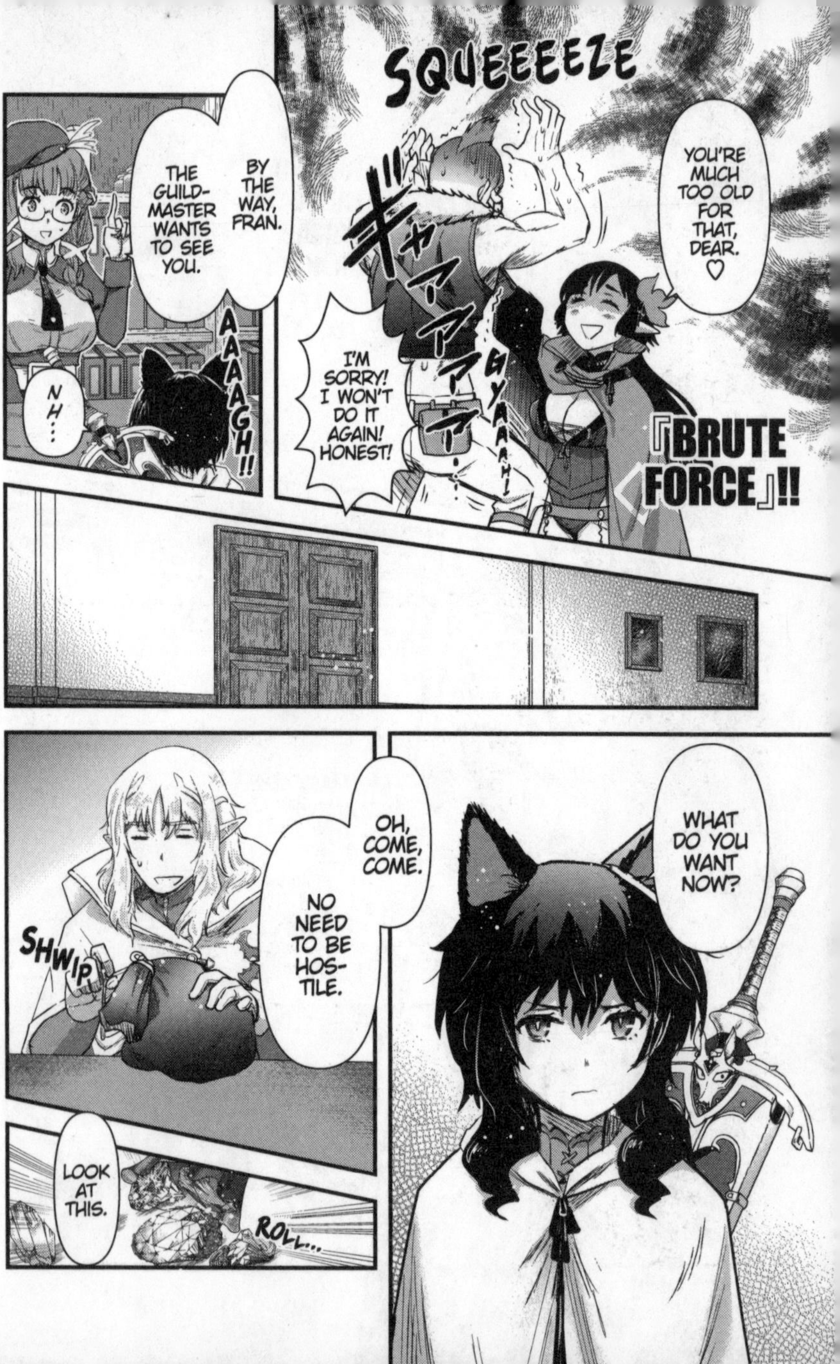
SQUEEEEZE
YOU'RE MUCH TOO OLD FOR THAT, DEAR. ♡
GYAAAH!
I'M SORRY! I WON'T DO IT AGAIN! HONEST!
『BRUTE FORCE』!!
BY THE WAY, FRAN.
THE GUILD-MASTER WANTS TO SEE YOU.
AAAAAGH!!
NH...
WHAT DO YOU WANT NOW?
OH, COME, COME.
NO NEED TO BE HOS-TILE.
SHWIP
LOOK AT THIS.
ROLL...

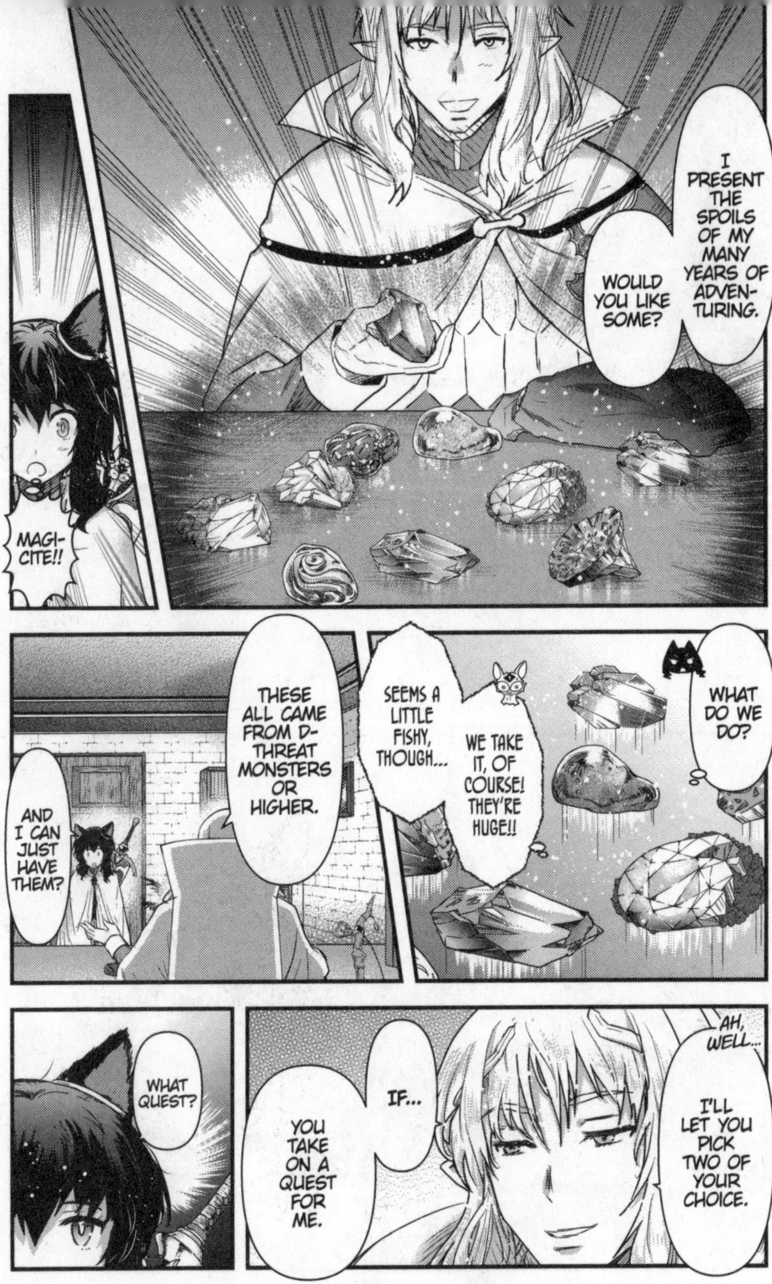
I PRESENT THE SPOILS OF MY MANY YEARS OF ADVEN-TURING.
WOULD YOU LIKE SOME?
MAGI-CITE!!
WHAT DO WE DO?
WE TAKE IT, OF COURSE! THEY'RE HUGE!!
SEEMS A LITTLE FISHY, THOUGH...
THESE ALL CAME FROM D-THREAT MONSTERS OR HIGHER.
AND I CAN JUST HAVE THEM?
AH, WELL...
I'LL LET YOU PICK TWO OF YOUR CHOICE.
IF...
YOU TAKE ON A QUEST FOR ME.
WHAT QUEST?

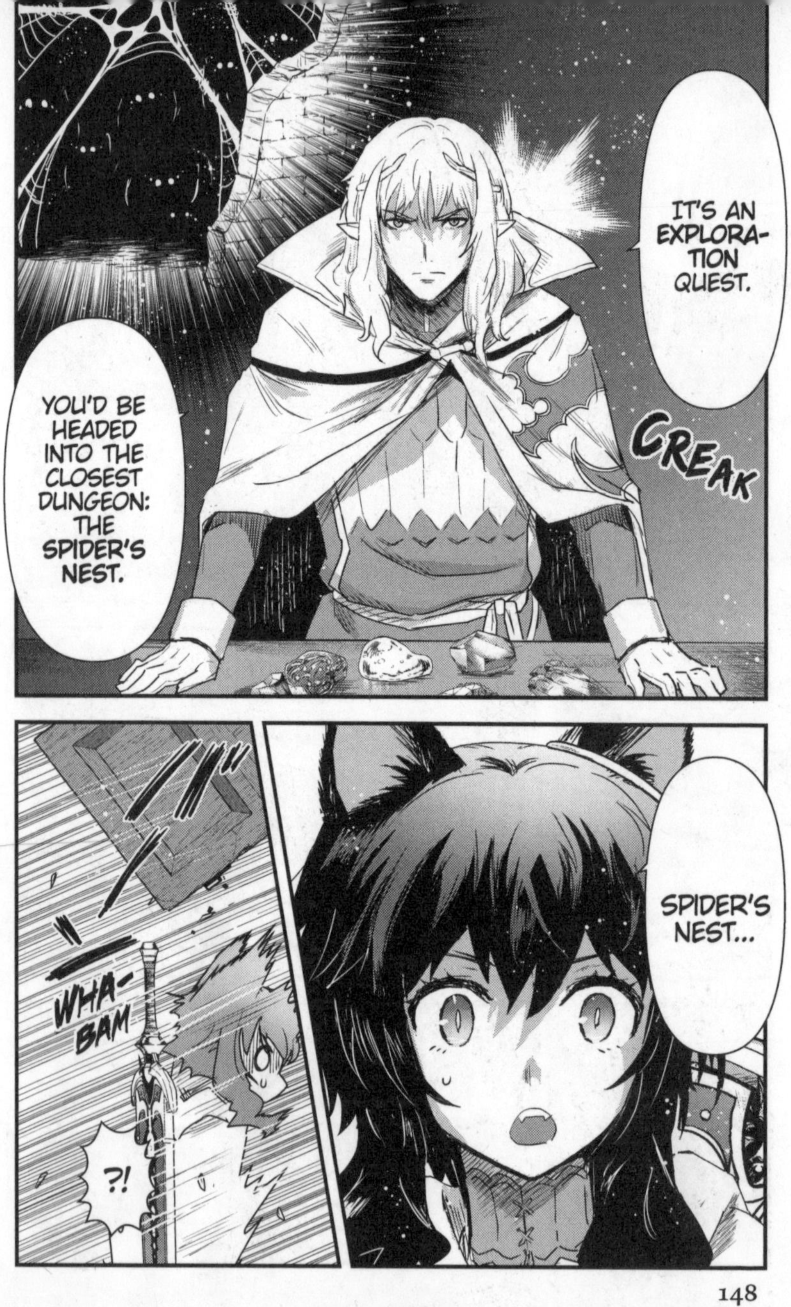
IT'S AN EXPLORATION QUEST.
YOU'D BE HEADED INTO THE CLOSEST DUNGEON: THE SPIDER'S NEST.
CREAK
SPIDER'S NEST...
WHA-BAM
?!

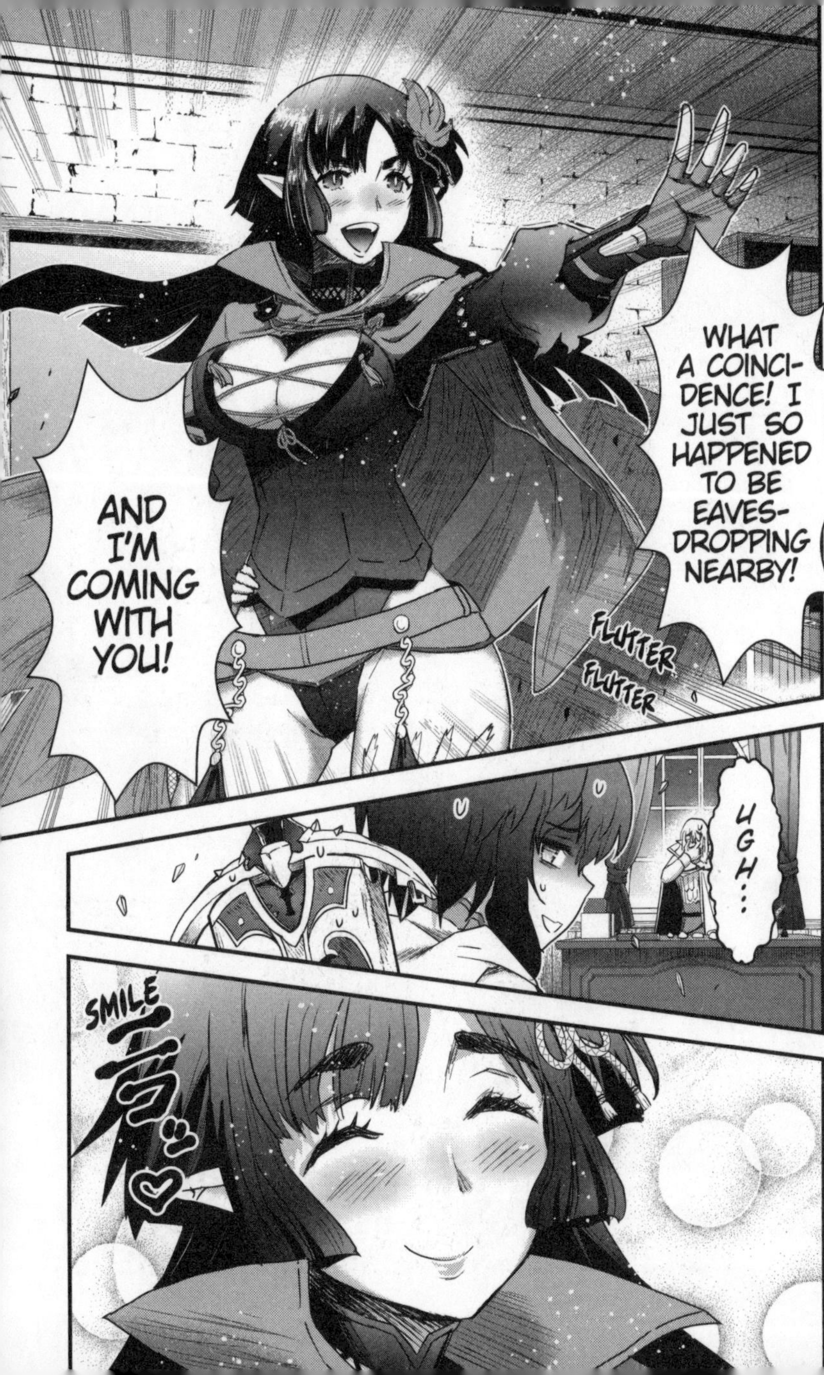
WHAT A COINCIDENCE! I JUST SO HAPPENED TO BE EAVESDROPPING NEARBY!
FLUTTER FLUTTER
AND I'M COMING WITH YOU!
UGH...
SMILE

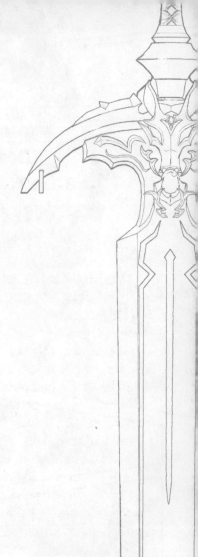

Reincarnated
as a sword

Reincarnated as a Sword
Bonus Story
Fran and Garbage Day

The Maid's Side

"Excuse me."

"Yes? How may I help you?"

I was out in the garden, lazing about, when a small beastgirl approached me. She looked to be about ten years old, and was dressed up like an adventurer. What did she want at this hour? As much as I treasured my impromptu break sessions, I needed to entertain her in case she filed a complaint.

"I'm here on a delivery quest."

"Oh, thank you very much. To whom is the delivery addressed?"

"To Dominic, from one Celeste."

A love letter to the young master?! Are you kidding me?! Why do you think I'm working for these financially bankrupt nobles?! I'd been working there five years, trying to catch Dominic's eye and get him to marry me. Broke as the family was, they were still aristocrats. I could get the benefit of their name, if nothing else!

"A-and may I ask who this Ms. Celeste might be?"

"The only child of the Myste Trade Association."

Damn it! This is the worst! She's rich and pretty!

The master would jump at the opportunity if he so much as caught wind of it. Should I dispose of the letter? No, that would be too obvious. Should I turn her away? No, she'd just come back sooner or later. But I had to stop this girl from making the delivery somehow. What should I do?

That's it! I'll stall her until she leaves!

Fran's Side

This is the place.

"Mmn."

One afternoon, Fran and I traveled to the noble district of town. We weren't out on a leisurely stroll. In fact, we were on a quest. We were to deliver a letter on behalf of a girl who'd fallen in love with a young man at a party—apparently, she was too embarrassed to talk to him herself. Delivering the letter also proved too great a task for said lovestruck maiden, forcing her to enlist the aid of adventurers.

Fran would've passed on the quest, but the rewards were far too tempting. The issuer was the daughter of a foodstuff trader who had access to exotic ingredients. When Fran learned about the potential for unique culinary rewards, she immediately applied for the quest.

Mail delivery's boring. Are you sure you're up for it?

"King Pork!"

King what?

"King Pork. That's the reward for this quest. It sounds delicious, and I want to try it. It's too expensive for us to buy normally."

Oh, okay.

To Fran, two kilograms of King Pork was worth more than its weight in gold.

Sure, I guess we can take it.

"Mm!"

And so we reached our destination. The recipient of the letter was the eldest son of a noble family, but you wouldn't be able to tell from how run-down his mansion was. The stone fence was broken in several places, and the gates looked like they hadn't been polished since it was built. These aristocrats weren't living the high life, despite their nobility. They weren't alone, though. There were other noble families who had no businesses or territories to manage and had to live in poverty.

Fran peeked through a hole in the wall and spotted a maid. The family was too poor to even hire a proper guard.

"Excuse me."

"Yes? How may I help you?"

The maid tottered over to us. We explained the purpose of our visit, but for whatever reason, she said she couldn't accept the letter."Why not?"

"The young master is the heir to His Countship. As such, he cannot simply accept any old communiqué. A test is required. Pass it, and I shall accept the letter for him."

"Bring it on!"

"Your trial will be difficult. You will have to clean the entire city!"

"What?"

"Pick up one hundred pieces of garbage! Oh, woodchips and other scrap don't count. But you're allowed to take more than a day."

153

"Mmn! Okay."

Wait, what? What did the letter have to do with picking up trash? Maybe she was just trying to turn Fran away. Meeting an heir to the count might be more difficult than I'd thought. I didn't think the maid would let us see him even if we cleaned up the city as she said. Still, Fran was up to the challenge.

We should probably think of another way to get in.

"Why? She said she'd let us deliver the letter if we picked up the trash."

I guess, but...

We couldn't exactly sneak into the mansion, so this seemed like the only way. We got down to work, starting with our immediate vicinity.

This is going to be harder than I thought.

The noble district was spic-and-span, which made sense, really. The district was probably cleaned on a regular basis. The maid must've known. No wonder she'd said we could take as long as we wanted. It was an impossible task to begin with.

Fran widened her scope and started cleaning up the business district. People stared at her, quite harshly. I figured cleanup in this part of town was left to the orphans and slum dwellers, with the guild compensating them for their trouble.

"Hey, you! Don't pick up trash on our turf!"

The slum dwellers were rightly upset at what they perceived to be Fran's invasion of their territory. She apologized and treated them to some skewers to make up for it. We were going to have to restrict ourselves to the noble district.

"What is it, Teacher?"

At this rate, it's going to take us a couple of days to finish this job. But I have an idea.

It came to me as Fran was handing out the orphans' lunch. If there was no trash, we would make our own trash to clean up!

We'll buy everyone skewers and hand those over to the maid!

Fran shook her head.

"She told us to clean up the city. It wouldn't be fair that way."

No?

"No."

That one hurt. When had I become so tainted? Or maybe Fran was just that pure.

Fran patrolled the noble district for trash with newfound vigor. She picked up whatever garbage was on the streets while also crawling into the tight spaces only children could reach.

"Ninety-seven!" Fran said triumphantly, as she held up a broken sword she found at the end of an alleyway. To her, it was like finding a legendary relic. Only three more to go. It was getting dark, though, so I thought we should retire for the evening. Suddenly, three men wearing leather armor appeared from the shadows and surrounded her.

"Hey, girl, that's a nice sword you have there."

"Heh heh. No one comes to this part of the district. There's nobody around to save you."

I didn't think there'd be punks lurking in the shadows of the noble district. Even with no eyewitnesses, an incident here wouldn't go unnoticed. The Knight Brigade would immediately start looking for answers, to ensure the safety of the city's affluent citizens. How could these idiots not know that? Then again, they were dumb enough to shake people down in the noble district.

What should we do? Rough them up a little and leave them?

Fran smiled.

What's up?

"Quest clear."

Ten minutes later, we returned to the mansion, where the maid greeted us with a scream.

"Wh-who are these people?! I said I wanted you to clean the city."

"I did."

"Why did you bring them here?!"

"I cleaned up the city's crime."

The maid fell silent at Fran's flawless logic. She was to blame for setting Fran off on a cleaning rampage to begin with.

"What kind of—"

"Oh, do we have a guest? My name is Dominic. I live in this mansion."

A handsome young man cut the maid off mid-sentence.

"Mmn. I have a letter for you."

"Oh? Why, thank you! Oh my goodness, it's from Celeste!"

And with that, our quest was finally completed. Dominic sure looked happy, though I couldn't say the same for his maid. Fran made sure the necessary documentation was in place before walking away. The maid frantically called after us, but we ignored her.

"Hey, get back here! What am I supposed to do with—"

All's well that ends well. Let's go claim that King Pork of yours.

"Mmn!"

How do you want me to cook it? Tonkatsu? Shougayaki? Maybe a simple pork steak?

"Curry it!"

Uh, curry? Are you sure? It's not every day that we get such fine ingredients.

"Mm! Curry's good enough as it is, so it'll taste even better with King Pork!"

Then I'll make curry and have tonkatsu and steak on top of it.

"Oooh! That sounds like the tastiest kind of curry! You're the best, Teacher!"

The quest had taken us the whole day to finish, but it was behind us now.

"Heeeey! What am I supposed to do with all this trash?!"

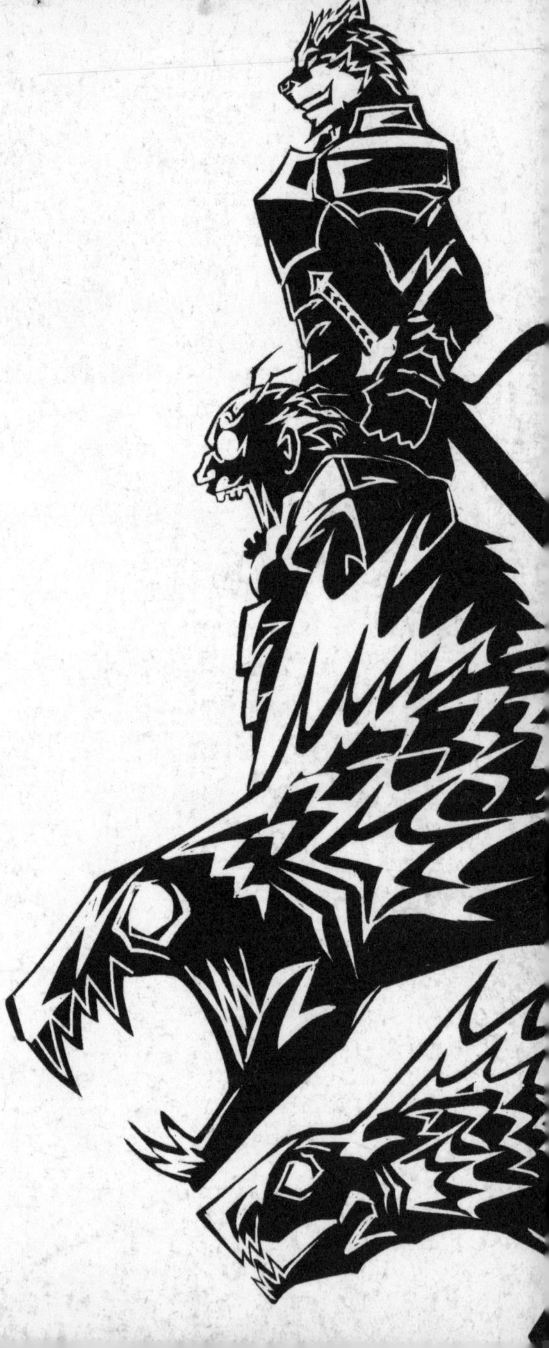

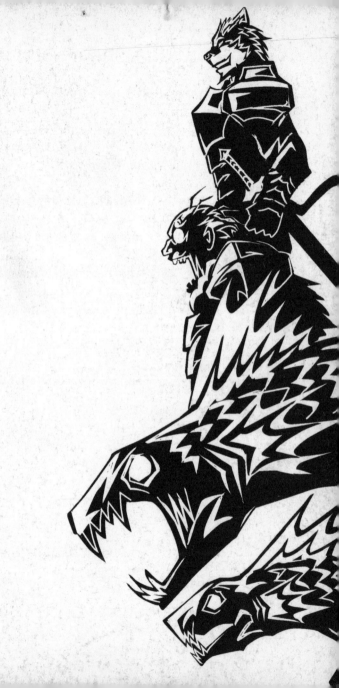